## ABOUT THE AUTHOR

Siddharth Dube was born in Calcutta in 1961. He studied at the University of Minnesota's journalism programme and at Harvard University's school of public health. He is now based in New Delhi where he is both a writer and a health policy analyst, currently working on a book about India's worsening AIDS epidemic. He has also worked for the health divisions of UNICEF in New York and the World Bank in Washington D.C. As a writer, he has published in *The Washington Post*, *The Financial Times* and India's *Economic and Political Weekly*. He was a visiting fellow at the Centre for the Study of Developing Societies in New Delhi while writing this book.

D0166746

# In The Land of Poverty

## MEMOIRS OF AN INDIAN FAMILY:
## 1947-97

## Siddharth Dube

Zed Books
London and New York

*In the Land of Poverty: Memoirs of an Indian Family, 1947-97* was first published by Zed Books Ltd, 7 Cynthia Street, London N1 9JF, UK and Room 400, 175 Fifth Avenue, New York, NY 10010, USA in 1998.

Distributed in the USA exclusively by St Martin's Press Inc., 175 Fifth Avenue, New York, NY 10010, USA.

305. 569
D81 i

Copyright © Siddharth Dube
Cover design by Ad Lib Designs
Typeset in Times New Roman by Megatechnics
19A Ansari Road
New Delhi 110 002
Printed and bound in the United Kingdom by
Biddles Ltd, Guildford and King's Lynn

The rights of Siddharth Dube, the author of this work, have been asserted by him in accordance with the Copyright, Designs and Patents Act, 1988

We gratefully acknowledge Jawaharlal Nehru Memorial Fund for letting us use the extract on pages 2 and 3, from *An Autobiography* by Shri Jawaharlal Nehru.

A catalogue record of this book is available from the British Library

Library of Congress Cataloging-in-Publication Data

Dube, Siddharth, 1961 -
JK     In the land of poverty : memoirs of an Indian family,  1947-
1997 / Siddharth Dube.
       p.  cm.
       Includes bibliographical references and index.
       ISBN 1-85649-597-3 (hc.). -- ISBN 1-85649-598-1 (pbk.)
       1. Poverty -- India. 2. India -- Economic conditions -- 1947 - 3.
India -- Politics and government -- 1947-I. Title.
       HC440.P6D83  1998                                      98-19800
       305.5'69'0954--dc21                                         CIP

ISBN      1 85649 597 3 Hb
          1 85649 598 1 Pb

To my father,
Basant Kumar Dube,
an incomparably great and good person,

and to my brother,
Bharat, for so unwaveringly believing in me and in this book.

# Contents

**Ram Dass and Prayaga Devi**

# Acknowledgements

Many people inspired and supported me – intellectually, emotionally, and often in both ways – in the exhausting years I spent researching and writing. I can only hope that with this book I give to them some small part of what they have given me.

My mother, Savitri, and eldest brother, Pratap, were, as always, the most admirable, staunch and caring companions I could hope for.

In Baba ka Gaon, Ram Dass, Prayaga Devi, Shrinath, Mata Prasad, Hansraj, Ram Saran and Mata Prasad Maurya, Durbhe and Phoolchand were by their bravery and goodness constant reminders to me of why it was essential to write this book.

I owe an enormous debt to Ashis Nandy, Amartya Sen and Scott Thompson for their early encouragement, without which I would not have begun this project; and to Saleem Kidwai and David Devadas – this book is theirs as much as mine – for their affection, guidance and help, not least with the unending translations from Awadhi.

My other dearest friends – Sohaila Abdulali, Tonuca Basu, Sheba Chacko, Brinda Chugani, Rosemary George, Suzy Goldenberg, Shilpa Hingorani, Inji Islam, Pichaya Manet, David Morrison, Rosemary Romano, Sankar Sen, Jai Singh, Sailaja and Tarun Tahiliani, Nilita Vachani and Kamala Visweswaran – made my life worth living with their love and generosity. Siddharth Gautam magically appeared – joyful and courageous as always – when I desperately missed him.

For their friendship and support, I am indebted to Shoba Aggarwal, Paul Desruisseaux, Robin Desser, Michael Dwyer, Gautam Khandelwal, Leena Labroo, Pankaj Mishra, Sanjay Pradhan, Arundhati Roy, N.C. Saxena,

Helen Saxenian, Jeremy Seabrook, Shashi Tharoor, Indu Vachani, and Jafar and Rajat Zaheer; and to my editors Renuka Chatterjee and Robert Molteno.

I am also extremely grateful to the United States Institute of Peace for the grant that underwrote much of this research, and to the Centre for the Study of Developing Societies in Delhi for hosting me as a visiting fellow.

# 1

# Introduction: This Naked, Hungry Mass

*'My mental picture of India always contains this naked, hungry mass'*

**Jawaharlal Nehru**
India's first prime minister

FROM 1919 to 1921, the central districts of Uttar Pradesh province were swept by a fierce peasant revolt. At the height of the conflict, thousands of impoverished peasants and landless labourers battled with *zamindar* landlords and the British colonial government, allies in exploiting the peasantry. The scale and ferocity of the revolt was such that it captured newspaper headlines in distant Delhi, British India's capital. The peasants' demands were radical. They sought nothing less than an end to their exploitation and oppression: the beatings and abuse by the landlords and their agents, forced and unpaid labour, the extortionate rents and illegal taxes that impoverished them. The province's British governor-general, apprehensive, warned of 'the beginnings of something like revolution'.

Though the landlords and the British administration were for a while in retreat, by mid-1921 they had used the police and army to crush the 'revolution'. The scores of thousands of landless labourers and petty tenants who had joined or been inspired by the revolt were once again condemned to brutal oppression and poverty. Their dreams of freedom evaporated.

Drawn into the revolt on the peasants' side was the young Jawaharlal Nehru, already a leader of the Indian National Congress. Decades later, Nehru wrote about his experience:

As a result of the externment order from Mussoorie I spent about two weeks in Allahabad, and it was during this period that I got entangled in the *kisan* (peasant) movement . . . Early in June 1920 (so far as I can remember) about two hundred *kisans* marched fifty miles from the interior of Pratapgarh district to Allahabad city with the intention of drawing the attention of the prominent politicians there to their woebegone condition. I learnt that these *kisans* were squatting on the river bank, on one of the Jumna *ghats*, and, accompanied by some friends, went to see them. They told us of the crushing exactions of the *taluqadars*, of inhuman treatment, and that their condition had become wholly intolerable. They begged us to accompany them back to make inquiries as well as to protect them from the vengeance of the *taluqadars* who were angry at their having come to Allahabad on this mission. They would accept no denial and literally clung on us. At last I promised to visit them two days or so later.

I went there with some colleagues and we spent three days in the villages far from the railway and even from the *pucca* road. That visit was a revelation to me. We found the whole countryside afire with enthusiasm and full of a strange excitement. Enormous gatherings would take place at the briefest notice by word of mouth. One village would communicate with another, and the second with the third, and so on, and presently whole villages would empty out, and all over the fields there would be men and women and children on the march to the meeting-place . . . They were in miserable rags, men and women, but their faces were full of excitement and their eyes glistened and seemed to expect strange happenings which would, as if by a miracle, put an end to their long misery.

They showered their affection on us and looked on us with loving and hopeful eyes, as if we were the bearers of good tidings, the guides who were to lead them to the promised land. Looking at them and their misery and overflowing gratitude, I was filled with shame and sorrow, shame at my own easy-going and comfortable life and our petty politics of the city which ignored this vast multitude of semi-naked sons and daughters of India, sorrow at the degradation and overwhelming poverty of India. A new picture of India seemed to rise before me, naked, starving, crushed, and utterly miserable. And their faith in us, casual visitors from the distant city, embarrassed me and filled me with a new responsibility that frightened me.

. . . Even before my visit to Pratapgarh in June 1920, I had often passed through villages, stopped there and talked to the peasants. I had seen them in their scores of thousands on the banks of the Ganges during the big *melas* and we had taken our Home Rule propaganda to them. But somehow I had not fully realized what they were and what they meant to India. Like most of us, I took them for granted. This realization came to me during these Pratapgarh visits and ever since then my mental picture of India always contains this naked, hungry mass.

In January 1995, three-quarters of a century after the revolt and almost half a century since India became independent, I travelled to the area of the revolt in central Uttar Pradesh (UP) province. My object was to write a memoir of one of the impoverished families who had fought in that revolt and of their experience in independent India. I had dreamt for many years of writing this memoir.

I was baffled by why poverty, hunger, ill health and a myriad other deprivations were still ubiquitous in India many years after Independence. The scale of poverty – the numbers of the 'naked, hungry mass' – has worsened so much in the past half-century that in 1997, even by conservative government estimates, the number of people unable to afford a survival-level diet equals the country's total population in 1947 of about 350 million. This is the largest group of impoverished people in the world. Even the proportion of desperately poor people is not substantially lower in the 1990s than half a century ago: at about 40 per cent of the population today in contrast to 50 per cent at Independence. And though many of the most dramatic manifestations of suffering long associated with India – bonded labour, large-scale epidemics, famines – have been largely controlled, this commendable progress is eclipsed by the failure to ameliorate the chronic deprivation and everyday hunger suffered by several hundred million Indians.

Equally puzzling to me was the fact that though the country today boasts a huge economy, a major industrial sector, the world's fourth largest army and diverse national achievements, India's record on raising human welfare, compared to most other developing countries, is miserable.[1] Levels of hunger, illiteracy, excess mortality and other indicators of deprivation are today far higher in India than in China, the Philippines or Indonesia. In 1947 living standards in China were much the same as in India, but 50 years later were twice that of India's. And though 20 years ago severe poverty was as pervasive in Indonesia as in India, only about 8 per cent of the Indonesian population is today absolutely poor, a proportion only one-fifth that of India. India's scores on human welfare are worse than those of every Latin American country but Haiti, and appear favourable only in comparison to those of the most impoverished and strife-torn sub-Saharan African countries.

Why has such acute and pervasive poverty persisted in India despite decades of fairly rapid economic growth, planned economic development and constitutional commitment to socialism? Did Nehru betray the impoverished peasants' faith in him, 'the new responsibility' that seized him during the 1919 revolt? Did the Congress party abdicate the many promises it made to the poor during the heady days of the nationalist movement? Why have the sheer numbers of the poor not ensured that India's parliamentary democracy would work to their benefit? Why has the persistence of mass poverty not emerged as a central political issue?

These questions were the beginning of my quest. Once embarked, I decided to frame the book around the true experiences of an impoverished family. I wanted to know, and to record for others, what the poor felt, what they thought, how they viewed the world and their own situation. History has almost always been written from the perspective of the wealthy and powerful. Thus, though the poor have long been a majority of India's population, they are almost entirely absent from the annals of Indian history, while there are scarcely any authentic records of their views and experiences. Yet, by sheer numbers, *the* history of India's poor is *the* history of India.

Moreover, very soon the generation of Indians who were adult at the time of the country's Independence will have died. The unique history of millions of people will vanish with the passing of this generation of the Indian poor. They have been participants and witnesses at one of the modern world's most extraordinary junctures: the constitutional pledge by the government of one of the first colonies to win independence that all its people were assured democracy and freedom from want. It is imperative that their history and their experiences in independent India be recorded.

What was the best way truly to represent in a book the views and reality of the poor? To me, there seemed to be only one satisfactory combination of methods. The first and most crucial step was to interview at length generations of one family and to reproduce verbatim their life stories. The members of this family would tell their own histories in their own voices. This was the most honest, exacting and powerful way I could think of to reflect their views. Because of my twin convictions that the poor or illiterate understand their circumstances very well and that 'outsiders' – however empathetic or skilled in research methods – can never comprehend realities radically different from their own, I rejected outright the option of placing myself as an observer-cum-narrator, or of writing their story in the first person or as a novel. These convictions were strengthened in writing this book. This family's testimony is ample proof that they comprehend their situation just as clearly as the educated and the well-off. And I could not have begun to grasp their view of life had I not relied on interviewing them and reproducing their testimony.

The second step was to place this family's experience within an analysis which explained two things: first, how the millions of other impoverished Indian families had fared in this half-century; second, the most important features and determinants of the many changes that have affected India in these decades, in politics, agriculture, the caste system and almost every other sphere. The need to locate this single family's experience within this broader context is self-evident. Focusing on the . story of one family ensures richness of detail and a sense of continuity, but the scale and complexity of poverty in India is such that a single family's experience can never be 'typical'. Also, the situation of this family or of the poor overall cannot be understood without analysing the patterns and determinants of politics, economics and social change. For instance, just the most obvious questions about this family – Why were they poor in 1947? Why are they poor today? – require an explication of a huge range of issues. These include, at the very least, the colonial political and land-ownership systems, the caste system, the nature of the Congress party and post-Independence development policies, the depth of the independent Indian state's commitment to equity and social welfare goals, the nature of subsequent land reform efforts, the pattern of agricultural and industrial growth, and national and provincial politics. Hence, this book melds the singular voices of this family with a broad analysis of India's 'political economy'.

In some chapters, the family's testimony is predominant, in others analysis prevails. Because the memoir is this family's, I have not edited their oral testimony beyond changes needed for effective translation or clarification. Their views and emphases and criticisms are intact and do not reflect my biases. If readers feel that this book is one-sided or too harsh – for instance, in the antagonism towards the upper castes, the landlords and orthodox Hinduism – they should remember that its purpose is to mirror an impoverished family's view of life. Similarly, in selecting which subjects to emphasize in the analysis, I have followed the emphasis placed by the members of the family. For instance, the issues of land reform and of the landlords' violence against the poor are persisting themes because this family considers them to be central to their poverty.

## Ram Dass

At the centre of this chronicle are Ram Dass Pasi and his village of Baba ka Gaon in the Pratapgarh district of UP province. Ram Dass was born in the mid-1920s to a destitute untouchable family of landless labourers, who were bonded to the village landlords. (The term 'untouchable' is used in this book in references before 1949, when the term and the social restrictions associated with it were declared illegal under the Indian Constitution. The preferred term now is scheduled castes, because these castes are enumerated on a government schedule.) Pratapgarh – located in the area of central UP known as Awadh – was the vortex of the 1919 revolt.

Ram Dass today, aged about 70, is a convivial man, self-assured and open in demeanour. Apart from his unusual dark grey eyes, in looks and

Ram Dass Pasi

dress Ram Dass is broadly similar to other poor north Indian village men of his age – short (about five feet four), slight-framed, strong-featured, mustachioed (a thick, carefully shaped bow of white hair), most often wearing a muddied cotton *dhoti*, brown *kurta*, short sleeveless jacket and cracked leather shoes. On special occasions, particularly in the evenings, he dons either a yellowish or lilac turban.

Ram Dass's father was from a village some 20 km to the north of Baba ka Gaon, called Ranipur, in Sultanpur district, which was part of the wealthy Amethi landlord's estate. Baba ka Gaon is Ram Dass's *nanihal* – his mother's village – but it became his family's home because his mother moved back to her parents' home once her mother-in-law had died and her husband and father-in-law still stayed away at work in Bombay for long periods. *My father used to go away for two years at a time and so where was my mother to go for refuge but to her parents?* Ram Dass and his elder sister were born in Ranipur, the rest of his siblings in Baba ka Gaon. In Bombay, Ram Dass's father worked as a labourer at the Khiljee Mills, a cotton-milling factory. He left Bombay in the early 1940s to return to Baba ka Gaon. He died in 1973, Ram Dass's mother in 1983.

Ram Dass was the second of five children. Only his youngest sister, aged about 50, survives. Puttu is married and lives in Dehra Dun, a prosperous UP town some 700 km north-west. She works as a labourer in a tea plantation. She is childless.

Ram Dass's elder sister, Prabha, died at the age of 40. Her husband and three children live in a village in Sultanpur district. Ram Dass says she died of some kind of paralysis. *We had no money, so where could we take her for treatment? So it was inevitable that she would die. There was a doctor in Gauriganj, where she lived, and he treated her, but these village doctors, what do they know about long, lasting diseases. At that time no one used to do* doctori dawai [Western, allopathic medicine].

Another younger sister, Bonda, died at the age of 25. She and her husband lived in a village adjacent to Baba ka Gaon. She had two daughters and a son.

Ram Dass's only brother, Ram Tehel, died of tuberculosis at the age of 22. When he fell sick, he was in Bombay with Ram Dass, working as a daily-wage labourer in small factories. *Because he was ill I told him to go back home to the village. I bought him as much medicine as we could buy. But he just withered away.* Only one of Ram Tehel's children survived, and on his father's death this son was brought up by Ram Dass and his wife. Kaalu, the son, now about 40, works in a welding shop in Faridabad, a large industrial town on the outskirts of Delhi. Kaalu has three daughters and a son, who live in Baba ka Gaon with his wife.

There are 18 people in Ram Dass's immediate family today, including his wife, two sons and their wives, eight grandchildren and four great-grandchildren. Ram Dass's wife, Prayaga Devi, is a few years younger than him. His sons, Shrinath and Jhoku, are aged about 45 and 35, respectively. The entire family lives in Baba ka Gaon, apart from Jhoku, who works in Dehra Dun.

Ram Dass says: *My first child was Shrinath. I had 12 children altogether, 1 girl and 11 boys. Apart from Shrinath and Jhoku, they all died after reaching 4 or 5 years of age. The child in Dehra Dun, Jhoku, is about number 8. The last two died at about 7 years of age. They died of small-pox. They didn't survive even though we gave them a lot of medicines. The earlier ones – I'm not a doctor, so how can I tell what they died of? It was just not in my destiny that they live.*

The history of Ram Dass's family is inextricably tied to the village of Baba ka Gaon – current population 500 – in the north-west corner of Pratapgarh district. This is the heart of the vast Gangetic plain, and at one of its meandering loops the Ganga passes just 60 km from the village. Baba ka Gaon is marked only on detailed maps of Pratapgarh district, but is located nearly equidistant between Lucknow, UP's capital, and Varanasi, both about 150 km distant. From either city, it today takes about five hours by bus to reach the rutted dirt track that leads to the village. Pratapgarh, the district capital, is two hours away. More convenient are the railway stops at Amethi or Gauriganj, market towns in Sultanpur district, both about an hour distant by jeep or horse-drawn cart.

Baba ka Gaon is about 4 km from the tarmac road that runs to Pratapgarh town from Ateha, the closest market to Baba ka Gaon. To get to Baba ka Gaon from this road, one must turn left at the large *peepul* tree 3 km from Ateha. The *peepul* tree, towering, ancient, waxy leaves glistening in the sunlight, has a broad cement base around its circumference on which a simple Hindu shrine with a vermilioned statue of the goddess Kali has been built of mud. A dirt track begins here, cratered with potholes and ditches, running past small ponds, airy groves of *mahua*

The Big Four – Ram Dass, Prayaga Devi, Shrinath, Hansraj

and mango trees, and several small hamlets. Everywhere there are young children – their ragged clothes and thin bodies so brown with dust that they appear to have sprung straight from the soil – herding cattle or goats, playing and screaming amongst the groves, collecting sticks for firewood, or dribbling back in twos and threes from school.

The track climbs imperceptibly on the way to Baba ka Gaon, entering the village at its eastern end. Baba ka Gaon is today shaped like a long, untidy oval. There are large trees and thickets of bamboo everywhere. Seen from a distance, they form a copse of variegated greens, making the village an oasis in the dusty summer months. Outside, a patchwork of fields, broken by mud borders a foot high and interspersed with clumps and groves of ancient trees, stretches into the expanse of the Gangetic plain.

On entering the village, the track breaks into two, the one to the right broad and sweeping, the other little more than a broken mud rut. The broader track goes to the area that has always been the preserve of the Brahmins and *Thakurs*, the upper castes. (The latter term is also commonly used in UP to refer to the men of the *Kshatriya* caste.) The houses on this side of the village are large – the size of colonial bungalows – built of fired bricks, with tiled roofs. Their high walls enclose courtyards and spacious rooms. Most have large amounts of open space around them,

**Baba ka Gaon**

where ancient trees grow. Ram Dass comments: *The* Thakurs *each have half or one acre of land for their houses. But people in my area don't even have space for a bed!* The buffaloes and bullocks tied in the courtyards are well fed. Outside, a particularly large home are parked a jeep and a tractor; another tractor is in a shed near another large home.

Of the 100-odd families today in Baba ka Gaon, the upper castes comprise 20 *Thakurs* and 3 Brahmins. All but two of these families live on this side of the village. Lower-caste people rarely venture here.

There are numerous temples in this section of the village, most in disrepair. Local legend maintains that there were once 52 temples in Baba ka Gaon, all in the upper-caste area. Of the older temples there are just eight left. The most important and best preserved is a simple ten-feet-high structure, built of mud, open on all sides and painted white, which sits under a magnificent *peepul* tree, virtually in the centre of the village; this is the Baba ka Mandir, a shrine for an ascetic who made this village his home many centuries ago.

A world apart from the upper-caste area is the side of the village reached by the rutted, narrow track. This poorer section is today home to both the middle castes and the scheduled castes, as huts have sprung up on the land that earlier divided the middle-caste area from that of the former untouchables, who were forced to live at some distance. *Where the middle-castes houses are it was all jungle till five or six years ago. Then during the land reform people began to make houses there.*

There are currently 41 families from the various middle castes.[2] The scheduled castes total 35 families. This side is also home to 7 scheduled tribe families. (India's indigenous communities are given protective discrimination benefits similar to those accorded to the former untouchables.) Two *Thakur* families moved to this area a decade ago, as they owned large plots of land here.

The majority of homes on this side are small huts, cramped close to each other, 50 of which would fit into the larger of the upper-caste mansions. Generally, the homes of the middle castes are better than those of the scheduled castes and the scheduled tribes. There is a handful of larger houses made of brick, and whitewashed. The best homes belong to the two *Thakur* families; they are capacious, solid and double-storeyed. *The two* Thakurs *whom you now see near my house have moved from the upper-caste area because they owned land here. They moved only 12 years ago or so. They have also been encroaching on other people's land.*

The huts are poorest towards the very southern end of the village, where untouchable families like Ram Dass's were once segregated. Most of these huts have just one or two tiny rooms. The walls are of brown mud and the roofs of thatch. Buffaloes and cows are tied close to the huts or in the open courtyards of the bigger houses. Mangy dogs and goats roam freely. But the huts and the small patches of land in front of them are spotlessly clean.

The men and women at this end of the village are visibly poorer, thinner and shorter than on the upper-caste side. These are the tiny but sinewy people who for a pittance load trucks, pull rickshaws and work on construction sites in India's cities and towns. In the village they are dressed poorly in faded clothes; the older men in *dhoti-kurtas* and the younger men in trousers and T-shirts, the women in sarees. Their huts have few possessions – generally, a bicycle, a few utensils, a *charpai* or two, a few religious posters and calendars, and sometimes a radio. Their children are with few exceptions bone-thin and stunted. Most are dressed in mud-covered odds and ends. Many of them are visibly sick, with eye infections, sores and boils. Flies settle thickly along the eyes of the infants.

At this end of Baba ka Gaon is a large pond flanked by trees and marshy land. The pond doubles in size during the monsoon, creating a pretty island out of the low-lying land on one end. It brims with a bewildering variety of water-fowl and wading birds – brown ducks, white cattle egrets, grey herons, dabchicks, and more – who call loudly, fly here and there, or poke diligently for food around the marshy shore. Especially in winter, when migrating birds come from distant northern lands, there is an air of excitement all day at the pond. The birds are virtually unafraid of humans, as Baba ka Gaon's villagers have for several decades prohibited their killing.

Ram Dass's family hut is amongst the last homes in this side of the village. *We built this hut in 1965. Earlier, it was a hovel. There were two rooms. We all lived in one room. And in the other room we used to keep the bullocks.* The new hut stands on the site of the old one. Built of mud and with a thatched roof of dried straw, it is indistinguishable from the other small huts which crowd around it. The path between the huts is narrow, just about broad enough to allow a couple of people to pass. At the edge of the path is a hand-pump.

A small verandah runs across the front of the house. Perhaps 20 feet long, the verandah is divided into two by a short wall. On one side are housed the family's two large, snowy-white bullocks; on the other side is a single *charpai*. The eaves of the roof come down very low, so that adults have to stoop sharply to enter the verandah; the low eaves keep out the rain and direct sun. Inside is a small room, little more than a corridor, which leads to a tiny courtyard, perhaps 12 feet long and 5 wide. The walls inside are far higher than the low-slung eaves would suggest, perhaps as high as 9 feet. There are three tiny rooms around the courtyard, each large enough to hold only the equivalent of two *charpais*. One room is a store, while the other rooms were built for Shrinath and Jhoku when they got married. (Following village tradition, on the marriage of their children Ram Dass and his wife began to sleep in the verandah so that the couples would have privacy.) A kitchen, whose entrance is raised about a foot higher than the courtyard, is where Ram Dass's wife sits and cooks and also serves food. Part of the wall facing the courtyard has a brick filigree to let the smoke out; this and the walls inside the kitchen are blackened with smoke.

As in much of rural India, there is an air of immutability about Baba ka Gaon. Most sights seem to date back centuries. The mud huts, rudimentary ploughs, the thick wooden wheels on the bullock carts, barefoot old men in muddy *dhotis*, women with their sarees pulled over their faces, dusty children herding goats – all these say that time has stood still, that nothing has changed.

But Baba ka Gaon has changed substantially. Ram Dass says: *If you had come 50 years ago you would have found the village very different. The village was half the size then. There are about 100 houses now in the village. There were far fewer then, about sixty. Every family has split into several families. As the families increase the number of houses grows.*

*The road to Baba ka Gaon was earlier along the same route, but then it was a little path as broad as two poles. The bullock carts would have to go through the fruit tree groves. They weren't good roads but at least they could be used all the time apart from the monsoons. The* Thakurs *would ride horses and their women would be carried in palanquins.*

*The village could not be reached during the monsoon till about four or five years ago because the path would be washed away. There would be waist-deep water in many parts! For weeks we couldn't even get to the closest markets. Because of the new, higher road at least the bullock carts and jeeps can always get within 3 km of the village.*

*There were no water taps 50 years ago, nor were there any hand-pumps. There were only three wells that we scheduled castes could use. The upper castes each had their own wells next to their houses. If the water in our wells finished, we could take water from the wells that were owned by some of the middle castes.*

*There are today many bicycles in the village, almost one in each home. I had seen cycles as a child when going to Pratapgarh or Amethi. I bought an old bicycle for Rs 30 when I came back from Bombay in 1962. Then in about 1975 I bought Shrinath, my eldest son, a cycle so that he could use it to go and study. I bought that one for Rs 105 as it was second-hand. New ones used to cost about Rs 150 then. Now they cost Rs 1200. The cycles used to be very strong then, like everything else.*

*I've never bought a radio. I've never been rich enough to buy a radio. Shrinath has never bought one either. But now he has a small one, which his brother Jhoku bought him from Dehra Dun. About half the families in the village now have radios.*

*But I listen to Shrinath's radio or to someone else's. I get all my information from the radio or from talking to others! I'm an uneducated man.*

According to official records, electricity has been supplied to Baba ka Gaon since 1993. But the reality is that, because the villagers refused to pay the large bribe of about Rs 3000 demanded by the linesmen, only ten families in Baba ka Gaon have electricity connections. Hence, though the village and the adjoining fields sport electric poles and wires the village is still not electrified.

Eight of the houses with electricity also have black-and-white televisions. Three of the *Thakurs* and one Brahmin have televisions; the rest belong to middle-caste families. The two tractors and single jeep in the village belong to the *Thakurs*. So do three of the four tube-wells for irrigation; the fourth belongs to a middle-caste family.

If Baba ka Gaon has changed substantially in the past half-century, the area and towns surrounding it have been transformed. *The roads to the towns were earthen. They had holes in them, and water would collect after even a small rainfall. If it rained hard the roads would be unusable. There were no cars. There has been a government bus line since the 1950s. As the road became better there were more buses. The proper road – levelled with small stones but not tarred – didn't come this side of the river. So we would walk to Gushannath, cross the Sai river by boat, and then catch the bus to Pratapgarh. It would take over three hours, but even today it takes nearly as long because the buses keep stopping for passengers! The tarmac road has been 20 years in some places, 10 in others. Now even the villages are being linked by road!*

In the past, wealthy landlords would use horses, palanquins or bullock-drawn carriages. The poor would walk or go on crude bullock-carts. The 20-km journey to Amethi, a nearby market-town and the seat of the landlord's estate in which Ram Dass's father was born, would take over two hours on foot, slightly more by bullock-cart. The pony-carts of today didn't ply then because the rutted dirt road could be managed only by bullocks.

Today, the bicycles and bullock- and pony-carts mingle with the rare government and private bus, the occasional jeep-taxi, and sometimes with tractor-drawn buggies. Most of the roads are cratered with deep potholes.

*Pratapgarh used to look like what Gauriganj is today. In Ateha, there was only one brick house – that of Noor Khan – the one on the corner, which now has the post office. The rest of the houses were mud and thatch hovels, like those of us poor people.*

*Because there were so few people, the bazaars were also little. There were just a few mud huts and a small weekly bazaar. They just used to sell local produce, clothes, and utensils. What else was needed? At that time no one had money to buy cement or bricks to make houses; it's not like today where everything is available.*

Pratapgarh, the district capital and formerly the seat of a large *zamindari* estate, some 50 km away, is now a typical north Indian town: dirty, congested with all manner of traffic, lacking the most basic municipal services. Any charm that it might once have possessed is now obliterated. There are innumerable shops, catering to almost any modern demand, be it photocopies, car repairs or video movies. Outside the town is the grand mansion of the Pratapgarh rajas, surrounded by mango orchards. Pratapgarh's population today is about 30,000.

Gauriganj, the jumped-up village that Ram Dass compares to Pratapgarh of half a century ago, is in neighbouring Sultanpur district, but only 20 km away from Baba ka Gaon, making it the closest large market. Gauriganj is still little more than a village today, boasting just one long road of shops and another shorter one with a hawker's market. There is a tiny railway station. The open sewers are choked with excreta and plastic bags. People defecate and urinate wherever privacy permits, the men most often along any convenient wall. A single fall of rain turns the roadsides and open markets into a quagmire of filth.

Ateha is the closest large village to Baba ka Gaon, about 5 km away. It is built at the junction of several roads. Centuries ago, Ateha was reputed to have been a fortified town, but there is nothing to show this today. There are some fine large houses, and an attractive mosque as well because of the large number of Muslims living here. The roads are potholed and cut by streams of blue-green sewage.

*Amethi was better than Gauriganj. People there looked richer. The traders were more reputed for their wealth. But even so, there was nothing in Amethi then; now it is a big town. It was totally barren and now look at all the shops.* Amethi, some 20 km from Baba ka Gaon, became a household name across India when it became the pocket borough of former prime minister Rajiv Gandhi. The town itself is no different to Pratapgarh – just smaller and, if possible, even messier and more choked with bullock-carts, tractors, jeeps and innumerable people. Its growth has been rapid because of the influx of government funds for the district. The handful of older buildings – including a mosque, a college and a few large homes belonging to traders – have been far outstripped by scores of new brick buildings, weakly built but two storeys high, that have gone up in every direction, seemingly without licence or planning. One positive legacy of its years as the constituency of a prime minister is the grand railway station.

Why did I choose Ram Dass and his family out of the many million impoverished families in India? And why Baba ka Gaon, Pratapgarh district or UP province?

India's size and social diversity mean that no one region, province or district can be typical. As I was picking just one area, I took pains to ensure that this area would not be unusually rich or poor, but would approximate the average. An obvious candidate was UP. With its current population of roughly 150 million, the province is home to about one-sixth of India's people. The northern, Hindi-speaking belt of which UP is the major constituent also contains the largest aggregation of the poor within India. In addition, for several decades the proportion of the absolutely poor in UP has been close to the national average. Within UP, I chose Pratapgarh because it is a fairly average district, neither unusually prosperous like the province's western districts nor as poor as the southernmost districts that border Bihar.

Apart from being quite representative of India's development experience, both UP and the area around Baba ka Gaon have been at the epicentre of modern India's emergence. From the early years of this century, the Indian National Congress flourished in the United Provinces of Agra and Awadh, as UP was then known, and the province became the core of the nationalist struggle. Mahatma Gandhi first enunciated his programme of non-violent aggression to achieve independence in Allahabad in 1920, 75 km from Baba ka Gaon. Allahabad was the birthplace of Jawaharlal Nehru. The demand for a separate homeland for Muslims, culminating in the creation of Pakistan, was led by UP's Muslims. The province became even more crucial to national politics after Independence in 1947, as the introduction of universal suffrage gave populous UP one-sixth of the seats in Parliament. Seven of India's 12 prime ministers have come from UP, five of them – Nehru, Lal Bahadur Shastri, Indira Gandhi, Rajiv Gandhi and Vishwanath Pratap Singh – elected from constituencies within about 100 km of Baba ka Gaon. Rae Bareli and Amethi, the pocket boroughs of Indira, Rajiv and Sanjay Gandhi, border Baba ka Gaon. What better site than UP and Baba ka Gaon to come to grips with understanding why the Congress, Nehru and his political dynasty, and independent India's politics, have failed to emancipate India's poor?

Why choose Ram Dass and his family out of the half-billion or more impoverished Indians? Much as in my choice of province and district, I made every effort to ensure that the family I chose would be fairly representative of the Indian poor.

The vast majority of impoverished Indians are of low or lower-middle castes, along with indigenous tribes and Muslims of low status. Three-quarters of the Indian poor live in rural areas.[3] Most are artisans, landless agricultural labourers or farmers with plots too small or infertile to meet their families' subsistence needs. Generally, the less land they own the more vulnerable they are to labouring for others at exploitative wages or renting land on adverse terms. In urban areas, a large proportion of the poor are recent migrants from their villages, seeking relief from their poverty. On arriving they compete against each other and the growing number of resident poor for any kind of job: begging, pulling rickshaws and carts, working as porters, labouring at construction sites, quarries or road construction, cleaning toilets and sewers, or working as menial help at roadside eating places. Generally illiterate and without appropriate skills, their employment prospects are so bleak that the luckiest are those who end up as domestic servants or as manual workers in factories. The migrants are generally men, who leave behind their families in the village. Only the most desperate of families move entirely to urban areas, with every able adult and child taking up whatever work they can find. But whether single or in families, the migrants often find that because of high unemployment rates and low wages there is no relief from their poverty. Crowded into the hutments and slums that now dot every Indian town and city, or surviving on the pavements, they discover that living conditions in the urban areas are often as harsh as the deprivations of the villages they fled.

Ram Dass's family is in many ways 'typical' of this vast multitude. They live in a rural area. Like large numbers of the rural poor, his family until recently owned no land at all and survived primarily by working for wages as agricultural labourers. They are of an 'untouchable' caste, who have always comprised a large and disproportionate share of the Indian poor. For aeons there was not one literate person in Ram Dass's family. Members of his family have generation after generation fled to urban areas to seek work. Some now live there permanently.

Ram Dass's family is also representative of that small percentage of the poor who progressed in this half-century from intense deprivation to being above the threshold of absolute poverty. I focused on a relatively mobile family for two reasons. The less weighty reason was to avoid the accusations that would have followed – to the effect that I was exaggerating India's failures – had I chosen a family that was still direly impoverished. (Of course, such charges are entirely misplaced because extreme deprivation is the common fate of at least 40 per cent of India's population.) The more important reason was because the experience of Ram Dass's family testifies that even families that rise above the threshold of absolute poverty still remain trapped in want and oppression.

There were other compelling (and beguiling) reasons to choose Ram Dass's family. Ram Dass and Prayaga Devi, his wife, are amongst the few surviving poor people of their age in Baba ka Gaon or in the other villages I visited in the area. They are both still fit, with their memory and senses undiminished. Both lived through the last two decades of British colonial rule, witnessed Independence and a full half-century of India's sovereignty. They are amongst the few remaining witnesses of the history of the Indian poor in the past half-century.

Moreover, Ram Dass was one of the few poor people in the area who knew of the 1919 Awadh revolt and, even more important, that his family had participated in the revolt. (He was born half a decade after it.) Another unexpected bonus was that a branch of Ram Dass's family lives in Amethi, the pocket borough of former prime minister Rajiv Gandhi, presenting an opportunity to compare whether the decades of being a 'VIP' constituency had benefited the poor there in comparison to those in Pratapgarh.

Ram Dass, Prayaga Devi, their two sons and their eldest grandchild are the core of this memoir. Their vision of life, their view of independent India, and their life stories are portrayed here. Like the millions of other impoverished Indian families, they suffer hunger, disease, the death of young children, illiteracy and every other conceivable deprivation. As untouchables, they disproportionately experience the cruelty sanctioned by the Hindu caste system against low castes. Landless, they are exploited and abused by the landlords they are bonded to. The members of this family speak of these things, they convey what it means to be poor.

They also talk of their unremitting struggle for survival and for social and political emancipation: their efforts to save their children and to educate them, the fight to acquire some land, their inspiration by radical leaders of the untouchables. They speak of their achievements, of the gradual changes in Baba ka Gaon, and of why the vast majority of the village's people are still impoverished and oppressed. They assess the politics and policies of independent India: the Congress party, universal suffrage, land reform, local self-government and progress on alleviating poverty. They enunciate their criticisms of such national icons as Mahatma Gandhi and Jawaharlal Nehru and leaders like Indira Gandhi. They speak of their betrayed dream that India's independence would liberate them from poverty and subjugation.

This memoir is a record of their experience and understanding of these developments. It is also an insight into why, despite their own efforts and the coming of Independence and democracy, Ram Dass's and many millions of other Indian families are still impoverished and possess only a grudging measure of social and political freedom.

# 2

# The Slaves of Slaves

RAM Dass was born in the Pratapgarh village of Baba ka Gaon six or seven years after Nehru's visits to the district – in 1927 or so. He has only a hazy memory of his parents telling him about the revolt against the exploitative rule of the *taluqadars* and *zamindars*, the mighty landlords of the region. He knows that his parents and several other relatives participated in the two-year-long struggle but remembers little about their involvement. He does not know about Nehru's visits to Pratapgarh nor of how the landless and the poorer peasants were eventually betrayed by Nehru, Mahatma Gandhi and other leaders of the Indian National Congress. But Ram Dass's recollections of his childhood and youth testify to the oppression and misery that Nehru glimpsed in his brief weeks in Pratapgarh.

*The* zamindars *were the slaves of the British but we were the slaves of slaves. Because of this we were so poor. We had only our miserable earnings from our labour for the* zamindars. *We would slave all day long for them and then get to eat a handful of grain at night. Our* zamindars *were* Thakurs. *There were three* Thakur *families who controlled this village. They shared ownership of the entire village and its lands. They were rich and powerful people. They had about 800 acres of land between them.*

*Because of the* zamindari *system, we had no land at that time. Everything was in the control of the* zamindars. *Everyone used to work for them. Even the land on which we built our houses was theirs. The administration was theirs, the land was theirs, everything was theirs. The* zamindars *would never work. They had to do nothing at all. They would just sit and eat!*

*Each of the* zamindars *had groups of people dependent on them, and they would either give us land to plough as sharecroppers or give us work as field labourers. We were bonded by tradition. We were like slaves, we would only work for one family. They gave us loans and then made sure that we were never free of the debt. At that time we were giving the* zamindars *Rs 10 for renting a half-acre field for the year. My family could sometimes afford to rent an acre or so. What would we earn? Nothing! There was no irrigation and productivity was low. But the* zamindars *would pay just a quarter of a rupee in rent to their overlords – the* zamindars *of Rajapur and Rampur – on a half-acre, even though we paid Rs 10 to them. They would give us land on either a rent or a sharecropping basis. The terms were up to their whims. They would give it to you for a year or two and then they would take it back, saying that they wanted to cultivate it themselves. Sharecropping was half of the threshed grain – you didn't share the husks. But then the* zamindars *started demanding half the husks too. They could demand anything they wanted because they owned all the land. Today a fraction of what you produce is enough to pay the rent. Then more than half of what you cultivated was not enough.*

*It was only sometimes that my family could afford to rent land from the* zamindars. *But even then we would need to work as labourers for them as we were so poor and the rent so high. The rest of the time we would do their field labour and be paid for the days they gave us work. For a day of hard labour they would give us one or one-and-a-half kilograms of grain. You took that back to eat with your family. And that was just one-and-a-half kilos – which an adult man could eat by himself! We would have to think what to do with this little bit of food: should we feed ourselves or our families or pay our debts? So how much could a person save, what portion of this food could they forgo eating so that they could buy clothes?*

*The* zamindars *could do anything. They could beat us, thrash us, torture us! How could we have gone to the police? None of us poor people ever went to the police. If we had, the* Thakurs *would have told us to get out of the village and they would have just kept all our possessions. Anyway, the police also belonged to the* zamindars! *The* zamindars' *attitude was: 'Obey my orders or leave my village.' You had to do what they wanted you to do, and if you didn't, you had to run away. If we uttered a word, they would take off their shoes and beat us. If we didn't understand their orders properly, they would beat us. And that's how time passed, my ancestors', my parents', and mine. We had to finish working for them and only then could we do our own work. We had to finish their fields before we could work on the land we had rented from them. Sometimes when we rented land, we would have planted the crops, tended and harvested them, and then the* zamindars *would come and take away the harvest! Or they would put their horses and bullocks in our field to graze. They would harass us in every possible way. And we couldn't find refuge because they even owned the houses we lived in. If you can't find protection in your own home, then where can you go? And if they were passing by from a distance and you didn't get up from where you were squatting, they would shout to you to come to where they were and then they would thrash you.*

*There were some* zamindars *who were kind. Not everyone was bad. The kindness was only in the way they treated you, not in how much they paid you. If some* zamindar *oppressed you too much, the kind ones would try to stop that harassment. And the kinder ones would not exploit you as much with the* begar *and* hari [forced, unpaid labour and ploughing, respectively]. *Others would make you labour the whole day and not even give you food after that! Not just the* zamindars *but all the members of their family would harass us. If you spoke to one of the upper-caste children not only would the child hit you but one of his elders would come and hit you. 'Hai! Give the damned creature a few blows!' Some villagers who were harassed a lot would just run away at night to their relatives or to a city. They would leave stealthily, because the* zamindars *wanted us to labour for them and wouldn't let us go.*

*Whoever is powerful, it is normal to be afraid of them, especially those who have you at their mercy. We were scared that they would beat us up or hit us because we were poor and depended on them. How could the poor fight the* zamindars? *How could people who have nothing to eat fight?*

Ram Dass's family had been subjected to this poverty and oppression for as long as he and his parents could recall. Aeons ago the untouchables were thought to have been the original and privileged inhabitants of the Gangetic plain. But that past was legend. The real past, the one his family recalled, was of their being condemned to the base of an exploitative social order.

Describing Awadh of the 1920s, Nehru wrote:

> It was, and is, the land of the *taluqadars* – the 'Barons of Oudh' they call themselves – and the *zamindari* system at its worst flourished there . . . In the greater part of these *zamindari* areas [Bengal, Bihar and the United Provinces of Agra and Awadh] there were many kinds of tenancies – occupancy tenants, non-occupancy tenants, sub-tenancies, etc. . . . In Awadh, however, there were no occupancy tenants or even life tenants in 1920. There were only short-term tenants who were continually being ejected in favour of someone who was willing to pay a higher premium.

The Persian terms *zamindar* and *taluqadar* originally referred to a large range of intermediaries between the ruler and the cultivator who played a role in revenue collection. Under the British, however, they became synonymous with landlord. The terms were essentially interchangeable across India, though in Awadh *taluqadar* referred to the grander *zamindars*; *zamindar* is used here to cover both senses.

Awadh's agrarian system had by the 1900s reached an intensity of exploitation of the peasantry in great part because of comparatively recent developments, dating back to the late 1850s. The British East India Company annexed the kingdom of Awadh – the largest of the Mughal successor states, in area and population substantially greater than most European nations – in 1856. Shortly after deposing the kingdom's Nawab rulers, the British Crown (which in the meantime had claimed the Company's Indian possessions) settled absolute proprietary rights in land on the larger of the *zamindars*, who combined the role of local chief and hereditary revenue-collecting intermediary. This strategy of coopting dominant local chiefs as junior partners and collaborators in their rule had already served the British well in establishing a *Pax Britannica* in the areas that they had annexed over the preceding century. But, as in those areas, the vesting of land proprietary rights with the chiefs fissured Awadh's rural society.[1]

The disruption occurred because though the larger *zamindars* had during the waning years of the Nawabi often raised themselves to the position of *de facto* rulers of petty principalities, they were not landlords in the European sense of owning extensive landed estates.[2] Under the Mughals and in the successor kingdoms, there was little notion of private 'ownership' of land. In practice rights to land were shared between peasants, who enjoyed hereditary occupancy rights that often approached *de facto* ownership, and village *zamindars*, who typically raised revenue from the peasants in their village and had a limited power to alienate land. Land was seldom sold or purchased as a commodity, and so long as the peasant paid the taxes and dues levied on him, he could not be evicted by anyone and typically could even repossess land on paying arrears. It was only on a small proportion of the cultivated area – the 'home farms' – that the village *zamindars* had an untrammelled right of ownership. The larger, elite *zamindars* rarely owned home farms, deriving their wealth from a share of the land revenue.

But to the British, logic and custom demanded that there be a clear owner of land, that this owner pay the land revenue, and that the owner's rights on the land be extensive and permanent so that he could work the land profitably. Rural Awadh, like most other parts of village India, was remade in the image of the contemporary English countryside. The *zamindars'* right to collect revenue from a given area was elevated into the absolute proprietary right of landlord. Not only did ownership of the vast bulk of cultivated land shift to the *zamindars*, but their power and wealth multiplied as the British soon made them the owners of inhabited sites, fallow and barren land, groves and orchards, water sources, river crossings, markets and roads. These landlords became the linchpin of the colonial order in Awadh, prosperous and loyal allies of the British.

Awadh was soon a paradise for landlords, a trend common to most of India during the century-and-a-half of British Company and Crown rule. In Awadh, some 200 large estates emerged. These land barons, like the Rajas of Amethi, Kalakankar and Pratapgarh, whose estates lay close to Baba ka Gaon, controlled scores of villages and, in some cases, thousands of acres of cultivable land. Next in the size of their estates were several thousand middling landlords. These included the wealthy landlords of Rajapur and Rampur, kinsmen who shared ownership of Baba ka Gaon as well as independently owning several other villages.

Below the large estates were thousands of village landlords. Some, such as the *Thakurs* of Baba ka Gaon, were 'under-proprietors' of the larger landlords, who left it to the village worthies to extract labour and exorbitant rents from the peasantry. But even the latter group were in effect powerful landlords, as they generally had absolute control over the land they rented from the larger landlords, which they did most often at a low rate fixed in perpetuity. Thus, the *Thakurs* of Baba ka Gaon were in essence owners of about 850 acres of land which they leased from the Rajapur and Rampur landlords and then rented at vastly higher rates to tenants.

In this agrarian order, the landlords, great or small, elite or village, did not play a productive role in either cultivation or exchange. They took no part in agriculture beyond renting out their land or having it worked by labourers. But even if the landlords did not add a paisa to the agrarian economy, the British were unflinchingly committed to them: the landlords had become their trusted intermediaries in revenue collection, policing and administration. The British faith was stated eloquently by a senior British administrator – soon to become the Governor-General of the province – Harcourt Butler, who asserted, 'For political purposes the *Taluqadars* are Awadh. In times of peace, and still more in times of civil disorder, their voice will be the voice of Awadh.'[3]

In turn, Awadh's landlords, like chiefs and princes across India, did not fail the trust put in them. They curried favour with the British. They jockeyed to win ever grander titles: Rai Sahib, Raja, Maharaja. And in the decades before India gained independence, they proved time and again that they were the imperial government's most loyal defenders against both peasant revolt and nationalism.

But while Awadh's newly elevated landlords prospered, the conditions of the mass of Awadh's peasantry became increasingly wretched as an outcome of the colonial land settlement. The settling of ownership of land on a tiny elite exposed them to extraordinary exploitation, trapping them in the worsening spiral of impoverishment that was the common fate of the peasantry across India under British rule. Though pre-British Awadh was far from idyllic – agrarian society was inequitable and stratified by caste, the *zamindars* were oppressive, the land-revenue demand high, violence frequent, and the mass of low-caste people condemned to being bonded serfs – the bulk of historical evidence indicates that the condition of the peasantry worsened greatly under colonial rule. The crucial difference between the two periods was that in the pre-colonial agrarian system rights to land and its produce were far more dispersed, restraining the *zamindars'* depredations. In contrast, under the British the *zamindars* acquired near-absolute power. While during the semi-feudal system prevailing earlier, they had to rely on force and social hierarchy to wring revenues from the peasantry, they now enjoyed ownership of virtually every inch of arable land, the legal power to fix rents and to eject tenants, and the backing of colonial state power. These changes brought to an end the old feudal system, with all its evident failures and inequities. In its place – in Awadh and across India – a complex and ugly mix of feudalism and colonial capitalism emerged. In this strange new system the *zamindars* were empowered to rule as despots.

And rule despotically they did. Secure as landlords, backed by British might, and undeterred by the rare and obsequious British demurral, they multiplied their demands on tenants and labourers, raising rents and imposing numerous illegal dues. In Pratapgarh district, rents were raised by as much as 50 per cent between 1862 and 1892.[4] But the burden on the peasantry was in fact far larger because the landlords imposed, over and above rent, a range of ruinous new dues that soon probably outweighed the revenue demand. One such exaction, *nazrana*, a large tribute or bribe required of tenants when they wanted to take out or renew leases, was so common and crippling that it often amounted to twice the recorded rent. The burden on tenants and labourers did not end there, for there were other dues like *ghodawan, hathyana* and *motorana* – levied when a new horse, elephant or a motor-car was bought by the landlord – and also *petpiravan*, a gift to the landlord when his wife conceived. In one documented case, charges were levied on the peasantry for a boil on the landlady's leg! The forms of exploitation were so multitudinous that one British administrator noted ruefully, 'In fact the Indian landlord seems to consider that a resident of his village should pay for permission to do any conceivable action, even for eating, drinking, and sleeping.'[5]

And as these new demands came on top of customary but onerous duties like *begar* and *hari* and the requirement that a number of agricultural products be supplied for free or below market price, far from even making a subsistence living most petty tenants and sharecroppers could not gain a return on their labour, sinking further into debt to the landlord. The overwhelming majority of Awadh's cultivators were soon reduced to tenants-at-will or landless labourers, or were evicted from working the land.[6]

Describing the condition of the poor in Awadh at this time, a British administrator wrote that the tenants endured

> for the most part, a dim, slow moving and too often a poverty-stricken and hunger-bitten life . . . a narrow round of struggle between the rent collector and the village usurer . . . Following them at the bottom of the scale (though not quite) were the tenants-at-will, the 'will' in question not being, as a rule, so much their own as their landlord's. These were tenants whose rents could be raised each year barring no holds, and the landlord, if he so wished, could evict them from their holdings at pleasure . . . [At the very bottom] there was the serf-bond cultivator who worked for high-caste tenants usually being indebted for life. This debt may have been contracted generations back, it did not matter.[7]

A primary outcome of the bolstering of the *zamindars'* position under British rule was the strengthening of the upper-caste domination of UP society, as the vast majority of the *zamindars* were upper-caste Hindus (along with high-status Muslims). Conversely, families like Ram Dass's from the untouchable castes shared in the worsening impoverishment of the lower-caste petty peasants and labourers. Their destitution made them ever more vulnerable to the severe forms of discrimination sanctioned by the caste system against the untouchables, who were ostracized and treated as neither fully Hindu nor fully human.

Ram Dass recalls, *Religion here consisted only of discrimination and untouchability. Centuries ago, if* Harijans [literally God's People, a term popularized by Mahatma Gandhi in the 1930s] *like me overheard the Vedas, they would be punished by having molten lead poured into their ears. When I was a child, neither women nor* Harijans *had the right to read, to be educated. If our family got a letter we had to go and plead with the* Thakur *or Brahmin to read it for us. We had to wait until they were free. Or we would work extra hard and finish all their work and then beg them. Even then, they would read it if they felt like it or otherwise they would shout, 'Get out, go away!' The upper castes would treat us untouchables worse than dogs! They would at least accept water served by the middle castes, but from us they would not accept water, nor would they ever sit with us. If by mistake we touched any of their eating vessels they would throw them away, but if a dog licked the vessels they would just wash them!*

*They call us dirty but they are dirty inside, in their souls. The outside dirt can be washed with soap, but the dirt from inside cannot be washed. Earlier we could not enter the temples in the towns and cities, though we could go to the ones in the village. We could not touch the wells used by the upper castes, even if the few wells in our part of the village dried. I only got angry about the discrimination if I was harassed too much or beaten. If there is a caged animal, and you irritate it, it will obviously get angry.*

Though the poor and those considered inferior are mistreated and isolated in most societies, the Hindu caste system was unique in the intricacy of social stratification, in the intense strictures against those considered polluted, and in the enormous proportion of people – about one-fifth of the Hindu population – who were exiled from society.[8] Hindus across India, particularly those of the upper castes, ostracized the untouchables because of the belief that any form of contact with these permanently polluted people would infect them.

The stigma of untouchability fell on groups associated with 'unclean' occupations such as scavenging, butchery, fishing, tanning, and toddy-tapping; castes who were considered an offshoot of a caste with an unclean occupation; those who kept pigs or ate pork or beef, or those who drank alcohol. Ram Dass's caste, the Pasi – one of the four major untouchable castes of UP – was considered untouchable primarily because of its association with the tapping and consumption of toddy. But even though over the centuries many untouchable castes often gave up entirely the occupations they were associated with historically, the mark of untouchability was impossible to erase. Thus, from well before Ram Dass's birth not one of Baba ka Gaon's Pasis worked as toddy-tappers. Across the province, the Pasis had over the past century begun working as field labourers, petty tenants and guards for the landlords. This did not dilute the stigma of untouchability.

The contempt they were held in and their exclusion from society did not mean that the untouchables were not an integral part of the economy. They were indispensable. They performed the bulk of the hardest labour, undertook the menial services that caste Hindus considered unclean, and were powerless to demand adequate returns for their work. As cheap labour and the performers of defiling tasks, the untouchables were essential to maintaining the way of life of the upper castes.

Caste made India's feudalism – whether the feudalism of Mughal or Nawabi rule or the amalgam of feudalism and capitalism that emerged under the British – qualitatively different to feudalism the world over. The intricate rules of the caste system, particularly the hereditary division of labour and the ban on marriage between castes, preserved the agrarian status quo and foreclosed lower-caste mobility. In addition, the caste system sanctioned preferential treatment for the upper castes even in the purely economic sphere. Thus, in Awadh and in most parts of India, upper-caste tenants were charged lower rents, were given better land, and were not required to perform forced labour for the landlords.

Consequently, caste was a powerful determinant of prosperity and class. The relationship between caste and class was never so perfect that castes were economically homogeneous. Amongst the upper castes there was a spread in economic status, and their members could range from fabulously wealthy landlords to petty tenants, though even the poorest were never as impoverished as those from the lower castes. But there was little variation towards the lower end of the caste hierarchy, whose members were virtually without exception poor. And for the untouchables, the 'pollution', ostracism and illiteracy sanctioned by the caste system irrevocably destined them to destitution.

British agrarian policy and the mechanisms of the caste system reinforced each other so powerfully that at the time of Independence the distribution of wealth and political power in UP approximated closely the caste hierarchy of Vedic Hinduism, which had blossomed centuries ago in this north Indian Aryan heartland. In orthodox Hinduism, the Brahmin, *Kshatriya* and *Vaishya* castes were the elite of society, signified by their ritual status as 'twice-born' castes. The *Shudra* castes were considered distinctly lower than the twice-born groups, and though they suffered ritual debasement, unlike the untouchables they were considered to be 'clean' and 'touchable'. (They are now commonly referred to as middle or intermediate castes.) The untouchable castes simply did not figure in the orthodox caste scheme and so were literally 'outcastes'.

The congruence between high-caste status and wealth was so great that about 90 per cent of the province's land was owned by upper-caste Hindus and high-status Muslims, though together they comprised just over one-third of the province's population.[9] In contrast, the middle castes were 42 per cent of the population but owned only 8 per cent of the land. And though the untouchable castes comprised about 23 per cent of the population – more than all the upper castes together – they owned just 0.9 per cent of the land.

## The Awadh Revolt

By the early years of the 20th century, Baba ka Gaon and the region surrounding it was a sea of poverty, broken by outcrops of prosperity and a few islands of immense wealth. Baba ka Gaon's population was less than two hundred. There were 40 or so homes. About half were miserable hovels, situated at a distance from the village. These were the homes of the untouchables, including Ram Dass's family. Most of the untouchables were bonded serfs of the village landlords.

In the village proper were another 15 poor huts, virtually all of middle-caste families. The majority were only slightly better than the hovels of the untouchable area. These were the homes of the landlords' pettiest tenants, though some were labourers. Although many of these families were impoverished, almost none were as destitute as the untouchables. About half a dozen of the huts were more solidly built, containing several rooms and small courtyards. These belonged to the best-off among the tenants, including two upper-caste Brahmin families.

The only signs of real prosperity in Baba ka Gaon were the homes of the three *Thakur* landlords. Each of the landlords controlled several hundred acres of land, which they rented out or had worked by labourers like Ram Dass's family. Like all other homes in Baba ka Gaon at that time, theirs were also built of mud and thatch, but were substantial and many-roomed, with carved wooden doors and windows: luxurious mansions in contrast to the huts of the other villagers. The landlords were well-dressed, had stores of grains, savings and jewellery, and were not affected by the famines that swept the area.

There was even greater prosperity close at hand, in the large brick mansions of the Rajapur and Rampur landlords, who shared control over Baba ka Gaon as well as independently owning about a dozen villages each. To the labourers and tenants of Baba ka Gaon, in awe and terror of the village *Thakurs*, the overlords were so mighty and distant as to seem unreal.

But even their mansions paled in comparison to the palace of the Amethi landlord, who controlled the extensive neighbouring estate, in which Ram Dass's father was born. This prosperous landlord, who boasted the title of Raja, lived in a fortified palace, sprawling over several acres of land, surrounded on two sides by thick jungle. The fort's carved gates were high enough to allow the landlord's elephants to pass. Inside were several palatial buildings, garnished with a largesse of spires and turrets. Outside the gates was a large barred cage to hold captive animals. The region was dotted with a handful of similarly luxurious mansions and palaces.

The peasant revolt that swept Awadh from 1919 to 1922 emerged from this background of poverty and inequity, much like the numerous other rebellions that broke out across India from the mid-19th century onwards.[10] Tenants and labourers united against the landlords, their agents, and the British colonial administration.

The beginnings of revolt were apparent by the end of 1919, first in Pratapgarh and then in the three adjoining districts of Rae Bareli, Sultanpur and Faizabad.[11] Independent *kisan sabhas* – peasants' associations – were organized by local leaders, which focused on the oppression by the landlords, particularly on the practices of *nazrana, bedakhli* and *begar* which to varying degrees affected tenants of all levels as well as labourers. Though large tenants were active in the early stages of the revolt, trying to secure occupancy rights and curbs on rent enhancement, tenants-at-will and labourers were the main actors in the revolt's later, violent phase, when they attacked the landlords' mansions and farms, and, in some areas, even property belonging to large tenants. As they composed the overwhelming majority of tenants-at-will and labourers, the lower-middle castes and untouchables (particularly the Pasi caste, to which Ram Dass belongs) were most prominent in this later phase.

The revolt was strengthened by the emergence of charismatic local leaders. Though most belonged to the region, there is virtually no record today of their names or of what eventually happened to them. The most influential of the leaders of whom there is some record was not a native of the area, but had lived there for decades: Baba Ramachandra, a Maharashtrian, was for a while an indentured labourer in Fiji and then became a wandering ascetic in Pratapgarh. Under Baba Ramachandra's leadership, the movement rapidly acquired a mass following – its popularity was such that some 100,000 peasants reportedly joined the association within weeks of its initiation.

Led by Baba Ramachandra, the peasants sought the support of the Indian National Congress, which was then essentially an urban-based, upper-class nationalist party, drawing most of its members from the intelligentsia, the professions and industry. The movement's influence and fame escalated when Nehru, the Congress' most promising young firebrand, and a number of UP Congress workers tendered their support in mid-1920. Together with Nehru and UP Congress leaders, Baba Ramachandra established the Awadh *Kisan Sabha*, which within a month had 330 branches across Pratapgarh, Rae Bareli, Sultanpur and Faizabad districts. By the close of 1920, the movement was demonstrably powerful and militant: in September about 50,000 peasants surrounded the Pratapgarh jail to press for the release of Baba Ramachandra, who had been arrested on a trumped-up theft charge; in December, close to 100,000 peasants attended the first Awadh *Kisan* Congress in Ayodhya, in the neighbouring district of Faizabad.

In these initial 18 months or so of protest, the peasants used demonstrations and social boycott of the landlords to draw attention to their discontent. Landlords who were considered to be especially harsh were denied the services of the barber, the washerman and others who were essential to their comfort.

The peasants soon became increasingly radical. At the formation of each *Kisan Sabha*, members vowed that they would not permit 'beating or abuse from anyone', would require a receipt for rent paid, would 'not pay illegal cesses [taxes], (and) not work as labourers without payment', and 'shall not be afraid of constables. If they oppress (us) we shall stop (them). We shall submit to no one's oppression.' After they returned from the enormous *Kisan* Congress in Ayodhya in December 1920, many groups of peasants refused to accept eviction orders by the landlords or to till their home farms. Clashes occurred frequently in the next few months between the peasants and the landlords' agents. The increasing radicalism of the peasantry and of local leaders like Baba Ramachandra, who began openly to advocate attacks on landlords' property, also revealed that the movement was no longer under the command of Nehru and the UP Congress leaders, who were opposed to any attempt to arouse political consciousness along class divisions.

In January 1921, the hitherto peaceable revolt exploded spontaneously into violence. The violence was sparked by the police firing on huge crowds of unarmed peasants who had come to attend demonstrations at two market towns in Rae Bareli district. Though less than ten people were killed, dozens were wounded. Subsequently, violence spread across the entire area, with large groups of peasants, in some cases numbering 10,000, plundering markets, attacking landlords and their agents, battling with the police, and burning and looting the landlords' crops. Many of the larger landlords fled their estates to their town mansions in Lucknow and Allahabad. In some areas, the rebels briefly set up parallel governments. The turmoil occupied national headlines, especially when Nehru visited Rae Bareli and other badly affected areas. In March that year, Sir Harcourt Butler, the province's governor-general, warned, 'You have seen in three districts in southern Awadh the beginnings of something like revolution.'

But the revolution failed. At the moment of their greatest strength, the peasants were betrayed by Nehru and Mahatma Gandhi. On behalf of the Congress, they exhorted the peasants to abort their struggle. Because the Congress' disavowal of the revolt came immediately after the violence of January 1921, Gandhi and other Congress leaders sought to portray their decision as being impelled by Gandhi's famed allegiance to non-violence. But, in truth, the peasant-Congress alliance had effectively ruptured months earlier. The UP Congress close links to the large landlords and Gandhi's conservatism in economic matters turned the Congress against the peasants, particularly because the peasants were becoming increasingly radical.

Visiting UP a few weeks after the upsurge in violence, Gandhi, by far the Congress' most powerful leader, issued public instructions to the peasants and their leaders. The instructions were phrased in such a way that they seemed to call for non-violence. But they were in fact a demand that the peasants end their struggle altogether. Gandhi instructed the peasants to abjure even non-violent methods of resistance – such as practising 'non-cooperation' by travelling without tickets on trains and offering 'passive resistance' by lying on the railway tracks – and to end their social boycott of the landlords.

In contrast, not only did Gandhi's instructions not require sacrifices from the landlords, they in fact displayed great sympathy for them. 'We may not withhold taxes from the Government or rent from the landlord' (Instruction 4) . . . 'It should be borne in mind that we want to turn *zamindars* into friends' (Instruction 6). 'We should influence our friends by kindness' (Instruction 3). Gandhi lectured a peasant audience in Faizabad in February, 'You should bear a little if the *zamindar* torments you. We do not want to fight with the *zamindars*. *Zamindars* are also slaves and we do not want to trouble them.' He urged them 'to suffer rather than fight, for they had to join all forces for fighting against the most powerful *zamindar*, namely the Government'.

Nehru, despite his florid espousal of the revolt in his autobiography, written decades later, acquiesced to Gandhi's views. In fact, at that time he probably shared Gandhi's condemnation of the radical turn that the peasant movement had taken. Thus, Nehru confessed in his autobiography that at a meeting with peasants in Faizabad he ordered those who had indulged in violence to put up their hands, even though he knew that the police were present and would arrest them. More than 1,000 men went to jail; many died there; and many were still there years afterwards – 'boys and young men, spending their youth in prison', Nehru later wrote – to burden his conscience when he was himself imprisoned by the British.

With historical hindsight, the rift between the peasants and the Congress was not surprising. The UP Congress, at that point dominated by the urban upper class and landed elite, had traditionally been allied to the province's large landlords. The peasant revolt forced the UP Congress' leaders to grapple for the first time with the dilemma that it could not build a mass base in the province if it continued to ally itself with the tiny and oppressive landed elite. Motilal Nehru, Jawaharlal's father and a Congress worthy at that time, revealed the ambivalence within the party: 'True it is that the Party stands for justice to the tenant but poor indeed would be the quality of that justice if it involves injustice to the landlord. The Party believes that it is only by serving the true interests of both that it can find a solid base for *Swarajya* and is pledged to stand by the one as firmly as the other in its hour of need.'[12] Though a decade-and-a-half later the UP Congress had turned against the grandest landlords – instead backing the smaller landlords and prosperous tenants, though not the mass of poor peasants and landless – in the early 1920s its leaders took the side of the landlords, great and small.

Gandhi's conservatism was another crucial factor in the decision to forsake the poorer peasants and labourers. So sympathetic did Gandhi seem towards the Awadh landlords that they passed a resolution in late 1921 supporting him and the Congress. Paradoxically, though in the decades ahead the uniquely charismatic Gandhi drew the mass of the peasantry across India into the nationalist movement, he always opposed the radical economic and social changes which were a precondition of measurably easing their poverty. Instead, as revealed in the Awadh revolt, Gandhi attempted to gloss over class tensions and to blunt radical agrarian demands, particularly land reform. He counselled mutual trust and understanding, but when forced to take sides sacrificed the interests of the poor, going so far as to destroy the *Kisan Sabha* movement in neighbouring Bihar province, which towards the end of the 1930s was gaining strength in its efforts to abolish the *zamindari* system and to help evicted tenants to reoccupy land. Gandhi's relationship with urban labourers was no different: he drew them into the nationalist movement but repudiated them whenever their demands threatened the Indian capitalists who were major financiers of the Congress.[13]

Consequently, the priorities of the poorer Awadh peasants and those of the Congress proved to be entirely incompatible. To the leaders of the Congress, the peasants' fiery revolt was a distraction from the Congress agenda of planned, mass civil-disobedience campaigns. Worse, the revolt had revealed itself to be class war directed against the major supporters of the Congress. In contrast, the impoverished peasants and labourers of Awadh were searching primarily for relief from their impoverishment and oppression by the landlords. At a meeting in 1921, an angry peasant told Nehru, 'Give us food, we do not want *swaraj*.'[14]

But without the Congress' support, the peasant revolt was doomed, too localized and isolated to withstand the might of the British colonial administration. The police and army moved against the peasants. The most influential peasant leaders were arrested, including Baba Ramachandra in February 1921. The landlords singled out and retaliated against peasants and labourers who had been prominent in the revolt. Reports of abuses against the peasantry carried out by the police or directly by the landlords' agents no longer made it into the national newspapers, in large part because the draconian Seditious Meetings Act was clamped on the worst-affected districts. In about a year the revolt had been squashed.

The landlords returned, unsubdued, to their exploitative rule. Though some colonial administrators had during the revolt spoken eloquently of remedying the abuses that had fuelled it, they made only pusillanimous efforts to do so in the following 25 years for which colonial rule lasted. The UP Congress was by 1936 publicly advocating the abolition of *zamindari*, but the alternatives it proposed would benefit the smaller landlords and the substantial tenants, and not ease one whit the impoverishment and oppression of the mass of peasants and labourers. The upshot was that, for the poor, Awadh's agrarian structure remained unaltered in its essentials right up to the time of Independence. Families like Ram Dass's were condemned to many more decades of oppression and extreme poverty.

## The British legacy of poverty

At the time of Independence, land ownership in UP was so inequitable that of the province's total rural population of roughly 12 million families, about 80 per cent were poor tenants, sharecroppers and landless labourers.[15] Even those with access to some land – the average holding was less than two acres – needed to work as labourers. The untouchable castes and those on the lower end of the middle castes composed this impoverished mass.

Above this mass were about two million cultivating peasant families. A large share had holdings of more or less economic size, with about half working an average of 16 acres each. The majority held their fields as tenants, though a few had small portions on *zamindari* title. Most worked their land through their own family's labour, although the most privileged of them would hire labour at peak cultivation times. The poorest of the cultivating peasants would themselves labour for others. The vast majority were of the middle castes, with a small share from the upper castes.

In contrast to this enormous group of labourers and peasants was a tiny elite of landlords. Numbering no more than 50,000 or 60,000 families, they owned or controlled virtually all the private land in UP, whether fields, groves, forests, village sites or marketplaces. The concentration of land control was so extreme that the province's top 20,000 or so families owned 60 per cent of the province's land. This elite was almost entirely of the upper castes, with a sprinkling of families from the high cultivating castes.

The vast proportion of this elite were village landlords, who controlled land in just one or two villages. The village landlords leased out most of their land and also operated as money-lenders. Most had home farms, and typically closely directed the cultivation of this by labourers. Almost all lived in the villages in substantial residences.

At the very apex of this elite were no more than a couple of thousand families, the grand landlords. They owned estates comprising many villages, which in some cases included several thousand acres of cultivated land. The scale of their holdings was such that the 390 grandest families owned nearly a quarter of the province's land. The grand landlords' land was rented out either to village *zamindars* – their under-proprietors – or by their bureaucracy of agents and retainers to tenants and sharecroppers. In contrast to a century ago, they also owned vast home farms, which were cultivated by tenants or labourers. Most were absentee landlords living in their mansions in Allahabad, Varanasi, Lucknow or the nearest district headquarters, though they typically also maintained mansions or palaces on their estates.

Conditions in UP were typical of British India and the princely states. Over 80 per cent of India's 360 million people lived in rural areas. A small number of princes, land barons and village landlords owned virtually all the privately held land, and prospered from the high rents, illegal dues and free labour they extorted from their tenants and labourers. But over two-thirds of the rural population owned no land at all.

The extraordinary inequity in land ownership was by itself a guarantee of pervasive and acute poverty. But the magnitude of poverty in colonial India was amplified as a consequence of several other factors. Chief amongst these was that the revenues raised by the colonial government and the profits of British firms in India were not reinvested in India but siphoned off to British coffers.[16] This colossal drain left hardly any surplus for investment in either agriculture or modern industrial development.

Particularly devastating for the living conditions of the mass of India's population was the stagnation in agriculture. The stagnation was a result both of government indifference – barring the production of agricultural raw materials, such as jute, needed for British manufactures – and of the inequity in land ownership. In the half-century preceding Independence, food-grain output fell behind even the modest 0.67 per cent per year increase in population, worsening India's capacity to feed itself. Between 1911 and 1941, per person food-grain availability shrank by nearly one-third.[17] Chronic hunger and famine became hallmarks of Indian life.

Nor was there substantial growth in other sectors of the economy to compensate for the worsening conditions in agriculture. On the contrary, indigenous Indian industries, such as textiles, had by the mid-19th century been destroyed as a result of deliberate British policy, which favoured their own manufacturing industry. The devastating result was a sharp rise in the proportion of the population dependent on agriculture, which increased from just over half the population in the mid-19th century to nearly three-quarters in 1921.[18] And though enclaves of industry later came up in port cities like Bombay and Calcutta, India's industrial base was tiny at the time of Independence.

By the close of nearly two centuries of British rule, the overwhelming majority of India's population lived in conditions of extraordinary destitution. At least one-third of the population was impoverished or destitute, and an even larger proportion poor. Over 80 per cent were illiterate. Hunger, famine and disease killed millions. As a consequence, average life expectancy was about 30 years; those from destitute families like Ram Dass's rarely made it to this age. Over one-third of all children died before their fifth birthday.

Some share of this poverty certainly preceded rule by the East India Company and the Crown. But despite this qualification, measured by the welfare of the mass of India's population, British rule was a disaster. By the most charitable assessment, the British colonial government had perpetuated the impoverishment of India's population. Judged more rigorously, it had probably worsened their poverty. Independent India began with this legacy.

Recalling his family's destitution at about the time of Independence, Ram Dass says: *That was the time of poverty. Poverty had weighed all us landless people down. Only the* zamindars *were wealthy and the only other people who used to eat well were those tenants who could afford to rent a lot of land. For them it was happiness and ease. But for those of us who worked as field labourers or could only rent little land, it was very difficult. Sometimes we would get work; at other times we couldn't find work. That's how we lived our lives.*

*The* zamindars *would still pay us only 1 or 1.5 kg of grain for a long day of labour. And some of the grain would be mud and stones! Because we were paid so little our whole family would work for them, even the little children. Sometimes when we didn't have food, we would go and ask a neighbour and sometimes even they wouldn't give us because they had none themselves. Poverty and hunger go together. The* zamindars *used to give us little, little bits of fruit from their fruit trees in the summer when there was no grain to eat. For the month of April we would live on mahua* [the succulent flower of a local tree]. *And then for two months in the monsoons, we would eat only mangoes. The* zamindars *would give us just enough to live on, to survive. There used to be famine here, whenever the harvest failed. We would go to the* zamindars, *who would say, 'We will loan you something, but you must give us so much more. If we give you 2 kilos we will take 3 kilos back from you.' And we would say, 'Take 3 kilos, because we have to somehow survive today, we have no choice.'*

*All year round we wore thick, coarse cloth. We would have only one piece of cloth. We wore it until it disintegrated. The women would have one torn saree and sometimes another good one. And those of us men who had only one* dhoti, *half we would wrap around our waist and the other half we would put over our shoulder. Those who had money being sent by relatives working in the cities had more to wear. It all depended – some people had more clothes, others just had rags. One has to endure not having enough to wear. Just like there are people who eat three times every day, while others survive on one meal a day. We didn't get any clothes from the* zamindar *we were bonded to. But the kindest* zamindars *in the village would give away their used or torn clothes to their labourers. The* jajmani [a patron–client relationship between lower castes, who provided specialized goods and services, and their upper-caste patrons] *would only be with the washerman or barber, and the* zamindars *would give them clothes and some land or some share of the crops.*

*Some people wouldn't bathe for weeks. There was water, but poor people didn't have the time to bathe. And then some people didn't have the habit of bathing. And some people didn't have clothes that they could change into. In winter, those who could afford to do so would get a piece of cloth stitched double and cover their shoulders with this. In both the winter and the monsoon you just had to manage, even though it was difficult in the cold and rain. And in the winter nights we would wrap rice stalks in old discarded clothes, and then hide under that. What did we know what a quilt was? We didn't even know what shoes were! Only at the time of marriage the bridegroom might have got a pair of shoes, which at his death would be given away to the barber or some other person. This pair of shoes would have to last from your wedding until your death.*

# 3

# Bombay I: 1949–1952

*AT the time of Independence we had lots of desires: that the* zamindari *system would end; that once our slavery ended we would be able to earn our living somehow. At that time we could not even talk. There was so much domination at that time that if we didn't get up from our* charpai *in respect even if we saw a* Thakur *from a long distance, they would come and beat us up.*

But the excitement of Independence and the traumas of Partition died down and there were still no changes in Baba ka Gaon – no revolutions, no emancipation for the impoverished, no attack on the landlords' power. Things were as they had always been. It was as if the British had never left, and the radical Nehru never become the new nation's prime minister. Ram Dass's family heard that in faraway Delhi and Lucknow the Congress leaders still planned to rid the land of the landlords, as they had promised the peasants during the struggle for India's freedom. But in Baba ka Gaon the landlords were as despotic as ever.

About a year-and-a-half after Independence, Ram Dass joined the ranks of impoverished people from Baba ka Gaon who left the village in the search for their own and their family's survival. He was about twenty-two. He left behind his wife and his first son, Shrinath, who was just 3 months old. They stayed with Ram Dass's parents. His father had returned to the village a year earlier from working in Bombay and Karachi.

*How could I live my life earning just this little bit from being a labourer for the* zamindars? *Here I used to get 1.5 kilos of grain as wages for a full day's work. So I decided to leave the village and find work in the cities. I went to Bombay, where my father had worked. I got much more money there, and so my family here used to live on that money. This was the only way to ensure that my family survived. I had no other choice.*

*And I had to pay off my father's debts to the* zamindars. *This consumed my entire wages for nearly three years. I was able to pay it from Bombay but I wouldn't have succeeded in paying it off if I had remained in the village. I kept sending more and more money because some of the* zamindars *would cheat and would say that we still hadn't paid off the debt. The accounting of the debt was entirely in their hands and they just told you how much you owed them. But luckily I had the postal receipts for the money I had sent from Bombay and finally they had to accept this. Whenever these people have a chance they would slit the throats of the poor!*

On an April morning in 1949, Ram Dass walked to Gauriganj alone, an hour-long trek across fields glowing with mustard and ripe wheat. The coal-powered train came at about midday, taking him to Allahabad. After a short wait in Allahabad, he caught another train to Bombay. The journey from Allahabad to Bombay – a distance of over 1,800 km – took more than two days and cost Rs 15, an enormous sum at that time, well over a month's wages in the village.

*I had only Rs 5 with me. I wasn't carrying any luggage. Just something to eat for the journey and the* kurta-dhoti *I was wearing. I was carrying things that people from the village had sent to their relatives in Bombay. There were a lot of people from the village working in Bombay. This was the first time I had left the region, and I enjoyed it.*

Bombay's population was less than three million in the year that Ram Dass arrived there. He disembarked at the then suburban Dadar station in the morning, entering a strange world of whistling and chugging trains and of hundreds of oddly dressed people rushing across innumerable platforms.

*I didn't feel any fear. I had no problem. At home they had given me the number of my uncle's tenement and the name of the area he lived in. It was in Bandra, number 63* chawl *and room 74. So I caught a train to Lower Parel, then kept walking and crossed the bridge. There I asked a shopkeeper the way to this* chawl, *who said go straight and then turn right.*

Ram Dass was one of hundreds of thousands of migrants seeking work in Bombay. For decades before Ram Dass made this journey, the poorest people of Awadh, like others across India, had been fleeing their acute poverty, particularly when famine or epidemic threatened to snap their always tenuous existence. They sought survival first as labourers in British colonies across the globe, and then within India, as employment picked up in activities like road and railroad building and the tea plantations. Many went to Bombay, as the port city had become a centre of trade and industry. Most of the migrants were men. Most, like Ram Dass, had never been further than their own or the neighbouring district.

*Poorer people from the village have been going for a long time to the cities to work as labourers – just the way they go out now. Now you don't find jobs easily. It was easier when I went to Bombay. Then people in the cities almost used to force you to work for them. Now they ask too many questions before giving you a job.*

*The* Thakurs *and Brahmins didn't leave the village. They had lots of wealth. The people who left were us naked, starving ones, who must earn daily to be able to eat, whether we labour here or in the city.*

*The middle-caste people could leave easily because most of them worked for themselves, but we scheduled castes were landless labour tied to the* zamindars *and had to go stealthily.*

Around the first decades of this century, Ram Dass's father and uncles emigrated to find work in Bombay and Karachi – the latter now in Pakistan – and several other cities. After many years of work in Bombay, Ram Dass's father finally quit the city in 1942 or 1943, sacked from his foreman's post at the Hirjee Mills because he had to take responsibility for a damaged mould.

*When we were children, we would send letters to him at the work address which was in Bombay 13. There was a box there and they would sort out the mail.* The letters would be written with the help of some upper-caste man in Baba ka Gaon. In Bombay, Ram Dass's father would find someone to read the letter out to him, as he was illiterate.

On leaving Bombay, Ram Dass's father returned for a few years to Baba ka Gaon, but even though he and his entire family worked as labourers for the landlords they could not earn enough to survive on. He then went to Rori, now in Pakistan, where he worked as a gardener. The violence and massacres that erupted during Partition in 1947 forced him to flee back to Baba ka Gaon.

Ram Dass spent from 1949 to 1952 in Bombay. He returned then for the first time to Baba ka Gaon, where he spent just over a year before returning once again to Bombay for eight years. These years in Bombay were a period of great ferment in Ram Dass's life. Through hard work he was able slowly to pull his family from the depths of destitution, though they were still impoverished. And in this city that brought together people from across India, Ram Dass's innate reluctance to resign himself to his bitter lot of being destitute and untouchable was strengthened by movements that fought for the emancipation of the untouchables.

For the first six or eight months in Bombay, Ram Dass could not find any work. He says he would never have taken on certain types of labour that he found demeaning, such as pulling rickshaws or goods carts. During this period, he lived with another uncle of his – his father's cousin – who worked as a gangman with the Western Indian Railways and had two rooms in a railway *chawl* in the central Mahalaxmi area of the city. *When I didn't earn my uncle used to feed me.*

At this time, many of Ram Dass's close relatives were working in Bombay, and in this alien land it was this far-flung network that enabled him to find work. Through his uncle in the railways, Ram Dass found work for two weeks in November 1949 laying railway tracks in a rural part of Ahmedabad district, in what is now Gujarat province. The job had been contracted out to a private firm, which hired the labour, including a large number of scheduled-caste men from Baba ka Gaon who were living in Bombay. Ram Dass was paid about Rs 20 for these two weeks of backbreaking work: very low wages – the equivalent of Rs 300–350 today[1] – but many times what he would have earned in Baba ka Gaon. *We are hardworking people anyway. We work the plough in the fields, even during the monsoons when the soil becomes mud. So our work in the village is even harder than what we had to do on the railway track. So it was not a problem for us.*

A few months later Ram Dass found his first long-term job, in which he eventually worked for two years. The job was with a contractor to the Western Railways, which had been given responsibility to clear the ash from coal locomotives and to load fresh coal. Ram Dass was one of about 30 labourers employed by the contractor at the 'Bamy-yard', a railway yard some 20 km outside central Bombay.

*We used to clean the ash from the engine and load the fresh coal from the wagons. The ash from the engine was sold. We would be paid one rupee each for unloading a wagon of coal. A wagon contained 20 to 22 tons. Six people would work together and would get five or six wagons done in a day. So our salary was about Rs 6 every day, but in the village at that time we would only have been paid one-quarter of a rupee!*

*Sometimes we would work all 24 hours. At peak periods, we would get just two to four hours rest every day, the rest of the time we would work. We would even unload at night. The contractor would sit there and watch and tell us to work hard because otherwise he would have to pay demurrage. We would unload the coal as soon as the wagons arrived. So we would get to sleep only a few hours, but on other days we would have very little work. The contractor was a Parsi trader. His accountant was an old Brahmin man. The minute we finished our work the accountant would shout at us to come and take our money. He was very good about this. We would say, 'We will bathe and come back,' but he would say, 'No, come now, don't you all go in different directions, come now and take the money but don't dirty the notes.'*

*The labour was all from UP. We were all scheduled-caste apart from a few backward-caste people. When working, we would look like black ghosts! We would have to scrub ourselves with soap. We would work barefoot. And just wearing an old torn* lungi *and vest. When we were unloading coke it was so hard we would get hurt and we would bleed. But one has to do these things to live. We were ready to do any hard labour. When your family is hungry you don't worry about the blood you shed.*

*When we unloaded the ash, it would be burning hot and we would have to cool it by pouring water over it. We would wear wooden slippers. Slippers made of rubber would melt and none of us could afford leather. And we would wear a cloth around our hands and neck to make sure that the hot ash would not fall on us. One person would fill in the ash, another would pour it. We would work with shovels. There wasn't too much danger with this work because the fire had been doused earlier.*

*If we just cleared the ash from the engines we would earn about Rs 60 per month, which wasn't enough. So all of us would work on unloading and loading the coal from the wagons for which we would get one rupee per wagon. And if I had some free time, I would go to work on separating the ash – the finer sections were separated from the bigger pieces and bits of coal by a sieve and these would be bought by different buyers. And for this work, which wouldn't take more than an hour, I would get Rs 5, much more than we were paid for unloading the coal. Even if we were eating we would stop and run to do this work because it was so well-paid. But you only got this work rarely.*

From his years of working at the yard and because several of his relatives have worked with the railways, Ram Dass knows intricate details of how trains switch tracks; how long it takes to stoke a coal engine; that there was a 'sick line' for engines that didn't work; the duties of railway employees and their work schedules; how wagons were detached and shunted; railway contracts and tenders; and the functioning of the various stations in Bombay, particularly which type of trains – goods or passenger – would stop where. Ram Dass says that railway staff are given housing because they must report immediately for duty whenever needed. *In the railways you can rest as much as you like but when you are on duty you have to work non-stop and for as long as necessary.*

In the early 1950s, when Ram Dass worked at the railway yard, it was little more than a mess of tracks criss-crossing a swampy, smelly tract that doubled as a garbage dump and a site for small tanneries. *It used to be so smelly, because of the tanneries, that you had to cover your nose when you came here. There were no shops. Nor did the road come as far as Bamy-yard. There was nothing else here but the railway quarters.*

Today, though the yard still functions, it has been engulfed in Bombay's pell-mell expansion. No longer is this a distant suburban area: it now lies at the heart of Bombay's industrial girdle. Surrounding the yard, and inexorably encroaching on railway land, is yet another of the city's horrific, disorganized slums, indistinguishable from other such poor neighbourhoods that spread thickly across Greater Bombay.

Diesel and electric engines move back and forth across the yard, occasionally towing carriages. The number of tracks has multiplied. The yard is enclosed behind high walls. But there is no dark mountain of coal waiting to be loaded, no labourers grimy with sweat and coal dust, and in place of the steamy whistle of the coal engine there is the brassy hoot of the electric locomotive.

On the pedestrian walkway that spans the yard are hawkers selling fruit, plastic bottles, mirrors, key-chains, food, handkerchiefs. Most have a space no larger than a shawl in which they display their wares. There are beggars everywhere. One old man, reduced to skin and bones and torn clothes, helplessly urinates where he is sprawled on his side, the liquid enveloping his lower body. Refuse spills down the steps of the walkway.

In the surrounding slums, grimy two- and three-storey buildings stand pressed against one another, their corrugated tin and tile roofs forming a bleak sea. Innumerable little shops offer food, cheap furniture, bricks, motor repairs. Tinny film music blares somewhere. There are no pavements. People wash their clothes at broken hand-pumps on the side of the road. On the road's edges are piled deep clumps of compost-like garbage, studded with plastic bags. Naked children defecate on the roadside, walking barefoot through the garbage and human excreta.

On the main road, which is a congested, diesel- and petrol-fume-choked highway to Ahmedabad city, garbage is piled high along the side of the large drains. The drains are about 15 feet wide, uncovered, with sewage a foot deep. The sewage is thick, dark, glutinous, filled with all kinds of rubbish: bloated plastic bags, dead animals, solid excreta, oil. Smaller drains feed the large ones. Adult men and women defecate in full view along the side of the drains, their embarrassment dulled by habit. They gaze blankly into the traffic.

Ram Dass says: *This poverty has always existed. People always lived in hovels. Now it's easier to beg because there are more rich people.*

*I had no particular pastimes in Bombay. I used to work, cook and eat. But when I had free time from work I used to go and walk around the city. I liked the atmosphere here in the city.*

Ram Dass's favourite place to visit in Bombay was the Prince of Wales Museum. He calls it *Kala Ghodha* – black horse – because this is the informal name given to the neighbourhood in downtown Bombay.

*I came to the museum with a friend the first time. We caught a tram to get here. And my wife also came to see it. I have been here many times. I like the old things in the museum the most. The first time I came here I was so astounded by it that I spent half the day here. I prefer it to the zoo at Rani ki Bagh where all the animals are in a lunatic asylum or in a jail. The zoo is for the pleasure of humans only.*

At the museum, Ram Dass's most treasured room is one which displays ancient Indo-Greek statuary. They belong to the Gandhara kingdom, which from the first to third centuries AD stretched across contemporary Punjab into Pakistan and eastern Afghanistan. Most of these stone statues are of the Buddha and their smooth, naturalistic forms radiate piety.

*I would also often go with friends and walk from the Mumbadevi temple to the Madhavbagh temple. We would eat our morning meal first, and then go home in time for the next meal. We would sit and listen to the devotional songs and I would do my prayers from far away because it doesn't matter from what distance you pray to God.* This area of temples in central Bombay was Ram Dass's favourite walking place. At one end is the Mumbadevi temple, dedicated to the goddess after whom the city is named. The temple is small, colourful, and has the usual mess of Indian temples around it – milling crowds, beggars, flowers and sweets to buy and offer to the gods. *In Mumbadevi there used to be a small pond, where people used to bathe. But it used to get very dirty because of the flowers thrown into it. Then the government closed it down.* On the other end of the area is the Madhavbagh temple, which in sharp contrast to the Mumbadevi is clean and secluded in a huge courtyard off the road. The temple is dedicated to Krishna. In between the two temples is a large flower market, where Ram Dass would often go wandering.

*I would also go with friends to the zoo at Rani ki Bagh, and Chowpatty beach too. I liked all these places. With millions of nice buildings, with nice people inside them, one can only like these areas. Of course I felt something inside me looking at these houses. In Bombay, there were rich people and poor people, there were all kinds of people. The ones who were rich then are still rich now. But if my heart is at peace, there is no envy. Someone whose heart is restless or fickle will not be content even if they have hundreds of things.*

*My first visit to Bombay was for three years and three months. I then went back to the village. I used to think about my wife and parents and children and village a lot. But there was no option. There were debts to repay both here and in the village. When man gets caught in the trap of labour, he has to continue working.*

*When my relatives would go to the village I would send clothes with them. I would also send money with them or through money orders. I used to eat well because I ate at home, and so I wouldn't spend too much money.*

*I used to live most of the time in a shanty. But, depending on work, I would sometimes stay on at the Bamy-yard; there was a huge shack where 30–35 people could sleep. There were 10–15 charpais on this side and an equal number on that side. It was nice and shady. All us labourers would cook with the coal from the yard. There was a tap there to bathe. And if we needed hot water for bathing we would go to the train engine and ask them for it. Everyone knew us here because we worked every day.*

*There was not much need for bedding because it is never very cold in Bombay. In the winter, all you need to do is put a sheet on the ground and then put another sheet over you. We were poor people and just slept like this.*

*I and the other people would spend Rs 20 on food, Rs 10 for tea and incidentals, and then send Rs 30 or more home. And that was a lot of money because when I was younger – say ten years before I went to Bombay – if anyone borrowed Rs 20, people would worry how that debt would be repaid. And the zamindars would rent out a small field at Rs 10 a year!*

*My eldest child was 3 months old when I first left. He had come here with his mother in 1951 for six months or so. My wife and he travelled from the village with my uncle. They stayed at the railway tenement in Mahalaxmi. For that time I moved back to the railway tenement because there was no privacy here at the Bamy-yard. But after a few months I sent my wife back and moved back to the yard.*

*My wife would come for five or six months at a time. When she was here I could not save anything. And I had to save because I was supporting about eight people at home.*

# 4

# *Zamindari* Abolition: 'The vision of a new heaven and a new earth'

RAM Dass spent most of 1952 and the whole of 1953 in Baba ka Gaon, before once again returning to Bombay. In his first months in the village he witnessed the legal abolition of the *zamindari* system, under an act passed by the UP assembly a year earlier. *We always thought that* zamindari *would end with Independence. Most of us thought that the* zamindars *would leave with the British and go to England!*

*The movement to abolish* zamindari *started much before Independence. We poor people didn't know very much earlier, we didn't even go to the market very much, we stayed around the village, but around the 1940s we started to learn that* zamindari *was to be abolished by the Congress. We used to hear about this in public announcements and meetings. Local officials like the* patwari [in charge of village land records] *used to tell us that* zamindari *would be abolished.*

*I had come back to the village in 1952 from Bombay. This was the time when* zamindari *was finally abolished. In the market place of Pratapgarh town, the public cryer had beaten the drum and when there was silence he shouted, 'The system of* zamindari *has been ended . . .' I heard this because I was in the bazaar. Ten or twenty men from the village were there and we rushed back and spread the news, saying that the drum had been beaten and this announcement made. The Thakurs in the village were very upset, saying that their rule had been finished.*

The succeeding years were to reveal that the act that abolished *zamindari* was never intended to benefit the millions of petty tenant or landless families like Ram Dass's. Of UP's rural population of 50 million people, the poorest half to two-thirds were left as bereft of cultivable land as earlier.[1] The failure to redistribute land in their favour was tantamount to condemning them to continued poverty and to unceasing exploitation by the land-owning upper castes.[2] In rural India, land has always been the primary source of wealth, as well as of power and high social status. Ownership of some land would have given the poor food as well as an economic asset with which to advance themselves materially. By making them free of the landed upper castes, village society and politics would have become more equalitarian. And because small farms are worked more intensively than large farms, utilizing more labour for every unit produced, redistribution would have sharply boosted employment prospects for the poor. In short, had the millions of landless, low-caste families like Ram Dass's been made owners of even tiny fields during the abolition of *zamindari*, their future in independent India would have been radically different to what transpired.

The shape given to *zamindari* abolition was the outcome of a prolonged drama, riven with intrigue. The drama was also tinged with grand irony, for despite having perpetuated the poverty and oppression of 'this naked, hungry mass', Nehru and the Congress succeeded in claiming that they were its champions. For Ram Dass and for many others of the oppressed, it was progress enough that the Congress had formally and legally ended the hated *zamindari* system.

During negotiations with Congress leaders in 1946–47, which led soon after to India's emergence as an independent state, the British mediated the accession to the Indian union of the several hundred princely states because they had enjoyed a semblance of semi-independent rule under British paramountcy. Despite popular resentment against the princes for their profligacy and brutal efforts to squash nationalist demands – 'personal autocracies, devoid even of competence', was how Nehru had once described them – the new Indian government assured the potentates of kindly treatment and continued privileges.[3] The princes retained their palaces, much of the extraordinary wealth in their treasuries, exemption from income and wealth taxes, immunity from prosecution, and they and their descendants were guaranteed generous government pensions in perpetuity.

Unluckily for the grand landlords of UP (and elsewhere), they were not governed by treaties with the British Crown, even though some rivalled the more splendid princes in wealth and dominion, and the British government did not mediate on their behalf. The barons bemoaned the fickleness of even the best-served masters. The Maharajkumar of Vizianagaram, who had made his home in Varanasi, wrote in a newspaper column in 1946, 'The *Zamindars* were not a political force because they had backed the wrong horse and always pulled the Britishers' chestnuts out of the fire for them and they were not wanted by the Congress and now they were not wanted by the Britishers. In a nutshell, the *Zamindars'* goose had been cooked for all time.'[4]

The reversal in the landlords' fortunes began in the early 1930s, when the British colonial government, buffeted by nationalist demands, expanded suffrage for the provincial legislatures, giving the vote to those with property or substantial income. Even though this enfranchised only the wealthiest one-quarter or so of UP's adults – in rural areas this covered just large landlords to superior tenants – the political calculus turned against the larger landlords, who proved woefully incapable of meeting the challenges of a competitive political environment.

The British had gambled on the hope that the grand landlords, the few thousand barons who were their major allies and who had benefited so richly from their rule, could be shaped into a conservative pro-British party which would counter the Congress' nationalist threat. That hope died quickly. The grand landlords failed to organize themselves into an effective political force. They instead formed two parties, both of which were riven by petty disputes, such as the demand by the grandest lords that lesser magnates never be allowed to supersede them in the party hierarchy. And though it was evident by now to the British government and to the more realistic of the landlords that agrarian reform could no longer be delayed, as tenants comprised 80 per cent of the electorate, the landlord parties failed to formulate policies that would win tenant support.

The failure was rooted in the landlords' haughty disdain of the peasant, whether tenant or labourer. Sir Jagdish Prasad, a mighty sugar-baron and luminary in landlord party politics, enunciated the view of his peers, writing in the *Landholders' Journal* in 1935 that the villager 'is a willing tool in the hands of any self-seeking, intelligent man . . . His political life is blank. He is completely ignorant of his rights and privileges. Any man with a little knowledge or power can lord it over him.'[5]

In contrast, the expansion of suffrage pushed the UP Congress to tailoring its agrarian policies to the needs of the smaller landlords and superior tenants and, consequently, to breaking with the grand landlords, once their firmest allies. (In practice, the line between smaller landlords and superior tenants was often fuzzy; not only were there some privileged tenants who functioned as *zamindars*, like the *Thakurs* of Baba ka Gaon, but, in addition, many smaller landholders had only a small share of their holdings on *zamindari* title, renting the rest from larger *zamindars*).[6] The shift in policy did not come easily to the Congress, in UP and nationally, dominated as it was by conservatives hostile to any attack on the institution of private property.

In particular, the process of charting the Congress' agrarian policy sparked a bitter confrontation between Nehru and Gandhi – already divided by Nehru's insistence that the party's leadership address the prickly question, 'for the freedom of which class or classes in India are we specially striving?' – with Nehru openly criticizing Gandhi for his unflagging defence of the landlords.[7] Thus, of the Mahatma, the man whom he called 'an extraordinary paradox', Nehru wrote in about 1935:

> To my surprise I have discovered during the last year or so that Gandhiji approves of the *taluqadari* [*zamindari*] system as such and wants it to continue. He said in July 1934 at Kanpur 'that better relations between landlords and tenants could be brought about by a change of hearts on both sides . . . He was never in favour of abolition of the *taluqadari* or *zamindari* system . . . I shall be no party to dispossessing propertied classes of their private property without just cause. My objective is to reach your hearts and convert you [Gandhi was addressing a deputation of big landlords] so that you may hold all your private property in trust for your tenants and use it primarily for their welfare . . . But supposing that there is an attempt unjustly to deprive you of your property, you will find me fighting on your side.'[8]

Such views were by this time anathema to Nehru, who declared, 'The *taluqadars* and the big *zamindars*, barring a few notable exceptions, are physically and intellectually degenerate and have outlived their day; they will continue only so long as an external power like the British Government props them up.'[9] To Nehru, the 'semi-feudal' *zamindari* system hampered agricultural and industrial 'production and general progress'.

Nehru's views on agrarian policy prevailed within the Congress. This was so because even many conservatives realized reluctantly that the imperatives of electoral politics called for strategies to attract tenants, as they were the largest bloc of voters. Moreover, it was clear by now that Nehru, despite his inspiring socialist rhetoric, was not proposing a radical redistribution of rural property.[10] Rather, Nehru's agrarian programme was aimed at curbing the power of the tiny number of grand landlords and conversely, aiding the smaller landlords and superior tenants, who were numerous and had the vote. This electoral calculation was obvious when in 1936 he wrote:

> The word *zamindar* is rather deceptive, and one is apt to think that all *zamindars* are big landlords. . . In the United Provinces, so far as I can remember, there are [nearly two and a half million persons] classed as *zamindars*. Probably over ninety per cent of these are almost on the same level as the poorest tenants, and another nine per cent are only moderately well off. The biggish landowners are not more than five thousand in the whole province and of this number, about one-tenth might be considered the really big *zamindars* and *taluqadars* ... Both these poor landowners and the middle landlords, though often intellectually backward, are as a whole a fine body of men and women and, with proper education and training, can be made into excellent citizens.[11]

Nehru's distinction between the large landholders and the others had a profound impact on Congress agrarian policy and, just over a decade later, on the shape of *zamindari* abolition in UP. In effect, the distinction allowed the Congress to attack the few thousand large landholders and the *zamindari* system (whose egregious aspects these barons displayed in abundance) while backing the interests of the smaller landholders, who comprised a major share of the electorate.[12] *Zamindari* abolition in UP was to spare these 'excellent citizens', falsely described by Nehru as being as impoverished as 'the poorest tenants', when in fact they controlled anywhere from fifteen to several hundred acres each, the higher end including the *Thakurs* of Baba ka Gaon, and to diminish the power of only 'the really big *zamindars* and *taluqadars*'.

Thus, despite persisting divisions, by the mid-1930s the UP Congress' agrarian policy was geared to benefiting the province's superior tenants and smaller landlords. Tenants were promised lower rent, secure hereditary tenancy rights, an end to *nazrana* and eviction, and the staying of all suits filed by the landlords against them. These promises also attracted a significant number of smaller landlords who rented land from others. Others amongst the smaller landlords turned to the Congress because they lacked the land and capital resources needed to meet the British revenue demands, and were consequently discontented with the existing agrarian system – including *zamindari* – and colonial rule. The Congress' resounding victory in the 1937 UP elections testified that its agrarian policies had secured the loyalty of the upper tenantry and smaller landlords. The two landlord parties together won less than one-fifth of the seats won by the Congress.

But despite tailoring its agrarian policy to this privileged minority and ignoring the needs of the many millions of poor tenants – at-will, sharecroppers and labourers, who lacked the vote and hence any political say – the Congress succeeded in luring the latter into the nationalist effort because its bold electoral slogans proclaimed the party's intention to abolish *zamindari* and to give 'land to the tiller'. The province's Governor, Sir Harry Haig, marvelled at the alluring power of the Congress election campaign: 'Meetings and processions, slogans and flags, the exploitation of grievances, promises which held out the vision of a new heaven and a new earth, stirred the countryside into a ferment such as it had never before experienced.'[13] By the eve of Independence, the Congress manifesto committed itself to *zamindari* abolition, stating that 'the reform of the land system, which is so urgently needed in India, involves the removal of intermediaries between the peasant and the state. The rights of such intermediaries should therefore be acquired on the payment of equitable compensation.' Giddy with these visions, few among the poorer peasants or landless thought it fit to ask just how thorough *zamindari* abolition would be or who the Congress would classify as 'the tiller' when Independence was won.

## Independence and the Congress' betrayal of the poor

Having bitterly castigated the British for beggaring India and her masses, and generated popular support for the nationalist cause by this charge, the Congress was duty-bound, on India's independence, to address the issue of alleviating poverty. As a result, India's birth as an independent nation was to the accompaniment of innumerable promises of welfare for her impoverished masses. In a radio broadcast on the eve of Independence, Nehru promised to 'plan wisely so that the burden on the masses may grow less and their standards of living go up.'[14] The Indian Constitution committed the state to securing for all its citizens 'justice, social, economic and political' and 'equality of status and opportunity'.

The abolition of *zamindari* was a centrepiece of these socialistic visions. Hence, immediately after Independence, Congress leaders in Lucknow, in tandem with the central government in Delhi, began work on fashioning legislation to end *zamindari* in UP. The legislation had to be passed by the state assembly because land and agriculture had been placed under provincial jurisdiction in India's federal system. The legislation took half a decade to emerge, as it was the focus of fierce contests between the conservatives and leftist groups in the UP and national Congress. Nothing less momentous than the future shape of UP's agrarian order was at stake.

The act that became law in 1951 showed clearly that the conservatives had exercised their dominant hold on the Congress. Indeed, the provincial government seemed extraordinarily eager to assure the landlords that their wealth would not be damaged. The province's conservative chief minister, Govind Ballabh Pant, went so far as to announce that the act would affect only the 390 grandest 'zamindars who controlled long purses and wagged long tongues'.[15]

Judged even by forgiving standards, the UP Zamindari Abolition and Land Reforms Act was only mildly reformative. Though it did reduce the concentration of land ownership somewhat and curb the most egregious excesses of the existing agrarian system, it did nothing at all to reduce the poverty of the millions in UP who possessed little or no land. Specifically, the act ended the power of the landlords to collect land revenue. Revenue was in future to be paid directly to the government. Also abolished were their powers and privileges; they could no longer demand *begar* nor the host of other customary or illegal dues they had long extracted from tenants and labourers. The government took over village land, market sites and other public-use land that had earlier been owned by the landlords.

The landlords remained owners of their 'home farms' and groves. They were also generously compensated by the government for the loss of rent revenues. Title to the land not classified as 'home farms' devolved from the landlords to superior tenants, those who possessed occupancy or hereditary rights. Tenants who lacked established occupancy rights as well as sub-tenants – those who rented from the superior tenants – were, in principle, to be given secure tenancies and the option of buying the land at a multiple of the rent they paid.

Though these clauses added up to quite considerable change in landowning amongst the top one-third or so of the province's population, with ownership devolving to superior tenants, the oppressive inequities of UP's agrarian order remained virtually intact when viewed from the perspective of the poor. This was because the act did nothing to redistribute land ownership in favour of the many million sharecropper, tenant-at-will and labourer families with little or no land – a vast majority of the province's population – as had been urged by the leftist groups within the Congress. The UP government committee preparing the act rejected ceilings and redistribution as politically impracticable, instead ruling that 'no limit be placed on the maximum area held either by a landlord or by a tenant. Everybody now in cultivatory possession, will continue to hold his whole area.'[16]

Moreover, though the landlord system had been abolished purportedly to give land to 'the tiller of the soil', the act's definition of 'tiller' and 'cultivator' did not require them to perform any manual labour, or even to live in the village, as long as they provided either supervisory or financial inputs. A result of political pressure from the landlords, this indefensible definition was legislated on the grounds that the upper castes were prohibited from performing manual labour by their caste traditions. In practice, the definition ensured that land would not be redistributed to the poor as it allowed landlords to continue having their extensive properties worked by others. (Conveniently for them, the act allowed a form of sharecropping!) The actual tillers got no land. In contrast, the leftists in the Congress had urged that 'personal cultivation' require 'a minimum amount of physical labour and [participation] in actual agricultural operations', a definition under which ownership of land would have shifted to the poor peasants and labourers who were the actual cultivators.[17]

The absence of a ceiling and the generous definition of 'tiller' were boons to the landlords, great and small. And as they wielded enormous power at the local level, with the collusion of pliant or corrupt land record-keepers they ensured that the few clauses in the act that threatened their interests were gutted. They converted tenancy relationships to crop-sharing arrangements, engineered the falsification of land records, and put land in the names of their relatives. Moreover, abolition had been so long in coming that many landlords had evicted scores of tenants – largely the sub-tenants and sharecroppers, who lacked written tenancy records – and greatly expanded their 'home farms' and groves. In the decade preceding *zamindari* abolition, tenants were ejected from more than one million acres, which the landlords reclassified as their home farms. By 1951, almost one-fifth of the total cultivated land in UP was classified as home farms and remained with the landlords.[18] As the wealthier landlords controlled a disproportionate share of the home-farm land – typically the most productive fields – they were the primary beneficiaries of the clause granting this land to them.

Another bonanza for the landlords was the clause giving them ownership of groves and orchards, which was done, once again, on the hollow claim that they were the 'cultivators'. The profits from selling the variety of fruit and other products from the groves were enormous, while the area under groves was very large. At the time of *zamindari* abolition, nearly one-tenth of Pratapgarh district was under groves.[19] The wealthiest among the landlords again benefited disproportionately as they had the largest and most valuable tracts of grove. Forty kilometres from Baba ka Gaon, the Raja of Pratapgarh retained the famed Lakhpera grove, so named because the 80-acre tract was reputed to contain 100,000 fruit trees. Ownership of such a grove was a guarantee of tremendous wealth in perpetuity.

Almost as if all this largesse was not sufficient, the act established rehabilitation grants for landlords paying less than Rs 10,000 annually in land revenue, on the grounds that they were not rich and needed government support to survive. This was extravagant fiction, since only the 390 grandest landlords were barred from these grants as a result, while several thousand exceedingly rich landlords, with estates that sometimes spanned scores of villages, received government aid.

Much as Chief Minister Pant had promised, only a few hundred grand land barons were affected by *zamindari* abolition, with their great empires left in tatters. But barring those few hundred, the terms of *zamindari* abolition were generous to other large landowners and munificent for the top one-third of UP's rural population who already either owned or rented substantial amounts of land. Thus, some of the grand landlords retained as much as 2,000 acres in a region where the average holding available per household was three acres.[20] Most of the several thousand large landlords emerged from *zamindari* abolition in nearly as favourable a position as earlier, owning extensive high-quality fields and groves. The primary beneficiaries of *zamindari* abolition were patently the smaller *zamindars* and superior tenants, who had since the 1930s been the Congress' most faithful supporters. The tenants now emerged as landowners. And both they and the smaller *zamindars* gained materially by cheaply buying up land being disposed of by the larger landlords. Their position relative to the larger landlords improved markedly, in terms of both political power and wealth. In sum, the concentration of land ownership had weakened, but only to the degree that large tracts of land passed from the hands of the grand landlords to superior tenants and small landlords.

The *zamindari* abolition act did not significantly ameliorate the harsh inequities of UP's agrarian order. The passing of land to the smaller landlords and large tenants was of no help to the poorer tenants, sharecroppers and the landless, whose immediate oppressors were, by sheer numbers, most often these landlords and tenants. As a consequence, not only did the poor receive no land but their exploitation continued. The poorest half to two-thirds of UP's rural population – millions of sub-tenants, tenants-at-will, sharecroppers and labourers from the lower-middle and scheduled castes – remained as impoverished as they had been under colonial rule, or, in the case of those evicted from the patches they had rented, even worse off.

## Why did the Congress betray the poor?

The incontrovertible fact that the abolition of *zamindari* in UP did not further the welfare of the mass of the province's people was a signal that the Congress' commitment to social justice and welfare was far, far weaker than suggested by its leaders' fiery speeches and the inspiring text of India's Constitution. Why did the Congress' pre-Independence promises of *zamindari* abolition and 'land to the tiller' – igniting visions of 'a new heaven and a new earth' in the millions of poor peasants drawn to the nationalist cause – end up leaving UP's agrarian status quo only slightly altered?

To a great degree, the pro-property and anti-poor nature of the *zamindari* abolition act was not surprising. Though the pre-Independence Congress successfully united a huge diversity of groups for the nationalist cause, its leadership was dominated by the propertied: the smaller landlords and large tenants in rural areas, and professionals, business people and industrialists in urban areas. On the occasions when it ran provincial governments before Independence, the Congress revealed that its policies, too, were aimed at the interests of the propertied, who after all comprised the electorate.

However, despite retaining its core base of support amongst the propertied, the Congress developed a socialistic visage during the early 1930s, as a consequence of the party's development from a narrow, urban upper-class affair into a mass movement. But the Congress' socialist pledges, whether in slogans or manifestoes, were always vague and equivocal, exemplified in the promises to abolish *zamindari* and to give 'land to the tiller'. Of course, this vagueness reflected the fact that the heterogeneous and deeply-divided Congress had not reached a consensus on many crucial economic issues, with its leaders resorting to woolly rhetoric to mask class tensions. But, in practice, in the pre-Independence period, the ambiguity helped the Congress leadership to represent themselves as the guardians of the interests of both the propertied and the propertyless.[21] (The inclusive ideologies devised by Gandhi and other leaders also served the same purpose of diverting attention from class or caste tensions.) After Independence, the absence of clear policy commitments allowed the Congress enormous leeway to diverge from its avowed socialist goals.

In the event, even this hazy commitment to socialism was considerably diluted by the time the Congress began to rule in New Delhi.[22] In the lead-up to Independence, the mildly Marxist Nehru and the diverse leftist groups in the Congress were in battle against Vallabhai Patel (who later became the home minister) and the conservatives who dominated the party machinery, as well as the provincial leadership. By late 1947, though Nehru remained unchallengeably the most powerful national leader, the party was effectively controlled by the conservatives. The rout of the left within the Congress was so complete that the Congress Socialists and Communists were ejected from the party, the radical Directive Principles of State Policy reduced to mere declarations of intent in the Constitution, and the right to property included amongst the legally enforceable Fundamental Rights. And in a development that severely circumscribed the potential for land reform, the Congress conservatives allied with the rural propertied to ensure that provincial governments, where the power of landowners was greater than at the centre, would be primarily responsible for agricultural policies and agrarian reforms.[23] Moreover, faced with the challenges of ruling India, beset at that time by mass refugee movements, conflict with Pakistan, and the integration of the princely states, the Congress government chose to concentrate on the task of ensuring political stability rather than to risk further unrest by broaching redistribution.[24]

Although by now it was overwhelmingly dominated by the propertied and conservative sections of the party, the Congress pressed ahead with *zamindari* abolition. But *zamindari* abolition was no longer viewed as an opportunity for redistribution but as a means of consolidating the party's political power in the provinces.[25] Consequently, the *zamindari* abolition act was shaped so that it would not attack the institution of private property nor the existing distribution of land, which favoured the Congress leadership and its core supporters. Rather, by withdrawing the revenue-collecting and overlord rights that lay at the root of the landlords' political power, the Congress ensured that the larger landlords could not emerge as a political threat. The strategy reaped rich dividends. Even the most recalcitrant grand and large landlords were forced into recognizing that the Congress was now the dominant political force in UP and at the centre; within a decade many had joined the party as crucial vote-brokers, putting their wealth and connections at the service of the Congress.

Similarly, across India, princes and land barons who had opposed the nationalist movement and the Congress now decided to join the party. With this development, in New Delhi and in provincial capitals across India, the Congress became irreversibly the party of property and of domination, not of redistribution.

In sum, despite endowing independent India with 'socialist' aims, the post-Independence Congress pursued conservative policies. Apart from the mild land-reform effort represented by the abolishing of *zamindari*, which in no province materially aided the poor, the Congress did not contemplate any other redistributive measures. To the contrary, it adopted colonial laws inimical to the poor. Chief amongst these was the Land Acquisition Act, which in the decades to come allowed the government to oust tens of millions of farmers and tribals from their land, and then use this land for dams, large industrial projects, nature preserves and, not least, luxury housing for India's elite.[26]

Equally important, neither of the two major Nehruvian initiatives – economic planning and development of heavy, basic industry through the public sector – were in any sense redistributive or socialist, though their association with Soviet-style socialism gave them the stamp of being intrinsically progressive.[27] Rather, the approach to planning adopted at that time, and continued through the 1960s, was framed on the 'trickle-down' reasoning that the achievement of self-reliant growth would automatically eliminate poverty. Within this theoretical construct, redistributive measures were unnecessary and could even hamper growth. In addition, the state-led industrialization of India aided the capitalists and boosted their political power. Since then, the not inconsiderable benefits of public-sector-led growth and the expansion of Indian industry have flowed almost entirely to India's industrialists and the urban upper and middle classes, not to the poor, especially as few jobs were generated for them.

The first years of Nehru's nearly two decades of tenure as prime minister did see the Congress moving to blunt the most offensive features of colonial India, notably the overweening power of the princes and the grand landlords in rural life, and that of British companies in industry. But these changes proved to be the sum total of the Congress' potential for transforming the economic and social order. The one clear opportunity available to Nehru and the Congress to ameliorate the poverty of India's masses – when the great landed elites were in disarray, private industry and commerce still puny, and the Congress in command of enormous public support – had passed, unexploited. The tragic legacy of this great failure was the perpetuation of India's mass poverty.[28]

But though Nehru and the Congress had been the architects of a conservative, pro-propertied India, they continued with their socialist rhetoric. At the annual Congress session in 1955, the Congress adopted a resolution, drafted by Nehru, saying:

> In order to realise the object of Congress ... and to further the objectives stated in the Preamble and Directive Principles of State Policy of the Constitution of India, planning should take place with a view to the establishment of a socialistic pattern of society, where the principal means of production are under social ownership or control, production is progressively speeded up and there is equitable distribution of the national wealth.

Two of the dominant leitmotifs of independent India were now solidly in place: that the mass of poor would remain impoverished, and that the Congress would combine radical rhetoric with policies that benefited the propertied.

### *Zamindari* abolition unfolds in Baba ka Gaon

Ram Dass witnessed the formal abolition of *zamindari* in 1952, but it was while he was away in Bombay for another decade that the changes legislated by the abolition bill actually affected Baba ka Gaon. *People in the village told me that in 1954 the government officials first came and did a survey of the land and how much there was, whom it belonged to and who was renting it, and then they left. They came with some other people, who were not officials, and started measuring the land like people possessed! They were here for only a few days. They stayed at the village headman's house.*

The process of giving title to tenants who possessed stable occupancy tenure, called *maurusi* in Hindi, was completed in 1956 in Baba ka Gaon. The village *Thakurs* were not much affected by this process, as very little of their land had been given out under stable tenancy rights.

But they fought fiercely against the second phase, in which the sub-tenants or subordinate cultivators – known as *shikmi* – were to be given title, as most of their land was worked by tenants-at-will and sharecroppers. As the *Zamindari* Abolition Act recognized the claims of these sub-tenants, the *Thakurs* risked losing ownership of this land.

*The* shikmi *was in 1959. There was a lot of tension at this time. Either you agreed to leave your land, or if you decided to stay you had to fight against the* Thakurs. *Much of the land that was supposed to go to the tenants didn't go. We couldn't retain possession of the land. The* Yadavs *got the most land and the* Mauryas *somewhat less, but us* Pasis *the least. It so happened that the* Yadavs *were cultivating the* Thakurs' *land slightly far away from the village, but the* Mauryas *and* Pasis *were cultivating land close to here. The* Thakurs *managed to keep most of their land here, though they lost some to the richest* Mauryas, *but the* Yadavs *managed to wrest the land that was at a distance because the* Thakurs *went there very little.*

*Only those people who already had some land fought, as they had the means to live! Whoever didn't have the means to fight left the land and just depended on God. There were no physical fights in our villages, though it did happen in other villages. If you decided to fight, the nayap* [a clerk in the lower courts] *came with the papers. He would tell people that your case was filed and would be heard at this time. People were asked if they wanted to compromise, which could be done here and now; and if not they could fight it out. The nayap used to collect all the people from the village. He would explain to everyone, 'Don't fight unnecessarily, you will waste your money if you do, only people who know they are in the right should fight the case.'*

*No one from the scheduled castes fought against the* Thakurs. *We were too poor and too scared. And only two scheduled-caste people got land in these years. My maternal uncle was one of them. Two acres were put in his name. But he lost most of this land later because he was blind and the* Thakurs *cheated him.*

By the close of the 1950s, by which time all the changes driven by the *zamindari* abolition legislation had been implemented, the agrarian situation in Baba ka Gaon and its vicinity was not remarkably different from colonial days. For all the passion it had ignited in the poor, and the feverish worry engendered in the landlords, *zamindari* abolition had proved to be nothing close to a significant reordering of the agrarian order. The concentration of land ownership had weakened somewhat, but measured by the power of the upper castes or by the numbers of landless, little had changed.

The wealthiest and most influential families in the area were still the large and grand landlords, the rajas of Amethi, Pratapgarh and Kalakankar and, some levels below them, the landlords of Rajapur and Rampur, the overlords of Baba ka Gaon. Though shaken by the abolition of their privileges, the shrinking of their estates and the loss of steady revenues, they were still wealthy – some fabulously so – and still rulers of much of what they surveyed. Most still owned several hundred acres as home farms, huge areas of groves and, in some cases, many hundred acres more of land now held in the names of relatives, servants and even fictitious tenants. The compensation they received from the government they invested in boosting production and profits from their farms and groves. Adding to their income were profits they earned from the large amounts of land that they did not manage themselves, which they gave out on sharecropping arrangements, which were still legal, or from surreptitious tenancies. They made sure that neither sharecroppers nor their tenants could ever assert tenancy claims. Thus, ensconced in their mansions, palaces or city pleasure-homes, the capable among them were ideally placed to begin to multiply their wealth and to capture power in this new India. Those who saw their wealth slip away in the next decades could, in honesty, only blame their own profligacy; the terms of *zamindari* abolition had been too favourable to them to blame their ruin on the Congress.

The prosperous *Thakurs* of Baba ka Gaon were in a similarly enviable position, as the abolition of *zamindari* had led to only a slight broadening of land ownership in the village. They were now outright owners of much of the 850 acres of land on which they earlier paid a nominal rent to the Rajapur and Rampur overlords. The land they owned was the best in Baba ka Gaon. They had lost control over the village public lands, some land under occupancy tenants, and a small portion of the land they had earlier given out to sub-tenants and to sharecroppers. But not only had they been well compensated for these losses by the government, they had also succeeded in illegally putting in their names a large chunk of the village's waste and degraded lands. And as they had large crop surpluses to sell, they also benefited enormously from the low taxes on agriculture.

But though the *Thakurs* were well placed, they were no longer the only controllers of cultivable land in Baba ka Gaon. Some of the former tenants and sub-tenants (two Brahmins and others from the middle castes) now owned ample holdings, in some cases as much as ten acres. And two former sharecroppers – both, extraordinarily, scheduled caste – also owned fields of an acre or two. Another blow to the power of the *Thakurs* was that the home-sites in Baba ka Gaon no longer belonged to them but to the government.

Though *zamindari* abolition had made owners of some former tenants, it had hurt a much larger number of families in Baba ka Gaon: smaller rent-paying tenants and sharecroppers from the lower-middle and scheduled castes, many of whom had been evicted by the *Thakurs*. A large number were reduced to working solely as labourers on daily wages, because the *Thakurs* and other new landowners were now wary of leasing out their land. Even those who were allowed back as sharecroppers had no hope of ever claiming tenancy rights, as the landowners made sure never to let them cultivate the same field for more than a year or so.

Wage rates remained as low as ever because an even larger proportion of the village's families were now dependent on wage labour. While the *Thakurs*' ability to demand that tenants and labourers provide them with *begar* or *hari* and other dues weakened somewhat because they were no longer the only landowners in Baba ka Gaon, these abuses continued for several decades. The local police, all drawn from the upper castes, were not inclined to enforce laws that had been imposed in distant Lucknow.

Though his family's destitution and oppression did not diminish one whit as a result of *zamindari* abolition, Ram Dass says he was not disappointed. Just the legal ending of *zamindari* was sufficient for him: even if the former landlords remained the *de facto* lords of Baba ka Gaon, at least they were no longer the anointed, legal lords. India's Independence had brought, in form, if not in fact, what Ram Dass had long dreamt of. He was content with just this grudging measure. *Maybe we didn't get any land from the ending of* zamindari, *but at least we escaped from slavery!*

# 5

# Bombay II: 1954–1962

RAM Dass returned from Baba ka Gaon to Bombay in early 1954. He lived in the city for another eight years, returning permanently to the village in 1962. In his second stay in Bombay he was particularly lucky with employment, finding jobs that paid relatively well and were not as gruelling as his previous job unloading coal and ash at the railway yard.

*I had gone to Baba ka Gaon for nearly two years, and the day I came back from there I went to the Mumbadevi temple to pray to the Goddess. And then I went to some relatives in Kurla who were my bhai ka mamia sasur* [brother's wife's maternal uncle], *and he said I'm going for my daily duty but don't leave, stay here for dinner. But then he came running back in the afternoon saying they are hiring people. I ran there with him and got a job! This was a dyeing factory in Worli. This factory closed some months later, but then both he and I shifted to Kamal Dyeing.*

Kamal Dyeing was a small factory which dyed textiles on contract. Employing a dozen people, it occupied a building the size of a large home in Love Lane in Byculla. Byculla was then a quiet industrial suburb. Today, the suburb is prime downtown property. There is no longer any trace of the Kamal Dyeing factory. In its place is a featureless apartment block.

*I felt very happy from my first day at the factory because I had found good work. Naturally one would feel happy. I didn't feel strange as I was used to factories because some of my relatives in Bombay worked in them. As I was a village person I used to be fascinated by the machines.*

Ram Dass worked on a machine called a jigger, of which there were six at Kamal Dyeing. *There were two rolling-pins in the water, two in the middle and two on top. There was cloth on it. And the colour had been made fast with caustic soda. It was passed over four times and the cloth would get coloured. There was a supervisor who would check the cloth. If it was too light, it was run over once more; if too dark, they would wash it with soap.*

*The factory officers used to talk to me nicely. If you worked properly and spoke properly then they would of course be nice to you. I used to work harder than everybody else.*

In his seven years at Kamal Dyeing, Ram Dass's salary increased from Rs 80 per month to about Rs 135, depending on the number of days he worked. In today's currency, this would be equal to roughly Rs 1,100, rising to about Rs 1,700, still an average salary for unskilled factory workers. *The amount I spent varied from Rs 10 to Rs 50 out of my salary. I would send the rest home.*

*In one month in 1956, five of my close family died: my maternal grandfather and grandmother, my brother Ram Tehel, my maternal uncle, and the 3-year-old son who was younger than Shrinath. First my son died. I was here in Bombay. And so I went home to the village and then I saw that my uncle and others had died. We had no land at that time, we worked as labourers. There we laboured and here we laboured. All of them there – my wife, my mother and father, my sisters – they all worked.*

*Shrinath, my eldest child, used to study at that time but I saw that though he was in the third grade he hadn't learnt anything. I thought I must educate him properly. And I said to my wife, 'Get him out of school, I will educate him in Bombay; I don't care how.' My wife said, 'What about the goat and cow: who will look after them if our son is not here to do this work?' But I said, 'Sell them and I will support you from Bombay.'*

*Shrinath stayed for two or three years in Bombay. We stayed in the Mahalaxmi chawl and the people there were very loving with him, not allowing me to pay for his food. He would sleep in a small bed. He would go to school alone.*

*Jhoku, the only other child to survive, was born in 1959; Shrinath was then 10 years old and studying here. Jhoku came here in the year of his birth, when he was 10 months old. He was very active and started walking when he was very young. When we went walking in Mahalaxmi a Dhobi man* [Dhobi is the washerman caste, also scheduled caste] *had made friends with him and would give him tea. Everybody liked Jhoku because he was fair and clean.*

*None of our other children ever came to Bombay. Most died in infancy and the rest when they were 4 or 5 years old.*

For part of his second stay in Bombay, Ram Dass lived with his uncle in a small two-room quarter at the railway *chawl* in Mahalaxmi. Ram Dass shared the quarter with his uncle and two other male relatives, though most of the other quarters in the *chawl* housed many more people, usually 25 people to a two-roomed quarter.

The *chawl* is a long, three-storey building on a surprisingly quiet, shady street off the Saath Rastha roundabout in Mahalaxmi. Its rear virtually touches the railway tracks and the Mahalaxmi railway station. From the top floor where Ram Dass and his uncle lived they could peek into the adjoining racecourse and watch the horses thunder past, though for a better view they would climb on to the bridge nearer the course. The building is honeycombed with small rooms, each not much larger than a walk-in closet. The rooms are dark and damp, seemingly without windows; they emit a heavy entrapped odour of fungus and cooking oil. There are no furnishings beyond bare bulbs, *charpais* and clothes piled one on another on hooks. The *chawl* is not unclean by the standards of low-income housing in India. But it is bleak, its symmetry broken only by the corrugated shacks that the ground-floor residents have set up to expand their living quarters. Only on the ground floor is there the usual mess and movement of urban India: emaciated cats slink through the garbage and plastic bags, a solitary television blares in the recesses of a shack, and adults play with little children.

*When I lived with my uncle and relatives, whichever of us four would come back earliest would cook. We used to cook well. Not like* dhabas *where they just put some chillies and spices. I had never cooked in the village but I learnt from my male relatives here.*

*My uncle died in 1956. When he died I shifted into the neighbours. They were so kind to me that they never took rent from me. They just used to take Rs 20 each month for food. For this I used to get two meals.*

*There were 22 people in my neighbours' rooms. We could all sleep because people used to work in different shifts. Four people slept here, six people there, another four here. And we would make bunks from the* charpais.

*I didn't have to do any housework when I stayed here. If I ever tried to clean the dishes, the neighbours would catch my hand and stop me, saying that they were younger and they would do it. The only work I would do was to collect the food rations.*

*The* chawl *was clean because it was run by the railways. There were bathrooms in the* chawl. *There was a bathroom for women on one side of the stairs and for men on the other. There were four bathrooms altogether. But you bathed in your own rooms – there was a tap in each. There was water in the early mornings but not in the evenings, so you would have to fill the water earlier for drinking and washing in drums but you bathed when the water was there.*

In 1961 Kamal Dyeing folded up . *I was a member of the union. When the factory closed down, the union helped us to get compensation from the labour court.* Ram Dass received Rs 1,662 in compensation – roughly Rs 20,000 today – money that he later used to buy the first bit of land that his family had ever owned.

A short while after Kamal Dyeing's demise, Ram Dass was introduced to a job at Bombay Union Dyeing Mills, a larger factory in the same neighbourhood, by a friend who worked there. *He took me there to get recruited. The officer asked me if I already knew the work and I said, 'Yes, I know how to operate the jigger machine. I can also work in the washing section and on the dyeing oven. I can also use the sewing machine.' I had learnt all these things because Kamal Dyeing was a small factory and we would be asked to fill in for workers who were sick.*

Bombay Union Dyeing, which shut up shop in 1995, covered several acres in the Lalbaug area of the city. The area is now part of central Bombay, but in the 1960s was an industrial suburb which housed the *grande dames* of Bombay's once-proud textile mills – Bombay Dyeing (a blue-chip firm not associated with Bombay Union Dyeing), Century Mills, Morarjee, Finlays, and others – many of them established here at the close of the 19th century. *Bombay Union Dyeing didn't do any weaving. They used to dye military uniforms. Big traders from Kanpur used to give them the cloth and they used to dye it. They used sodium to make the colour fast. It was made yellow by salt and then Congo Red was added to make it red. There were a lot of angrezi* [English] *words for the colours – white, black, rose, pink, orange.*

The factory's high steel gates would open each morning at seven to let in the several hundred people who worked there. At the front of the factory compound was an ornate three-storey mansion, on the ground floor of which was the office, while the next two floors were the wealthy factory owner's home.

Nearly 100 yards behind the mansion was the factory: a gargantuan metal hangar, tens of thousands of square feet, with steel-beamed ceilings that towered into the air and an enormous work-floor that shrank the huge dyeing machines into insignificance. The ceiling was a network of large channels and pipes. Outside this main building were several other buildings, small only in comparison to the main one, which housed the boilers and other machinery.

At its peak, which was around the time Ram Dass worked there, Bombay Union Dyeing employed about 600 workers, including some 350 temporary workers. Ram Dass was employed as a temporary worker for a little under a year. *When I was leaving, they said come back and we'll make you permanent. But I didn't come back to Bombay because I had to look after things in the village.*

*Most of the workers were from different districts in UP. But there were also Maharashtrians. Some workers were educated, others weren't. But at that time who was educated? We didn't have enough to eat so how could we study?*

*It was very hard work in this factory. But if you're used to working since your childhood you don't get tired. And if I can drive the plough, why should I get tired by this? It was only eight hours here, but farming is a full-time job. This life was much simpler; you leave here and go home and cook your food. But with farming your worries don't cease even when you're asleep.*

*We would come at 7 a.m. We took a half-hour break for lunch at 11 a.m. I brought food from home. We left at 3.30 p.m. Then the second shift would start. There were 36 jiggers here, but I would usually work on No. Nine.*

*For safety we would just wear vests and shorts. We would bring our clothes and change here. Anyway the clothes would get covered with colour. And it used to be hot in the factory because of the steam. And it used to be so noisy that we would communicate by gestures. Of course the conditions were bad here compared to the village. But we got more money and we also got used to it. It used to be difficult, but to earn money one has to endure difficulties.*

As with his other jobs, Ram Dass recalls every detail of the processes at Bombay Union Dyeing: how the material was bleached, dyed, boiled, steamed and wrung; how it went from one machine to another; and which workers were responsible for which tasks.

Until close to the end of Ram Dass's years in Bombay, he and his family were amongst the poorest 20–30 per cent of India's population. They were landless, heavily indebted and scheduled-caste, characteristics that defined the deeply impoverished in rural India.

In the decade from the early 1950s, according to national surveys and several studies, poverty worsened across India. At the beginning of the 1950s, somewhat less than one-third of India's rural and urban populations were considered deeply impoverished, unable to afford a survival-level diet and other essentials of human survival. This minimum expenditure level was set as the poverty line. Most analysts agree that poverty worsened in the half-decade that followed, largely because of poor harvests, so that by 1960–61 about half of India's population was estimated to be below the poverty line. Another one-third of the population was considered poor, but able to ensure the minimum diet and other essentials.[1]

With Ram Dass's earnings in Bombay, during the 1950s his family moved from a situation of sheer destitution to being close to the poverty-line threshold. Most estimates for that period set the poverty line for a family of five at roughly Rs 100 per month in rural areas and Rs 125 per month in urban areas. In his penultimate year in Bombay, Ram Dass earned Rs 135 per month at his Kamal Dyeing's job, and somewhat less the following year as a temporary worker at Bombay Union Dyeing. But Ram Dass was supporting several children and adults – his parents and wife could earn little in Baba ka Gaon, where wages had not increased for decades – and had spent a large amount of money in trying to treat his brother's tuberculosis. Moreover, a major part of his earnings were absorbed by paying off his father's large debts to the village landlords.

Ram Dass's 11 years in Bombay were a period of great change for him and his family. Before he went to Bombay, neither he nor his wife had ever travelled more than a few dozen kilometres away from Baba ka Gaon. In these years, Ram Dass became the primary earner for his extended family, which, for most of this period, included his parents, his wife, a younger brother sick with tuberculosis, and several children. Many of his closest adult relatives, and most of his children, died in these years. For the first time Ram Dass had some savings, and had succeeded in paying off his family's inherited debts to the village landlords.

In Ram Dass's recollections of these years, two things stand out as having been of crucial importance. One was that he learnt to read and write. Ram Dass was virtually illiterate when he arrived in Bombay, capable only of signing his name and reading a few Hindi words. As a child he studied for a year at the government-run primary school in Devapur, a kilometre from Baba ka Gaon, defying the upper-caste stricture against untouchables being educated. Nevertheless, Ram Dass was forced to leave the primary school because his family's destitution meant that he had to start working as a labourer for the landlords.

*I went to school for a year, because my father wished me to do so. My father was angutha chhaap* [illiterate: literally, to use one's thumb imprint as a signature] *but because of going to school for this one year, I could write my name and read a little bit even before coming to Bombay. But on the way to school the* Thakurs *used to mock me, saying 'Oh Mr Clerk, namaste. Mr Clerk, salaam.' They had so much power that we untouchables could not go to school and the atmosphere at school was such that we could not study there. I could go inside the school but could not get water to drink there – we had to ask someone to serve us – could not touch the bucket nor the serving vessel for water. We were considered so low by the upper castes that even the dogs could eat or lick their leftovers, but not us!*

In northern India at the time of Ram Dass's youth, untouchables were barred by the upper castes from attending schools. The few who did attend, like Ram Dass, encountered only virulent hostility from both teachers and students. Most often, untouchable students were made to sit outside the classroom and their work was corrected by the teacher from a distance. Untouchable students were often not allowed to speak or to answer questions, for teachers feared that even this was a means of pollution. In some places the upper-caste ire was so strong against untouchables who dared to seek education that the upper castes destroyed their homes and crops. As a result, only a minuscule percentage of the untouchables ever attended school or were literate. In UP in 1931, about half a per cent of untouchable men were literate, though nearly 30 per cent of Brahmin men were.[2]

*I learnt how to read Hindi when Shrinath began to go to school in Bombay; he was in the third grade. There was a friend of mine who taught Shrinath everything – every accent and letter of the alphabet – and I learnt with him too. I am poor at writing, but I can read. After learning how to read I bought the Ramayana. And I also had some books with devotional songs written in them. And these had the explanations written in simple Hindi.*

Extraordinarily for a person of his age and origins, Ram Dass also knows some English. *In Bombay Union Dyeing, the master dyer would send me to the store to bring the colours for the dye. So I had to learn English. I learnt it slowly from a reader* [a book which has both English and Hindi in it]. *Because of this I could go and choose the colours.* Ram Dass can now spell his name in English – he says it letter by letter. He knows a handful of English words which he uses while speaking Hindi; they range from such common words as 'police', 'wagon' and 'train' to complex ones like 'pollution' and 'demurrage'; he pronounces the last as 'damrage'. He can also slowly read unfamiliar English words. *I would have even started writing English if I hadn't gone back to the village. And I can also understand English numbers.*

*Education is very important. It is the only wealth that cannot be taken away from you. I had decided years ago that even if I had to beg, I would educate my children. I saw that we are all uneducated, and that only educated people progressed and got jobs. Now many of us are educated and ensure that our children are in turn educated. Slowly and gradually there will be progress.*

## The true leader of the untouchables

The second great change in Ram Dass's life was his introduction to Babasaheb Ambedkar, the great untouchable leader. For Ram Dass and virtually every other of India's former untouchables, Bhimrao Ramji Ambedkar – respectfully known as Babasaheb or Baba Ambedkar – is a demigod. From the 1920s until his death in 1956, Ambedkar led the emancipation of the untouchables, secured for them a remarkable range of civil rights protections, committed the independent Indian state to programmes for their education and employment, and sparked in them an enduring sense of self-respect and an awareness of how future gains could be secured through electoral politics.

*By the time I went to Bombay people didn't believe in caste and untouchability as much as they used to when my father and uncle lived there. When they lived there, us Harijans would not be given tea in the roadside tea and food stalls. My father and uncle could not enter the stalls, just as they couldn't enter the temples. When they went to the tea stalls they had to carry their own mugs and buy tea and sit far outside. People knew what caste my father and uncle were from and would tell others that these are untouchables. They would find out their caste because there were lots of people in Bombay from our village and from places close to it. And anyway people of our Pasi caste had to give attendance at the police station every day because we were considered criminal castes, so even people from Bombay knew our caste.*

*But because of Baba Ambedkar's work, the Harijans started being served at the roadside stalls. This was just two or three years after Independence. According to the law passed by the government, whoever wished to eat at public hotels could do so freely.*

*I heard about Babasaheb Ambedkar from my scheduled-caste friends from Maharashtra who worked at Kamal Dyeing and Bombay Union Dyeing. They would teach us about life in Bombay, warning us about the dangers of the city. They were as poor as us and more or less all illiterate. They came from villages and said their oppression was similar to ours. And they came here for the same reasons as us.*

*My two good friends' names were Devji and Tano. They were at Kamal Dyeing. One of them worked on the next machine and so we got to know each other. When we stopped working together, we lost touch, but whenever we ran into each other we would ask with affection how the other was. I would speak to them in Marathi, which I had learnt a bit because of listening to it everyday.*

*The difference between their situation and ours was that they were less scared than us. They could fight back against their landlords. But we were very scared of the Thakurs. I'm not sure whether they owned any land or not, but like us they also worked as labourers in their village. They told me about Ambedkar, about his concern for the untouchables and the poor and how he had studied why people were forced to live so poorly.*

*Baba Ambedkar made us aware of the Dalit's power in elections.* ['Dalit' is Marathi for 'oppressed'. Coined by Ambedkar, the term was widely adopted by the former untouchables in the 1960s as an expression of pride and assertiveness.] *That whether you are a Raja or a Dalit you have equal votes! That on this one day of voting you have power equal to any upper-caste person! He assured us this much, and just this much is enough.*

*Ambedkar would come and address rallies and say don't give up hope, continue the struggle, work hard and continue to fight. Continue to fight and continue to work. He said if you stop working no one will notice you.*

*When the meetings would happen it would either be declared a holiday, or a lock-out or a strike. There used to be big meetings in the park, and we would get to know about this and go there. Either Ambedkar or other big leaders would come. There they would explain all this to us, that we should continue to fight our own battles but that we must work to meet our everyday needs. They would say continue your fight, don't close the factory down and then whatever happens legally you should accept.*

*I saw Babasaheb at a large public meeting in Bombay in 1956. I had also seen Nehru and other political leaders. It was too far at the meeting to see Babasaheb closely. The man was there, far far away. And there were lots of police with sticks in their hands, and you weren't allowed to talk; the police would say you should only look as this is what you came here for. And we people were not educated at that time and were very scared of the police. In fact, village people thought that even guards were police because of the turbans they wore!*

*Ambedkar died in 1956. Us scheduled-caste people were all very unhappy when he died. The local scheduled-caste people took out a procession on his death. We just went and watched. Because we were outsiders we were more vulnerable to getting harassed by the police, which is why we rarely joined processions.*

Self-respect, the outlawing of untouchability, a panoply of affirmative action programmes, special representation in Parliament and state legislatures, political organization across India: Ambedkar's extraordinary legacy to improving the conditions of the former untouchables spans all these and other hard-won victories. Because of his popularity among the scheduled castes across India, Ambedkar is, with Gandhi and Nehru, arguably the only pre-Independence leader who even today evokes allegiance nationally, though from very different constituencies. As important as the other two, Ambedkar embodies what all former untouchables can aspire to achieving. Overcoming the oppressive disabilities of being an untouchable in turn-of-the-century India – he was born in 1891 in modern-day Maharashtra province to a Mahar family – Ambedkar acquired professional qualifications on a par with those of the most eminent upper-caste leaders of the independence movement.[3] He gained a doctorate in economics from Columbia University in New York, a D.Sc from the University of London, and was admitted to the Bar from Gray's Inn in London. As a statesman, he was independent India's first law minister and a primary architect of the country's Constitution.

But despite this political legacy and his personal achievements, Ambedkar is, bafflingly, absent from the records that purport to explain modern Indian history and politics. In these records Ambedkar has been relegated to the shadows, much as untouchables were for millennia banished from the sight of Hindu society. Thus, British historian Percival Spear's classic account of modern India, written in the early 1970s, mentions Ambedkar once, though even this reference is omitted from the book's index. Some fifteen years later, the *New Cambridge History of India*, a study of post-Independence politics, written by American political scientist Paul Brass, again gives Ambedkar a single mention. Avowedly revisionist writers are as much at fault: Indian historian Sumit Sarkar's account, *Modern India 1885–1947*, mentions Ambedkar just twice, while a comparative lightweight like Motilal Nehru (Jawaharlal

Nehru's father) gets five times as much attention, and industrialist G.D. Birla perhaps twenty times as much.[4]

Ambedkar's exclusion from the historical record stems in part from the exclusive obsession of analysts of pre-Independence India with elite nationalist politics, particularly the Congress and its charismatic leaders. In the case of some writers prejudice is a factor, as Ambedkar's origins as an untouchable and his harsh condemnation of Hinduism have alienated many upper-caste Indians. But a crucial yet too often overlooked reason is that in a supremely ironical twist of history, much of what Ambedkar achieved for the untouchables has been credited – in India as much as abroad – to Mahatma Gandhi, who, despite his own abhorrence of untouchability, opposed Ambedkar's demands for political and civil rights for the untouchables.

The irony is underscored by Eleanor Zelliot, one of Ambedkar's most important biographers. She writes:

The Constituent Assembly of independent India passed a provision legally abolishing untouchability on November 29, 1948, nine months after the death of Mahatma Gandhi. As the measure was approved, the house resounded with cries of 'Mahatma Gandhi ki Jai' – victory to Mahatma Gandhi ... Present at that session of the Constituent Assembly as chairman of the drafting committee for the constitution was Dr B.R. Ambedkar, an untouchable ... The irony of the moment was lost on those present – a legalistic measure was taken in the name of Gandhi who had no use for legalism, coupled with lack of recognition for Ambedkar, the Untouchable who drafted the measure and who had bitterly fought Gandhi to secure legalistic approaches to the problem of untouchability.[5]

The view that Gandhi was the Mahatma who led the untouchables to freedom is anathema to many former untouchables, whether those like Ram Dass who were adults in 1947 or today's youngsters. For them Gandhi was certainly a Mahatma and a leader in the fight for independence but he was not their leader, an honour reserved almost exclusively for Ambedkar. Ram Dass says, *Gandhi was a leader of only the upper castes. During the Round Table Conference in England, he would keep saying we are all one people, but this is just the usual stance of the upper castes who keep saying we are all one when it suits them. But the rest of the time they beat the lower castes.* (The Round Table Conference of 1931 marked a milestone in negotiations between the British government and Indian nationalist parties, but was also the first of many bitter confrontations between Gandhi and Ambedkar.)

Though both Gandhi and Ambedkar condemned untouchability, their approaches to tackling the problem were fundamentally irreconcilable. Their relationship was marked by hostility and angry public criticism of each other. Gandhi questioned Ambedkar's right to assume the mantle of untouchable leadership. Ambedkar accused Gandhi of being a stooge of the upper castes.

Gandhi's approach to untouchability was essentially that of a reformer of Hinduism. His abhorrence of untouchability did not lead him to reject the caste system, which he considered crucial both to Hinduism and to reconstructing Indian society once independence was won. (Gandhi did repudiate his belief in the merits of the caste system in the last years of his life, but this change went virtually unnoticed because of the many decades in which he had upheld the system.[6]) Instead, Gandhi focused on bringing about a voluntary 'change of heart' on the part of the upper castes so that they would end their oppression of the untouchables, accept them into the *Shudra* 'touchable' category of castes and, hence, allow them full participation in Hindu society.

Because he viewed untouchability only in spiritual and religious terms, Gandhi saw no need to address the material deprivation the untouchables suffered, nor any role for government to aid their progress through compensatory policies. To the contrary, Gandhi argued that the untouchables should continue with their traditional menial and despised jobs, such as scavenging, as long as society accorded them as much respect as that given to Brahmins. Ambedkar called this idea of Gandhi's 'an outrage and a cruel joke'.[7]

Gandhi's stature and the strength of his condemnation of untouchability was such that he unquestionably did greatly advance the cause of turning public opinion against untouchability. In cleaning his own toilet and insisting that all the inmates of his ashrams do so too, Gandhi challenged the prejudices of many upper-caste Hindus, the majority of whom found his views on untouchability discomfiting and radical. Moreover, Gandhi did his best to keep the issue of untouchability at the top of the Congress agenda, despite objections from Nehru and other leaders that it diverted energy from the task of winning independence.[8]

But many untouchables, whether highly educated like Ambedkar or without formal schooling like Ram Dass, found much in Gandhi's views on untouchability to be patronizing and offensive. Particularly galling was that in Gandhi's scheme they were essentially objects of pity. The upper castes had to act by becoming penitents and purifying themselves through serving the untouchables. This condescending attitude was embodied in the name of the organization started by Gandhi in 1932, the Harijan Sevak Sangh or the Servants of the Untouchables Society. The Sangh soon had no untouchable members, an anomaly Gandhi countered by asserting that it was an organization for the expiation of the guilt of caste Hindus.

And in Gandhi's concept of service to the suffering untouchables, there was little room for the politically conscious untouchable – like Ambedkar – pressing for substantive social and economic change. Indeed, Gandhi earned their ire because of his insistence that he and other Hindu reformers could by themselves adequately represent the untouchable cause and knew better than leaders like Ambedkar how the untouchables could be emancipated. At the Round Table Conference in 1931, Gandhi argued, 'I claim myself in my own person to represent the vast mass of the Untouchables ... There is a body of Hindu reformers who are pledged to remove this blot of untouchability ... Those who speak of the political rights of Untouchables do not know their India.'[9]

But to Ambedkar and other untouchable leaders, Gandhi's programme of religious reform and humanitarianism seemed calculated to subvert their demands and to be an effort to ensure that the social order – and hence the social and material privileges of the upper castes – would not be disturbed. Ambedkar wrote:

What is the object of this Harijan Sevak Sangh? Is it to prepare the Untouchables to win their freedom from their Hindu masters, to make them their social and political equals? Mr Gandhi never had any such object before him and he never wants to do this, and I say that he cannot do this. This is the task of a democrat and a revolutionary. Mr Gandhi is neither. He is a Tory by birth as well as by faith . . . His main object, as every self-respecting Untouchable knows, is to make India safe for Hindus and Hinduism. He is certainly not fighting the battle of the Untouchables. On the contrary, by distributing through the Harijan Sevak Sangh petty gifts to petty Untouchables he is buying, benumbing and drawing the claws of the opposition of the Untouchables which he knows is the only force which will disrupt the caste system and will establish a true democracy in India.

Ambedkar was equally angered by Nehru, who consistently dismissed the demands of untouchable leaders as a distraction from the independence effort. 'Turn to Pandit Jawaharlal Nehru,' he wrote. 'He draws his inspiration from the Jeffersonian Declaration; but has he ever expressed any shame or any remorse about the condition of the 60 millions of Untouchables? Has he anywhere referred to them in the torrent of literature which comes out from his pen?'

Ambedkar's radical vision of the untouchables' future was that the untouchables would, through self-respect and organized action, make themselves equal to upper-caste Hindus in every way. Reform of Hinduism, the religion which had reduced the untouchables to the status of despised slaves, would not gain this future for the untouchables. Consequently, early in his political career, Ambedkar turned to securing the political, economic and legal rights that he felt were essential to the untouchables' emancipation. The British receptivity to these demands, especially for a separate electorate for the untouchables, stemmed in part from their calculation that the array of separate electorates would both appease and weaken Indian nationalist pressure.

Ambedkar's efforts in the early 1930s to gain for the untouchables special electoral representation as a minority (akin to that already granted to the Muslims in 1906 and subsequently to other communal and special interest groups) pitched him against the combined might of Nehru and Gandhi, who were adamantly opposed to allowing either reserved seats or separate electorates for the untouchables. Their opposition stemmed from much the same reasons that had led them to repudiate, a decade earlier, the revolt by Awadh's impoverished peasants.

To both Nehru and Gandhi, Ambedkar's demand for a separate electorate threatened the Congress' claim that it represented every Indian, and certainly every 'Hindu', in the nationalist effort. The Congress' power would diminish greatly were the untouchables given a separate electorate. Gandhi's outrage, in addition, stemmed from his belief that in politicizing the untouchables' demands, Ambedkar was threatening the unity of Hinduism as well as stoking a class war where the exploited lower castes would revolt against their upper-caste oppressors. In desperate protest, Gandhi began a 'fast unto death'.

Horrified at the prospect of being held responsible for the Mahatma's death, Ambedkar gave up the demand for separate electorates. But Gandhi's recourse to what was in effect blackmail immeasurably embittered Ambedkar, who wrote angrily: 'Mr Gandhi, the friend of the Untouchables, preferred to fast unto death rather than consent to them and although he yielded he is not reconciled to the justice underlying these demands.'[10]

Ambedkar's battle with Gandhi and Nehru was not entirely in vain as, in lieu of a separate electorate, he wrested agreement that the untouchables would be given reserved seats in Parliament and the state legislatures in about the same ratio as their proportion to the total population. This was the genesis of programmes of protective, compensatory discrimination for the untouchables. In 1935, the untouchable castes were listed on a government schedule for special privileges and preferential policies, hence the term Scheduled Castes. The groups listed on this schedule were entitled, in addition to reserved seats in all legislative bodies, to reserved places in government jobs and seats in schools and colleges. In independent India, the protective programmes secured during British rule were to grow into a vast machinery of protective discrimination for the untouchables, the world's largest such scheme.

Surprisingly, in the immediate post-Independence period, Ambedkar was given a central role in the Constitution-making process as well as being made independent India's first law minister. This brief period of co-operation between the Congress and Ambedkar stemmed from the recognition by Nehru and other Congress leaders that the untouchables remained alienated from the Congress. As the head of the committee drafting the Constitution, Ambedkar ensured that the programmes and safeguards for the untouchables secured from the British were incorporated into the Constitution, and a number of new rights added. However, some of his most crucial proposals for the emancipation of the untouchables were rebuffed. The most important of these was his demand that the government undertake an ambitious land-reform programme to benefit the untouchables. The Congress government's repudiation of this measure or of any other form of redistributive land reform, which would have transformed the condition of the overwhelmingly landless untouchables, was tantamount to permanently perpetuating the untouchables' thrall, an outcome proved by the experience of the past half-century.[11]

As a result of Ambedkar's influence, the Indian Constitution incorporated a large number of justiciable Fundamental Rights aimed at preventing caste discrimination or the practice of untouchability by the state or by individuals.[12] Article 17 abolished 'untouchability' and its practice in any form. Other articles prohibited discrimination on the grounds of religion, race, caste or sex in 'access to shops, public restaurants, hotels and places of entertainment', or in 'use of wells, tanks, bathing ghats, roads, and places of public resort', or in admission to educational institutions. Article 23 outlawed *begar* or forced labour, to which the scheduled castes were most vulnerable. Article 25 guaranteed entrance to Hindu religious institutions. In 1955 the central government passed the Untouchability (Offences) Act, which made the imposition of disabilities a crime punishable by a fine of up to Rs 500, imprisonment for up to six months, cancellation or suspension of licences and of public grants.

Ambedkar resigned from his post as law minister in 1951 over irreconcilable differences with Nehru. The record of the last years of Ambedkar's life is dominated by his dramatic conversion, along with nearly a million other former untouchables, to Buddhism in 1956. His conversion set in motion a movement that endures until today.

Ambedkar's decision to convert to Buddhism and to encourage other scheduled caste people to do so was the culmination of decades of wrestling with the problem of untouchability and its relation to Hinduism. In the early 1920s, Ambedkar was against conversion as a means of attacking caste discrimination, but within a decade was convinced that the untouchables could only be free – and the caste system destroyed – if they left Hinduism. Ambedkar explained the imperative of conversion by likening the caste system to a four-tiered wall on which the Brahmins were at the top and the untouchables at the bottom: if the bottom tier were pulled out, the whole structure would collapse.[13] In 1935, Ambedkar had declared, 'I was born in the Hindu religion; but I will not die in the Hindu religion.'[14]

To Ambedkar, Buddhism was the ideal religion for the untouchables to convert to: it was of Indian origin, casteless and egalitarian. It was also anti-Brahmin, and Brahmin opposition had been a primary cause of Buddhism's virtual extinction in India by the 10th century. Moreover, Buddhism's recent record in India was distinguished by concern for the untouchables. Buddhist groups in southern India were by the 1900s encouraging untouchables to convert to their 'democratic religion'.[15] Typically, Ambedkar emphasized the religion's stress on equality, justice and humanity, not its philosophical or mystical aspects.[16]

Ambedkar died less than two months after converting to Buddhism. His death dislocated the conversion movement, but even so the overwhelming majority of his fellow Mahars – several million in number – and smaller numbers from other scheduled castes in Maharashtra had soon converted to Buddhism. Conversions became increasingly widespread across India, and the 1961 Census reported a roughly twenty-fold increase in the number of Buddhists. The strength of the conversion movement was all the more remarkable because converts were barred from the affirmative action programmes for the scheduled castes on the specious grounds that untouchables leaving Hinduism for other religions did not need special safeguards as they were no longer 'untouchable', and that caste Hindus would no longer discriminate against them. The decision by millions of scheduled caste people to forgo these benefits reflected the extraordinary respect they accorded to Ambedkar, as well as the revolutionary spirit he encouraged in them. In independent India, empowered by the vote and by the constitutional safeguards against untouchability, they joined Ambedkar in his most revolutionary act – the repudiation of Hinduism, the religion that had bound them for millennia.[17]

*Some of us Harijans thought that we should create our own religion. But Babasaheb said why don't we choose a religion that suits us. He didn't like the Hindu religion – because of untouchabilty, of not being allowed to go to temples, of not being treated as humans. He would say to the upper-caste Hindus, 'If we are not humans, why should we stay in your religion? If by sitting even far away we pollute you then why should we stay in your religion?'*

*If you read Baba Ambedkar's works he makes references to the various Hindu scriptures pointing out that they are often worthless from a moral and social standpoint. The Ramayana is full of such instances. For example, if you read it carefully, you will see that it says that the upper castes should beat untouchables, poor villagers, the drum, animals and women as much as possible, that this is their fate. Because we were all illiterate, the Brahmin priests could fool us into believing such rubbish!*

*In Hinduism, we do whatever the upper castes say, we believe whatever they insist. We are oppressed and have to agree to their point of view. The priests take a lot, they are always demanding things, they tell us to offer something here and something there, they demand money for all their services. You even have to wash the feet of the priests. But in Buddhism people only have to greet each other as equals and to bless one another.*

*In our village no one changed from Hinduism to Bodh Dharma at the time that Babasaheb left Hinduism. If someone else had maybe I would have also. If large numbers change, then you have more confidence to do so as well. We were too bound by tradition. But recently even in our area a few people have changed to Bodh Dharma. There is now a Bodh temple near Baba ka Gaon.*

*The Hindu religion has improved. All because of Ambedkar. Where we earlier could not sit with others or have tea at a hotel, now we can do this. The older people of the upper castes still have these prejudices, but the younger ones have learnt to behave better.*

*Ambedkar spoke for us. He saw to it that the lower castes and women were educated. If Ambedkar had not been there we would not have been helped by the government, and my son Shrinath wouldn't have been able to go to school. Because of Ambedkar, we Harijans got job concessions. If Baba Ambedkar wasn't there, none of us untouchables would be awake and aware today. We would have not got anywhere.*

# 6

# The 1960s

IN 1962, Ram Dass returned from Bombay to settle permanently in Baba ka Gaon. *I came back here because I had to look after the family. If I was not here, my children would have had to look after the animals and couldn't have gone to school. So I thought if I come and stay here, they would be able to study and would be happy. And I had already finished paying off my family's debts to the zamindars, so we were more free of them than earlier.*

*By 1962 there were some differences in the village. There was an improvement of at least 25 paise in a rupee. Though the zamindars were still very powerful, their ownership of property had become less. Earlier they owned everything, even the land that we built our houses on. Nobody else owned anything. Then their property became somewhat less and other people also began to own land.*

*I had the money given to me when the Kamal Dyeing factory closed. The Thakurs that my family worked for here offered to sell me half an acre of land. This was land that my family had in the 1940s tilled for ten years as sharecroppers and that should have become ours in the shikmi. But anyway I paid Rs 400 for it. Then this Thakur told me that he would transfer the title to me later because it would be cheaper this way. But he didn't transfer it. Sometime later he died. Then the* Thakur's *brother denied that I had paid for the land, saying, 'Can you prove that you paid him?' I was so angered with this cheating that I just said, 'God is my proof but keep your land!'*

*How could I fight them? The* patwari *was a Brahmin and despised me for being of low caste. And the* Thakurs *had money with which to bribe him and I had none. You can't trust these big people! If they get hold of any money that belongs to the poor, it never comes back. They are cheats in everything. They will slit your throat! Because of their cheating I was left with just one-seventh of an acre. But even this little bit of land gave my family some means to live. And my family and I were sharecropping one more acre. And we would also work as labourers for the* Thakurs *and the middle castes.*

No longer bonded to the *Thakurs* by debt or the force of custom, Ram Dass was able to search for other ways of ensuring his family's survival and welfare. *I started to do some business, buying cattle from villages and towns, and selling them here. I would first use them for a while and would sell them when I found the opportunity. I would make Rs 25 or Rs 50 profit for each bullock as I would have trained them to pull the plough or the bullock cart. I would keep two bullocks at a time because I could use them for ploughing my land and I could also rent them to others.*

*The cattle fairs were sometimes held as far away as Kanpur, Unnao or Gwalior. I wouldn't go to the very distant fairs because I had my field to look after. There were thousands of bullocks and cows brought there for sale. They were of many different breeds. The Gwalior bullocks are very large, much taller than a man, spotlessly white and quiet. They are good workers. But the ones I like best are the bullocks from Kheri. They are the best workers even though they are very small. But they are as bad tempered as they are hardworking! They try to hit everyone and they fight with the other bullocks! I only had one pair of these. One died, and the other refused to work with any other bullock so I had to sell it.*

*At the fairs there would be lots of people from my area – Pratapgarh, Allahabad, Rae Bareli – and we would walk back together until we had to take our separate routes. We were like the caravans of Baghdad! We would walk at least 30 miles a day. We'd make the cattle walk for an hour and then give them a half an hour break. They would get to graze when we stopped to rest or eat. The journey was quite safe; there were animal thieves, but as we were about 30 of us, no one would attack us. We would take turns to stay up at night. The thieves would steal but they weren't violent, so if they saw you awake they would not do anything. And we used to camp near villages because we could buy fodder and could take help from the villagers.*

*Now I don't have enough time or I would still do this business. You can make quite a lot of money, though of course you can also lose everything if the animals get sick.*

## Nehru rediscovers land reform

The major characteristics of Congress government rule had been established in the early 1950s, and there was no break with this pattern of development in the 1960s, despite Nehru's death in 1964. His successors as prime minister, Lal Bahadur Shastri and Indira Gandhi, amplified his policies. Thus, much as in the previous decade, the record of Congress rule in the 1960s was dominated by the rituals of radical rhetoric and symbolic attempts at redistribution on the one hand, and the continuation of economic policies that overwhelmingly benefited the upper and middle classes, both rural and urban, on the other. Not unexpectedly, Ram Dass's family remained impoverished throughout the decade, while both the numbers and the proportion of the poor increased.

Indeed, the Congress' major redistributive effort of the 1960s – the imposition of ceilings on agricultural land and redistribution to favour the poor – was an extraordinary travesty in both conception and results. After the abolition of *zamindari* in 1952, the Congress governments in New Delhi and the provinces turned away, relieved, from the unsettling issue of agrarian reform. They were compelled to return to the issue at the close of that decade because the Congress had suffered electoral defeats to parties promising radical land reforms.[1] To counter their appeal, the Congress central government, under Nehru's guidance, promised reform that seemed intrinsically radical: the imposition of ceilings on the amount of land that could be held by an individual or family, with the 'surplus' land redistributed to the poor. Strikingly, this measure had been rejected by the Congress leadership just a decade earlier, during the contests over the shape of *zamindari* abolition, for being politically unfeasible. The Congress' rediscovery of the policy, of course, was not prompted by a sudden burst of radical energy. Rather, in the course of the 1960s the Congress governments in New Delhi and the provinces were to demonstrate how even ostensibly radical policies could be reduced to being harmless.

The need for land redistribution was incontrovertible. The inequity in land ownership across India was enormous, with the rural rich continuing to own vast properties. An elite of less than half a million families – about one-half of one per cent of the rural population – owned well over ten per cent of the cultivable land, with average holdings of 80 acres each. The next million owned roughly as much, with holdings that averaged 37 acres.[2] In contrast, more than one-tenth of India's rural families were landless. The next poorest quarter owned less than half an acre each. If an average ceiling of 20 acres per rural household had been applied at this time, roughly 55 million acres would have been 'surplus'. Redistribution of this huge amount of land would have had a tremendous impact on reducing poverty. But, as events unfolded, less than five per cent of this land was declared surplus; and not all of this was redistributed![3]

In UP, the scope for redistribution was as great, as the abolition of *zamindari* had not reduced the enormous inequities in land ownership, and quite possibly had increased them.[4] At the beginning of the 1960s, one-fifth of UP's 13 million rural families were landless. Another quarter of the rural population – including Ram Dass's family – owned less than one acre each. Together, this mass, verging on half the province's rural people, owned just 1.6 per cent of the cultivable land! In contrast, the top ten per cent owned well over half the land, with a sizeable number of this elite each still controlling thousands of acres of land.[5]

But despite these obvious inequities and the scope for alleviating poverty, Nehru's government lacked commitment for land redistribution almost as much as the provincial Congress governments, which were transparently dominated by the rural landed. This was obvious from the mildness of the central government's land ceiling directives to the provinces.[6] They were so extensively shot through with exemptions and loopholes that even if enforced they would have left untouched the majority of large landowners. Thus, the directives recommended that the ceiling laws exempt 'efficient' or 'mechanized' farms, however large, along with cattle breeding and dairy farms, sugarcane farms owned by sugar factories, orchards and plantations. Also exempted were farms owned by religious, charitable or educational institutions, or co-operative societies.[7]

The ineffectual proposals were weakened further at the provincial level, where virtually no Congress government was prepared to countenance land redistribution. Though most of the provinces adopted ceiling legislation in 1960–61, almost all expanded the myriad exemptions recommended in the central directives. As a result, landowners needed little ingenuity to be able to retain control of their holdings, however extensive.

In UP, resistance to the land-ceiling effort came from a large and politically dominant section of the population. The number of families owning large holdings of fifty, one hundred or even several hundred acres had expanded several-fold since the abolition of *zamindari*, as the smaller landlords and the more prosperous tenants had purchased land being sold by the large *zamindars*. With this new congruence of interests, these *Thakurs* and Brahmins, with a sizeable sprinkling of elite cultivating and higher-middle castes, emerged as an extraordinarily powerful force against agrarian reform.

This group's power stemmed not just from their ownership of sizeable properties but also from their nearly absolute control of the Congress in UP. The UP Congress, which ruled the province from 1947 in an unbroken innings of two decades, had, from well before Independence, drawn its main source of support from the smaller landlords and substantial tenants. But by the close of the 1950s many of the erstwhile land barons had also joined its top leadership, deserting the landlords' Praja Party which had been routed in the 1952 elections.[8] Others from amongst the former barons led the challenge to Congress by conservative opposition parties including the Jana Sangh, today's Bharatiya Janata Party (BJP). But whether within or outside Congress, whether erstwhile grandee or former superior tenant, the province's new and old landowners were united in their opposition to land ceilings or other redistributive agrarian reforms. From positions of power in the legislature and administration, they and their kin ensured that their holdings would never be whittled away. They were almost always able to ensure that the laws passed by the state legislature were too weak to threaten their interests. On the rare occasions when threatened by particular aspects of a law, they used the corrupt and pliable bureaucratic system to gut the policies or even to twist them to their advantage.

The land-ceiling act that came into force in UP in 1960 was a first victim of this opposition. The act was so mild and so riddled with exemptions – most proposed by the central government – as to seem farcical to even generous observers. It imposed nothing more threatening than a generously high ceiling per family of five members of 40 irrigated acres or 80 unirrigated acres; an additional 8 acres were allowed for every additional family member. Under this ludicrous formula, a landowner could retain 128 acres of land in addition to limitless orchards and land covered by other exemptions.[9]

Given the abundant exemptions, the UP government itself from the start expected very modest results in terms of the amount of land that would be declared surplus: nothing more than 400,000 acres, just about one per cent of the province's cultivated area. But the results fell far short of even this modest goal. Just 20,000 acres were redistributed, of which fully half were unfit for cultivation.[10]

Because it was apparent that the act would not be enforced, given bureaucratic collusion and the patent lack of political commitment, landlords flagrantly put large amounts of land in the names of servants, dead relatives, fictitious people, and even pet dogs, cats and elephants! Others retained thousands of acres of land by establishing bogus co-operatives or charitable, religious or educational trusts. Many cheated the public exchequer by claiming huge sums as compensation for land that they never gave up.

Events in Baba ka Gaon transparently revealed just how weak the redistribution effort was. No land was redistributed to the poor; to the contrary, the village *Thakurs* secured for themselves title to all the degraded land around the village – about 30 acres – as well as the rights for fish-farming in the large pond outside the village!

The land-ceiling effort in the 1960s was nothing short of a farce. The sense of burlesque was accentuated by the fact that by the close of that decade India's central and provincial governments had together issued such reams of agrarian reform legislation that they could claim that no other country had developed such a voluminous body of agrarian laws so quickly. No matter that the laws were in their entirety so toothless that a Planning Commission review noted caustically, 'In no sphere of public activity in our country since Independence has the hiatus between precept and practice, between policy pronouncements and actual execution, been as great as in the domain of land reform.'[11]

## The landlords prosper with the Green Revolution

By the mid-1960s, 15 years of government threats – though never implemented – to appropriate and redistribute their land had given those with large landholdings ample opportunity to disguise their holdings in any number of ways, ranging from legal exemptions to illegal transfers. With their tens or hundreds of acres securely under their control, UP's landowners were ideally placed to reap the benefits of the 'Green Revolution' in agriculture, which began to spread in the province at this time. Within a decade, those with large holdings had grown even richer; those with five to ten acres had prospered, but millions of land-poor and landless families like Ram Dass's remained as hungry as ever.

The boom in agriculture in UP and several other northern provinces brought to an end a century of near-stagnation in agricultural growth in India. In the first four decades of the 20th century, food-grain output in India grew by a yearly average of only about one-third of one per cent.[12] The dismal performance of agriculture stemmed from the inequities of land ownership, insecure tenancy, and the paucity of government funds for irrigation and other necessities of agriculture. And because food-grain output fell behind even the modest one per cent annual increase in population, India's capacity to feed itself worsened significantly in the first half of this century. By Independence, the availability of basic foodgrains was one-fifth lower for the average Indian than half a century earlier.[13] Chronic hunger and famine were hallmarks of Indian life.

During Nehru's regime, the central government lacked a coherent agrarian policy, with its energies devoted to furthering industrial growth. There was little consistency in the policies attempted – community development, agricultural extension, land reforms, improved irrigation and even co-operative farming were all tried without vigour and then discarded.[14] Agriculture continued to perform poorly, and through the 1950s and 1960s the shortage of food-grains forced the Indian government to rely on the US government for several million tons of food aid each year, a dependence fraught with political sensitivities and uncertainties.

No less than in colonial days, India's reputation abroad was such that to many the word 'India' evoked only images of bone-thin or pot-bellied children, and of gaunt, half-naked adults.

On Nehru's death, first Shastri, Nehru's successor, and then Indira Gandhi paid greater attention to the agricultural sector. The impetus behind this was several years of acute food shortages in the mid-1960s, which both slowed economic growth and stoked public anger. Worried by the prospect that the Congress would be trounced in the 1967 elections, Mrs Gandhi sought a 'quick-fix' solution to the shortage of food-grain.[15]

The thrust of Mrs Gandhi's strategy was rapidly to boost food-grain production by concentrating government resources on high-potential districts – essentially those with good irrigation – and on large and medium farmers. Within these districts (almost all in northern India), the government identified the large and medium farmers, and then showered them with easy credit, assured irrigation, extension services and price support for the output, so that they would succeed in adopting the new high-yielding grain varieties. In effect, a commercial enclave was being created within the vast, technologically backward and neglected agricultural sector. The strategy succeeded admirably in its limited goal of rapidly raising total food-grain production. With this success, Mrs Gandhi accomplished for the rural propertied what her father had wrought a decade earlier with the urban elite: furthered their business interests through favouring them with government finances and support. Under the Congress, there was to be socialism in neither urban nor rural India.

The approach chosen by Mrs Gandhi suited not just the propertied in rural areas, but also the urban elite and middle classes, because it forestalled the need for a redirection of government finances from industry to agriculture. But the rural poor suffered in numerous ways as a consequence. The exclusive concentration on boosting production through larger farmers meant that alternative strategies that would have improved production, employment and equity, such as land reform and making small farmers viable, were ignored. Rural inequity worsened because of the growing prosperity of the large and medium farmers, and the unchanged position of the landless and small farmers. And because large farms use more capital and less labour per unit of produce than small farms, rural employment grew much less than it would have if land reform had taken place and the increases in production come from smaller farms. Yet another egregious outcome was that, although the Indian government soon had vast stocks of 'surplus' food-grain, purchased from the Green Revolution districts and farmers, the rural poor could not afford to buy this food and remained as hungry as ever, though tons of grain rotted or were eaten by rats in government warehouses. (Anyway, it was only in rare cases that the government's public distribution system ever serviced rural areas, especially in poorly administered provinces like UP.) This was a particularly ironic outcome, because for the Indian government, public and the world in general, the 'surpluses' were taken as evidence that hunger was now a thing of the past in rural India. In fact, foodgrain production had grown barely faster than population.[16]

In UP, the Congress government had by the late 1960s substantially increased allocations for agricultural development, particularly for minor and major irrigation projects. By the close of that decade, the Green Revolution approach resulted in astonishingly large increases in wheat yields in western UP, paralleling the earlier success of Punjab and Haryana. Almost entirely because of the enormous wheat production increases in western UP, Punjab and Haryana, the national production of wheat doubled between 1962 and 1973.

In Pratapgarh, the Green Revolution technology reached large farmers at the very end of the 1960s, essentially because the provincial government focused its efforts first on the western districts, which had since the turn of the century been far better irrigated than the central or eastern areas of the province. But by the early 1970s the Green Revolution had taken such firm roots in Pratapgarh, in part because the area irrigated by canals and minor irrigation sources had increased several-fold since Independence, that in the following decade the district recorded amongst the largest increases in food-grain output of any of India's several hundred districts.[17]

In the early decades of the spread of the Green Revolution, in Pratapgarh as elsewhere in India, the landlords and medium farmers cornered almost entirely the benefits of rising agricultural productivity and profits. Many of the larger farmers were former landlords, who invested the compensation received from *zamindari* abolition in acquiring

Green Revolution technology. By the close of the 1960s, virtually every district in UP boasted a number of capitalist ex-*zamindars*, their 30-, 40-, 50-, or 100-acre holdings lush with the latest high-yielding varieties of wheat or paddy.[18] The growing profitability of farming strengthened their resolve to fight any attempt at land reform, while at the same time their prosperity once again bolstered their local political power.[19] The medium farmers, generally of the middle castes, were also well placed to share in the benefits flowing from the Green Revolution. Though few were substantial landlords, most owned enough to prosper and to sustain upward mobility through their access to Green Revolution technology.

## And the poor got poorer

In 1960–61, about 40 per cent of India's rural population and about 50 per cent of the urban population were estimated to be below the absolute poverty threshold. By the close of the decade, rural poverty had worsened, with as much as another 10 per cent of the rural population moving below the poverty line. Urban poverty levels remained essentially unchanged. The worst hit were the poorest 10 per cent of India's population, whose incomes fell by perhaps one-fifth from already rock-bottom levels.[20]

The worsening poverty came despite a fairly sustained national economic growth rate of about 3 per cent per year. As the rate of population growth had increased to 2.5 per cent per year, the increase per person of 0.5 per cent per year left only limited room for improvements in the well-being of the poor. But far from poverty being reduced by even this amount, it worsened as a result of growing inequality between the upper-income groups and the poor. Thus, rather than economic growth 'trickling down' to the poor, as India's politicians and policy-makers had insisted would occur, the gains of growth were in the 1960s hogged by India's tiny upper-middle-income and rich classes. A major cause of the increase in rural poverty was the spiralling prices of food grains, which hit the landless and those with too little land to produce enough for their needs. Ironically, food prices climbed despite the boom in national grain production, testifying to the power of the rich farmers' lobby.

Even in the few dozen districts where the Green Revolution technology was widely adopted by large farmers, the incomes of the impoverished did not rise until many years later. Most of the poor were landless, so miracle seeds, canals and tube-wells were of no relevance to their fortunes. Those who sharecropped or owned a little land were so impoverished that they could not afford the new seeds, nor the fertilizers and pesticides that had to be used.[21] In Baba ka Gaon, for instance, the *Thakurs* began to adopt the high-yielding grain varieties by the close of the 1960s. Because virtually only the *Thakurs* had access to credit or sufficient savings, even the few middle-caste families owning five to ten acres did not adopt the high-yielding varieties until a decade later. The *Thakurs* prospered. But though their extensive fields were soon lush with the bounty of the Green Revolution, their power over the landless labourers or marginal farmers who toiled for them, including Ram Dass, his wife and his parents, was such that wage rates did not rise at all for nearly two decades.

Ram Dass and his family were most probably below the poverty line through this decade, though not as destitute as they were before Ram Dass had gone to Bombay at the end of the 1940s. Their main source of income was from Ram Dass and Prayaga Devi working on daily wages as agricultural labourers for the *Thakurs*; the wage rate had not risen since Independence, nor was there any increase in the number of days for which they could find work. And together with Ram Dass's parents, they cultivated the tiny sliver of land that they owned, and sometimes sharecropped another half-acre of land. This did not provide enough food for the family's annual needs, and as a consequence they were badly affected by the rise in food prices. Their income was occasionally supplemented by the trade in bullocks that Ram Dass had started. A major factor contributing to their poverty in this period was that the number of earning family-members was outweighed by dependents, even though Shrinath, Ram Dass's elder son, and Kaalu, his orphaned nephew, both in their early teens, helped in the fields and in looking after the younger children.

# 7

# The Messiah of the Poor: Indira Gandhi

INDIA seemed poised on the brink of apocalypse in the late 1960s. The major cities were torn by strikes and mass agitations by industrial workers, many fuelled by shortages of food grains and other essential goods. Bihar and eastern UP were swept by a prolonged drought that threatened to become independent India's first fully fledged famine. Fierce 'Maoist' revolts had begun in north Bengal's Naxalbari area and in several tribal districts of Andhra Pradesh, where the Left led 'land grab' agitations. Fractured by social instability and economic failure, India's future seemed bleaker than ever before in the 20-odd years since Independence.

For the poor, in particular, there could not have been a grimmer time since Independence. Poverty had worsened substantially in the previous decade. At the same time the upper and middle classes had prospered visibly: industrialists, professionals and government officials in urban areas; landlords and substantial peasants in the regions touched by the Green Revolution. With Nehru's death, even the Congress' ritualistic pro-poor rhetoric had dimmed. Looking at the dismal record of the decades since Independence, there was little reason for the poor to persevere with their dream that in independent India they would be freed from poverty and oppression.

Yet, in one of the most dramatic turns in Indian politics, concerns about poverty re-emerged strongly at the very end of the 1960s. The next decade witnessed a renewed attempt at land reform and the initiation of an impressive range of anti-poverty programmes. The Congress strove to win back its reputation with the poor. Politicians of every ideological persuasion were forced to adopt the rhetoric of social justice and poverty eradication.

This perplexing twist in Indian history was precipitated by none other than that enduring enigma of modern India, Indira Gandhi. Within short years of emerging as a political force in the mid-1960s, Mrs Gandhi had pushed poverty higher on the national agenda than it had arguably ever been before in independent India's history. But, eventually, her record on tackling India's poverty was as discredited as the record of her political career. In the two decades in which she dominated Indian politics – from her rise to power following the death in 1964 of her father, Prime Minister Nehru, to her assassination in 1984 – Mrs Gandhi's stature amongst the poor fell from being their messiah to being their dreaded nemesis, and then settled at the unhallowed level of the run-of-the-mill politician who used populist appeals for political gain.

Mrs Gandhi began her first term as prime minister in early 1966 with economic policies that continued the conservatism of Lal Bahadur Shastri, her predecessor. Shastri had abandoned the idea of economic planning, with its socialist underpinnings, in 1965, and Mrs Gandhi extended the 'plan holiday', declaring herself to be a 'pragmatist'. She followed up this declaration by devaluing the rupee by half, under pressure from the US.[1]

But within a year, Mrs Gandhi had ostensibly forsworn her conservative economic world-view. The impetus for this was the Congress' rout in the general elections of 1967, which saw its share of the 518 seats in the Lok Sabha, the crucial lower house of Parliament, fall from 371 to 281.[2] The disavowal threatened the Congress' 'one-party' rule of India. To stem the erosion of confidence – support from the urban middle class, the poor and Muslims had visibly declined – Mrs Gandhi set the party in an aggressively populist direction on economic policy and set about reinventing herself as the messiah of the disadvantaged.[3] These tasks were accomplished with the dramatic flair and charisma that were soon established as her great political strengths.

The urban working and middle classes were one target of Mrs Gandhi's new-found populism. Her pledges to them were in their entirety little more than a hodgepodge of symbolic changes, rather than real social and economic transformation. They ran the gamut from nationalization of banks and businesses, and curbs on industrial monopolies, to pride in India's growing military power, and then to ceilings on urban income and property, attacks on ostentation, and abolition of the privileges and 'privy purse' pensions still enjoyed by the former princes. Announcing the nationalization of the major banks in 1969, she promised this to be 'only the beginning of a bitter struggle between the common people and the vested interests in the country'.[4] But as these moves failed to rouse much support, prior to the 1972 general elections Mrs Gandhi drew the poor to the centre of her political strategy. She adopted the thrilling, resonant slogan, *'Garibi Hatao!'* – Abolish Poverty – as the main plank of her manifesto.[5] The rural and urban poor, at 40 to 50 per cent of the population, had the potential of being a vote bank that would surpass any that her rivals, in the Congress or elsewhere, could seek out.[6]

Having captured the public imagination as a heroine of the masses – a task eased immeasurably by being Nehru's daughter – Mrs Gandhi called national elections for March 1971, a year earlier than scheduled, to gain a popular mandate for her rule. The election results proved the extent of her success in remodelling herself and the Congress. The Congress won 352 of the 518 seats in the Lok Sabha, nearly as much as the undivided Congress had enjoyed before the 1967 electoral debacle. (In 1969, the Congress had split, leaving Mrs Gandhi's conservative rival, Morarji Desai, with the rump party, the Congress-Syndicate.) Scheduled caste support was crucial to Mrs Gandhi's victory; of the constituencies reserved for scheduled-caste candidates, the Congress won two-thirds. Mrs Gandhi's remarkable victory was interpreted as her having won the allegiance of the poor, across regional, religious, caste and ethnic lines, with the *Garibi Hatao* slogan.[7]

Mrs Gandhi's triumph was cemented when the Congress swept 70 per cent of the assembly seats in elections in 16 major provinces. As the architect of the Congress Party's recovery and with clear Congress control in Parliament and most provincial legislatures, she now wielded unchallengeable power. There was little to prevent her from fulfilling the promises of social and economic justice which had brought her victory:

there was little resistance within the Congress; the opposition parties had been trounced; and the often-conservative Supreme Court could be overridden by parliamentary majorities. Those who had voted for Mrs Gandhi expected action from her.[8]

Ram Dass says: *Nothing much happened to me from Mrs Gandhi's promises of Garibi Hatao. My family was left as poor as we always were. And neither was I optimistic that much good would come. There used to be orders from the government: Hatao, hatao, hatao. But who will remove poverty? The orders came from the government but they just stayed on paper.*

The results of Mrs Gandhi's multitudinous promises to eliminate poverty were painfully modest in UP. This was so even though Mrs Gandhi had every reason to pursue the goal of *Garibi Hatao* with special keenness in the province, as it was the Nehrus' home, the site of Mrs Gandhi's election as a member of Parliament (from Rae Bareli), and historically the foundation of Congress power.

Certainly, judged by appearances, the *Garibi Hatao* effort should have resulted in a substantial amelioration of poverty. In New Delhi, within Mrs Gandhi's first months in office, anti-poverty efforts had been raised to the level of being an integral part of the planning process. For the first time in independent India's planning history, the traditional emphasis on economic growth was matched by a stress on the need for overt redistribution of assets and of the benefits of growth.[9] The chief elements of the *Garibi Hatao* strategy were a renewed effort to lower and enforce land ceilings as well as the launching of massive anti-poverty programmes. The reasoning behind this double-pronged approach was that land ceilings would structurally transform rural society and loosen the upper-caste stranglehold, while the poverty programmes would provide the poor with assets and a minimum standard of living.[10]

But the appearance that Mrs Gandhi and her regime were committed to a revolutionary assault on the structural causes of poverty was illusory. As the unchallenged head of the central government, there was nothing to prevent Mrs Gandhi from ensuring, at the very least, that the central government's policy recommendations to the provinces on land reform and other related matters were truly progressive. That even this did not transpire revealed Mrs Gandhi's commitment to social justice to be far weaker than was suggested by her fiery rhetoric.

Of course, she was only following in the established mould of Congress leaders in the constant interplay of radical rhetoric and conservative policies.

The chasm between rhetoric and practice was especially transparent in the central government's recommendations on land reform, the major initiative of the *Garibi Hatao* strategy. Though the recommendations were less generous than those issued under Nehru a decade before, they were still so compromised and rife with exemptions as to be incapable of real transformational impact. A ceiling of 10 to18 acres was proposed for the best irrigated land, but farmers with private irrigation were permitted to own more, a resounding victory for the larger farmers' lobby. Each family could own an additional 27 acres of single-cropped irrigated land, as well as 54 acres of dry land or orchards. The exemptions allowed were just marginally less liberal than in the farcical ceiling law of the 1960s. Exemptions were continued for plantations, charitable or religious organizations, co-operatives, and agricultural universities or institutes.[11] The only exemptions revoked were for 'well-managed', 'mechanized', or sugar-cane farms!

Not surprisingly, given the liberal exemptions and scope for classifying prime land as 'single-cropped', the government expected to acquire only four million acres of land, about one per cent of the total cultivated area. In contrast, if the stricter ceilings and less generous exemptions proposed in a government planning document had been adopted, over ten times that amount would have become available for redistribution. The planning document estimated that redistribution of this amount of land would lower the number of people below the poverty line from 40 to 33 per cent.[12]

Events in Lucknow confirmed just how unthreatening were the central recommendations. There, extraordinarily, without significant dissension, the provincial Assembly adopted the central recommendations virtually *in toto*. The relative quiet in the Assembly was not a sign that the Congress and opposition ranks were no longer dominated by substantial landlords. To the contrary, in interviews before the legislation was debated, over 100 legislators, across party lines, admitted that they opposed land ceilings because their personal holdings would be affected.[13] But when it came to voting, the legislators did not oppose the legislation simply because they knew full well that the loopholes and exemptions in the law could so easily be exploited during implementation that they – and their kin and supporters – could escape with their illegal landholdings entirely untouched.

Sure enough, there was soon ample proof that this was indeed the reason for the lack of opposition: the provincial government projected that the enforcement of the ceiling legislation would result in at most 400,000 acres being declared as surplus, no more than that expected under the first ceiling act of 1960. Eventually, implementation of the act was so poor that only 200,000 acres were declared surplus and about half of that allotted. By government calculations, about 200,000 families benefited, but in reality a sizeable share of even this small number of families was either not able to secure control over the plots alloted to them because of the ire of the landlords, or found themselves owners of barren or unproductive slivers of land.[14]

Ram Dass comments: *There were some small improvements. A little land was distributed to the poor. Till then, of the 80 families in the village only about 10 owned land. Almost none amongst the scheduled castes had any land. This did change because of Indira Gandhi's* Garibi Hatao. *But till today, it is only the* Thakurs *and some of the middle castes who have enough land. The rest don't even have enough to feed their families from. Poor people were supposed to get enough land to live on. At a minimum they were to get enough land to make full use of a plough and pair of bullocks. This was about three acres. But in practice, people got two-thirds or one-third of an acre, or even less. My family got one-third of an acre.*

*All the landless people in the village got titles to land, but some were never able to take possession and others were able to take possession of only a little bit of the land alloted to them. The* Thakurs *threatened that they would cut us into pieces if we tried to take posssession! They harassed anyone who protested. And they filed legal cases against our taking over the plots, and we poor people were ensnared in these cases for years. Many of the poorer people just gave up sooner or later. Some of them don't even know till today where the land is that they had been allotted!*

*Even with the allotments made from the village land, the* pradhans [heads of the elected village council], *who were always* Thakur *or* Brahmin, *put the land in the name of their own relatives!*

*Three landless families in Baba ka Gaon have land on paper, but they will never get possession. One is a* Pasi *and another two from middle castes. The law is that whoever has title should be given possession. The laws are very clear and strong to say that action should be taken if people aren't allowed to take control of the land given to them. But who is going to enforce this, who is going to take action? No officials came to ensure that things were being done properly. The ones who are supposed to implement are the ones who benefit from the law not being implemented! For all her promises, Indira Gandhi was always so busy visiting hundreds of countries that she never had time to see the poverty at home or to see whether her laws were working!*

## From messiah to nemesis: the Emergency

On 26 June 1975, provoked by a court ruling countermanding her 1971 election to Parliament and facing popular discontent – including, earlier that year, a 'land-grab' attempt by activists on her expensive four-acre farm on Delhi's outskirts – Indira Gandhi imposed Emergency rule on the ground that India's security was 'threatened by internal disturbances'. (Though the imposition of Emergency is allowed by the Constitution, it had until then been used only during wars.) Power was concentrated in her hands, Parliament effectively suspended, and fundamental rights abrogated.

Mrs Gandhi evoked the welfare of the Indian poor to justify her recourse to Emergency rule. In an address to the nation that morning on All India Radio she insisted, 'I am sure you are conscious of the deep and widespread conspiracy which has been brewing ever since I began to introduce certain progressive measures of benefit to the common man and woman of India.' Just days later, on 1 July, she proclaimed a Twenty-Point Programme of economic and social reforms. This was a smorgasbord of promises to the poor – who were assured that land reform laws would be implemented 'with redoubled zeal', rural debt liquidated, bonded labour abolished and minimum agricultural wages enforced – and to the urban working and middle classes, who were proffered tax cuts, 'better quality' cloth, and an assault on the ill-gotten wealth of the urban elite.[15] And some months later, to demonstrate the depth of her allegiance to social justice, Mrs Gandhi amended the preamble to the Constitution so that the Indian state was henceforth described to be 'socialistic'.

But despite Mrs Gandhi's constant invocation of the poor, by the close of the 22 months of Emergency rule few amongst the poor still regarded her as their heroine. The campaigns of forced sterilization and slum clearance begun by Sanjay Gandhi, Mrs Gandhi's 29-year-old son and heir-apparent, left her reputation tarnished almost beyond repair, as it was inconceivable that they were pursued without her concurrence. The campaigns – which singled out population as the cause of India's poverty, and the poor as a blight on the urban landscape – also betrayed Mrs Gandhi's retrograde attitude to the poor: that though they were a valuable vote bank, they were also the root cause of India's troubles.

In viewing 'over-population' as the cause of India's myriad problems, Mrs Gandhi and Sanjay Gandhi echoed a fear that had been heard for centuries, ironically from well before the start of the high population growth rates that began in India only at the close of the 1920s. In his famous late-18th-century treatise predicting that population growth would outstrip food supplies, the English demographer Malthus devoted an entire chapter to the Indian subcontinent, arguing that the poverty, chronic hunger, starvation and general misery on display there proved his theory of over-population. And in the 1920s, shocked by the poverty of the Awadh peasants – 'this vast multitude of semi-naked sons and daughters of India' – Nehru, schooled at England's most hallowed centres of learning, reiterated Malthus' reasoning, writing that: 'The land was rich but the burden on it was very heavy, the holdings were small and there were too many people after them.'

Both Malthus and Nehru were guilty of simplistic determinism. Nehru paid little heed, at least in that comment, to how inextricably the poverty of India's peasants was rooted in the gross inequities of land ownership and in their exploitation by landlords and colonial government. Malthus' theory was, of course, later disproved by the experience of the Western nations, where progress in agricultural techniques kept food supplies far ahead of population growth.

Certainly, by the 1970s, every visible measure showed that India's demographic situation deserved official attention. At Independence, India's population was 350 million; a quarter of a century later, the 1971 census showed that the numbers exceeded 500 million. But the approach of compulsion and forced sterilization pushed by Mrs Gandhi and Sanjay during the Emergency revealed a total disregard for the complex forces that lie behind rapid population growth.

Thus, neither Mrs Gandhi nor Sanjay considered that the government was itself to blame for the population pressures, through having patently failed to build an effective family planning programme, which would advise couples and bring contraceptive methods within their reach. Nor did they consider that fertility rates would remain high as long as the poor continued to face very high risks that their children would not live to be adults. In UP in the early 1970s, more than one-third of all children died before they reached the age of five, clearly a powerful incentive for parents to spread the mortality risks by having several children. Nor did they stop to contemplate the many other variables, well known to demographers by then, that encouraged high fertility in impoverished, patriarchal peasant societies like India. Among this welter of factors were such potent pressures as illiteracy, the limited scope for women to make decisions about how many children to have, and the reliance of poor rural families on children to work and to support them in their old age. Clearly, the fact that all these variables still encouraged high fertility reflected the root failure: that 25 years of Congress rule had failed to improve the conditions of the poor.

But ignoring these complexities, and the possibility of favourably influencing these variables through government welfare efforts, Mrs Gandhi and Sanjay settled on an approach that fused Malthusian reductionism to 'blame-the-victim' prejudice. Family planning became one of Sanjay Gandhi's favourite causes, and he pursued it with the fascist zeal that was soon revealed to be his hallmark. The fascist approach was not surprising in an individual who was convinced he knew better than everyone else what was good for them and for India, beginning his extra-constitutional reign in the Emergency with the statement, 'I firmly believe that the best ideology for the people is my ideology.'[16] Under his direction, the government's family planning programme was transformed into a crusade to enforce male sterilization through vasectomy operations. The crusade was most aggressively pursued in the Hindi-speaking northern states, whose chief ministers vied with each other to curry Sanjay's favour. The chief minister of UP unilaterally raised the target for sterilizations from 400,000 to

1.5 million.[17] In UP and in several other states, the chief ministers imposed sterilization quotas on civil servants, the police, health and family planning staff, and even teachers. Many thousands of junior government employees had their pay withheld for months; others were denied promotion and many more dismissed from service because they failed to produce evidence that they had induced a requisite number of men to undergo sterilization. Given this chain of pressure, it was inevitable that brutal abuses of the poor would occur.

Ram Dass recalls: *The* nasbandhi *happened in the region around Baba ka Gaon too. No one from the village was sterilized, but this was only because there was no way that a vehicle could get to the village! This road hadn't been built then. And we lower-caste men would rarely go to the market – and if we ever heard the noise of a jeep we would run into the fields and hide!*

*But in my paternal uncle's village in Sultanpur district, all the lower-caste men had to hide the entire night in the fields. One wasn't even safe in one's home because the government officials would raid the houses. Anyone who got caught was taken away in a jeep and sterilized! They even caught my uncle, even though he was about 60 years old. He and another* Harijan *– a boy who wasn't even married – escaped from the jeep and hid for 15 days in the fields.*

*It wasn't a bad policy in itself that men with three or four children should have the operation for sterilization. But you cannot force people. And it was directed only at the poor. The government officials never touched the* Thakurs *or Brahmins even though they have at least as many children as us! And the officials would catch hold of poor people and sterilize them even if they didn't have any children. They didn't worry about the age of the man, they were just interested in the numbers.*

The sterilization programme developed into a wholesale cycle of abuse and tyranny. Much as in the area around Baba ka Gaon, government officials across north and central India raided villages, rounded up the poor, and dragged them away for forcible sterilization. In cities, police routinely arrested slum and pavement dwellers and municipal sweepers and took them directly to sterilization camps.[18] The intense pressure to fill quotas of 'acceptors' resulted in careless surgery and many deaths.[19]

Defiance provoked worse repression. In rural areas, communities who resisted were punished by having all their men rounded up and sterilized. In urban areas, demonstrations against forced sterilizations and slum clearance led to police shooting – killing more than 70 in the UP towns of Muzaffarnagar and Sultanpur (the latter just 60 km from Baba ka Gaon) in October 1976; and between 6 (the police count) and 400 (the unofficial count) at Delhi's Turkman Gate.[20] Many of the abuses were never recorded, nor is the scale known even today because in early 1976 a blanket ban was imposed on criticism of the family planning programme. But the pall of fear that developed permeated the entire northern area.

The rural and urban poor were the primary victims of the slum clearance and sterilization campaigns. But Indians of every class were soon opposed to the Emergency, as in one way or another they too suffered from the suspension of democratic processes and the abuses inherent in dictatorial rule. By the end of the Emergency, some 200,000 people had been arrested or ordered to be arrested. A large number of these were political leaders, but many others were the victims of personal vendettas, or those who had offended Mrs Gandhi, Sanjay Gandhi, or their cronies. India was rapidly enveloped in a miasma of fear and repression.

After nearly two years of rule by her and Sanjay Gandhi's fiat, Mrs Gandhi announced national elections for March 1977. Her decision was evidently based on the assumption that the Congress would win: the economy was in good shape; she continued to believe that the actions taken during the Emergency enjoyed support, especially among the rural poor; and reports from the intelligence agencies predicted a sweeping victory for the Congress.

The 1977 elections were fought on the single issue of the Emergency. The results exposed the depth of Mrs Gandhi's hubris. She was routed in her Rae Bareli pocket borough. Sanjay Gandhi was trounced in the Amethi constituency, just across the district border from Baba ka Gaon. The Congress won only about one-quarter of the Lok Sabha seats, winning just two of these from the Hindi-speaking belt. The Congress' share of the vote in UP shrank from the 49 per cent won in 1971 to 25 per cent; nationally, it declined by nearly 10 percentage points.[21]

Belying its glorious beginning, the record of Mrs Gandhi's first decade of rule as prime minister was a singularly unflattering one. In that short period, she had tarnished Nehru's legacy, earned an unsavoury reputation for nepotism and dictatorial abuses of power, and hastened the Congress' decline in New Delhi and in virtually every province. Most galling, perhaps, was that she had been disavowed by the poor, whom she had assumed to be a compliant vote-bank.

The most spectacular loss of support for Mrs Gandhi was from the scheduled castes, particularly in the hard-hit northern Indian states. The repudiation was particularly apparent in the constituencies reserved for schedule-caste candidates, of which the Congress won just a quarter, with most of these victories in the south. Ram Dass comments: *Because of the* nasbandhi, *poor people voted against Mrs Gandhi. We all voted for the Janata Party because we were so fed up with what had happened during her rule. We were all very happy when she lost the elections!*

## The poor at the close of the 1970s

The ascension of the Janata Party and its allies to power in New Delhi and, after assembly elections in June that year, in eleven provinces, marked a watershed in independent India's history: nothing less momentous than the end of the Congress' 'one-party' dominance of Indian politics. But, however important as history, this pivotal turn was to hold few, if any, benefits for India's poor, putting an end to even the mild reformist thrust initiated by Mrs Gandhi so fulsomely a decade before.[22]

As in New Delhi, the Janata government in UP was a combustible alliance of disparate parties, drawn together momentarily by their opposition to Mrs Gandhi. But taken together, the constituents of the Janata effectively aggregated the support of large and medium peasants, many made prosperous by the spread of the Green Revolution. A large proportion were from the elite cultivating and higher-middle castes. Signalling the emergence of these castes as a major force in the province's politics, in 1977 UP had its first non-upper-caste chief minister in the middle-caste Ram Naresh Yadav.

Given its base of support amongst the medium and large peasantry, Janata rule differed in important ways from that of the Congress regimes, which had come to power with the backing of a more diverse range of rural and urban interests. One consequence of the Janata's more purely rural backing was greater emphasis, both in rhetoric and practice, on public investments to promote agriculture and the rural sector over industry and urban interests. A second consequence, with profound repercussions for the rural poor in UP, was that the 'rural tilt', as Janata leaders described their preferential policies for rural areas, was matched by a neglect of distributional concerns. The difference between Congress and Janata approaches towards issues of social justice and poverty was particularly apparent where agrarian reform was concerned. In the case of the Congress, because of the party's historical commitment to agrarian reforms, the central leadership in New Delhi would periodically force Congress governments in Lucknow to proclaim the government's commitment to this goal. Of course, the experience of the previous three decades had proved that the commitment would not be implemented, in great part because the central government's commitment was itself weak, and in part because the UP government generally lacked the political strength to tackle the powerful.

But under the Janata there was a conscious policy decision to bury the issue of agrarian reforms. In the Janata-designed Five Year Plan (1978–83) for UP, agrarian reform merited less than three of the document's 1,500 pages. Of these pages, the subject of ceilings and redistribution received three paragraphs, to the effect that 'much of the work has been completed'. The message was evident: there was no scope left for redistribution.[23] In UP, Janata rule put an end to the discussion of land reforms as a goal of public policy.

At the close of the 1970s, the percentage of the population estimated to be below the poverty line was only imperceptibly lower than at its beginning, and no lower than a quarter of a century earlier.[24] This was so even though the economy grew at a fair clip, with the national product expanding at an average of 2.3 per cent each year. But these gains were negated by the worsening distribution of income. And in a new development for India, the huge number of poor people went hungry despite the stocks of wheat and rice overflowing from government granaries.

Like most poor families in UP, Ram Dass and his family remained as impoverished through the 1970s as they had been in the 1960s. As in that decade, they owned only the one-seventh of an acre of land that Ram Dass had bought on returning from Bombay; this small field could provide them with only an insignificant amount of food grains. (It was as late as 1982 before they got possession of the one-third of an acre of land from land reform.) Ram Dass and his wife, his mother (his father died in 1973), his older son and his orphaned nephew all worked as field labourers for the *Thakurs*. Their wages did not increase despite the burgeoning 'Green Revolution' harvests from the *Thakurs'* large fields. The 1970s drew to a close with every sign that Ram Dass's family would never be able to extricate itself from the deprivation that it had long suffered.

# 8

# Shrinath

IN 1978, Shrinath, the elder of Ram Dass's sons, was employed as a teacher in the primary school system operated by the UP government. With this, Ram Dass's family began a slow climb out of poverty, though it was to be nearly another decade before they were no longer impoverished and could meet all their basic needs.

The manner of their emancipation spoke volumes about the limitations of India's development since Independence. For more than three decades, Ram Dass's family had remained deeply impoverished, and tyrannized by the village landlords, despite their every effort to progress. In these decades, the numbers of impoverished and destitute people in India had nearly doubled, increasing by about 100 million. The Congress party, which had ruled in Delhi and Lucknow for three unbroken decades, had emerged as a force to further the interests of the propertied. The 'socialism' promised by Nehru, Indira Gandhi and other Congress leaders had never even begun to be delivered, and the paltry redistributive efforts initiated since Independence had only marginally aided a small proportion of the impoverished, or ameliorated their oppression. In Baba ka Gaon, neither the number nor the proportion of impoverished families had diminished.

**Shrinath**

Thus, if families like Ram Dass's moved out of poverty, they were the exception, and their limited emancipation came because of good fortune and extraordinary endeavour.

Ram Dass says: *If I hadn't worked very hard as a labourer and educated Shrinath, it would have been impossible for him to become a teacher. It was very difficult for me to send Shrinath and Jhoku to school. But I had this conviction that I should make them study however poor I was. So I worked harder so that they could study. I bore a heavier burden. I told Shrinath that you will have to wear torn clothes like me but at least you will be able to go to school. When there were four days left to pay the monthly school charges for slate and chalk of Rs 5, he would tell me, 'Dada, I need this money on this day,' and I would try to arrange for it. I would sell some grain that we had stored, or borrow money from someone.*

Shrinath is known to all the lower-caste people in the village as 'Masterji'. 'Masterji' is more a honorific than a nickname, for Shrinath is held in high esteem for accomplishing what was always regarded as impossible for Baba ka Gaon's scheduled castes – completing secondary school and, even more wondrous, becoming a teacher. He teaches at a primary school close to Baba ka Gaon.

Shrinath's learning and reputation for integrity have made him one of the most respected middle-aged men amongst the lower castes in Baba ka Gaon. By example, he has encouraged other scheduled-caste families in the village to educate both their boys and their girls, so much so that an unusually large proportion of the younger scheduled-caste population of the village is literate. Shrinath's eldest son was the first scheduled-caste person in Baba ka Gaon to gain a Bachelor's degree, and his eldest daughter the first to complete the eighth grade, which is typically the highest grade that even upper-caste women study in rural UP.

In his mid-40s today, Shrinath looks quite like Ram Dass, but is more reserved, almost sombre. He talks rarely, preferring to listen closely to others. He smiles less readily than his father, but when he does laugh it is rich and full. His face generally wears a faraway expression. His mother, laughing, says: *Sometimes he is so lost in his reading that you can pass your hand in front of the paper and he still won't notice you.* Most often, Shrinath wears a *kurta*-pyjama of white or brown *khadi*.

While working in the fields, which he does every morning before school and on returning in the late afternoon, he wears a *dhoti*, wrapped high above his knees. In the slush and mud of the monsoon, he dons a vest and old, small shorts, which look incongruous on him.

Shrinath studied first at the primary school in Devapur, 2 km away, at which Ram Dass had studied for a single precious year decades earlier. When Shrinath joined the school, there were already four or five other scheduled-caste students from Baba ka Gaon there.

*I didn't even learn the Hindi alphabet in the two years that I spent at the school! The teachers were all from the upper castes and wouldn't bother to teach us lower-caste students. They would pay attention only to the upper-caste children. Everyone knew which caste you were from because we all came from nearby villages, and the teachers could always find out because they wrote down your caste at the time of admission. This is done even now. As we scheduled-caste people usually do not have a last name, unlike the upper castes, everyone would know that we were scheduled-caste. The untouchability of my father's time had diminished somewhat. At least we didn't have to sit far away from the other students. But still we weren't allowed to touch the drinking-water vessel or mug. Even though India had been independent for ten years, the old prejudices had not changed.*

*Since my father was living in Bombay and saw that my progress was next to nothing, he called me to Bombay in 1959 or so. I stayed there for three years. We were taught very well. A different teacher used to come every hour to take the new class and we were taught every subject. I came back to the village in 1961, and then went back to Bombay. But in 1962 I had to shift back to school here because the factory my father worked in was being closed down and he was going to come back to the village.*

Shrinath went back to the Devapur school, joining the fourth grade. *It was difficult. There was a great difference in the education between here and in Bombay. I was happy that I had studied outside, where I had gained so much. Here I was just lying around not learning anything.*

*The discrimination had become less. And I was a very good student, especially because I had learnt so much in the Bombay school. In class four, I was the best student. And because of this I got a lot of appreciation from the teachers. And in particular there was one good* teacher who lived close to our village and he gave me a lot of help. His name was Ram Dev Upadhaya. Despite being a Brahmin, he did not discriminate against me at all. All people are not the same and some are very compassionate. After eating dinner, I and some other students would go to his house. He used to say, 'You all come, I will teach you for one or two hours. And if there is some problem in understanding we will solve it together.'

I was at the Devapur school until I finished the fifth class. I then went to the secondary school in Sanghipur, which is about a 40 minutes walk from here. I was taught there well. I had a very good mathematics teacher there, Chedi Lal-ji.

When I was in school the monthly fees used to be Rs 7 per month. It was very difficult for my family to pay this. We would postpone paying it for a few days but then we would eventually have to pay. And there used to be a fine for each day you were late with the fees.

I could not study enough at night because I was worried about how much lamp-oil I was using. We didn't own a lantern but had a chimney lamp. Our poverty was so much at that time that I would stop studying because I wanted to save the lamp-oil. I used to study until midnight or even later, but then my parents would finally tell me, 'Go to sleep because you're using too much oil.'

One day when I was a child I was studying during the monsoons. It was raining heavily and it was dark and so I was lying in the doorway of the hut. There was also a strong wind and to protect the flame in the lamp from going off I used a book as a wind-break. I fell asleep and the book fell onto the flame and caught fire. And my pillow caught fire! And it was only when my hand started burning that I woke up!

I would wake in the morning and go to brush my teeth. Then I would cut a huge bundle of fodder for the cattle. This was from the fields of the zamindar. Then I would have a bath, eat my breakfast and walk to school. There were no bicycles. There was no real road either. You had to walk past the canal and through the fields.

School used to start at 10 but we had to arrive 15 minutes earlier because there was a prayer and attendance. At 10 the study would start and we would go to our classrooms. The clothes we had were far worse than what the children wear today. We would only wear dhotis and shirts. Some would wear a pyjama. It was very rare for boys to wear *pants. But in Bombay I wore pants. In the village I had one* dhoti *and this I would wear for about one week before washing. When I worked in the fields I would wear underwear. It was only when I joined class six that my parents got a pair of pyjamas and* kurta *stitched for me. When these began to tear, only then did I get another one.*

In 1973, Shrinath graduated from the twelfth grade after passing the Intermediate examination required of all students. He was nearly 20 years old. *I was interested in studying further, but it was very expensive to do this. And my family's situation wasn't good at that time. We had income only from labouring, and just a tiny plot of land from which we could get some grain. My father was alone, my brother was very young, and there were lots of people in the family. My grandfather and grandmother were very old. I stayed at home for one year, working as a labourer and in our field. Then I applied to the government training course for primary school teachers. I got into the course after two years. I got in on merit as I had scored 56 per cent in the Intermediate exams. There were reservations for the scheduled castes and if I had got less I would have got in on that quota. But even after completing the course I didn't get a posting to a school until 1978.*

Under a government affirmative-action programme to raise the number of scheduled-caste teachers in the government school system (virtually all the primary schools and a majority of secondary schools in rural India are funded and operated by provincial governments), qualifications are somewhat relaxed for applicants from these castes. As with other affirmative-action programmes for the scheduled castes, roughly 18 per cent of all job openings are reserved for them. When Shrinath applied to the training course that precedes hiring, so few scheduled-caste persons were educated that the vast majority of posts reserved for them would go unfilled and would be allowed to lapse. At the time that he graduated from school a quarter of a century ago, says Shrinath, teaching still remained the exclusive preserve of the Brahmins and other upper castes, and he cannot recall there being a single scheduled-caste teacher in the surrounding schools then.

With Shrinath's employment as a teacher, Ram Dass's family began a slow climb out of poverty. Shrinath began on a salary of Rs 300 per month; by the end of the 1980s this had increased to roughly Rs 3,000. By saving carefully from this income, in the early 1980s Ram Dass and

Shrinath bought slightly over one acre of good land. In 1983, the family got two-thirds of an acre of infertile land from the land-ceiling effort begun by Indira Gandhi a decade earlier. But until at least half-way through the 1980s, Ram Dass's family remained deeply impoverished, probably close to the threshold of absolute poverty. Ram Dass, his wife and Shrinath, as well as Shrinath's wife and teenage sons, continued to work as labourers for the *Thakurs*. Hansraj, Shrinath's eldest son, recalls that until about 1985 they all went short of food, did not have money for clothes, and often could not pay his school fees.

Coincidentally, the turning point in the well-being of Ram Dass's family came at about the time in which the proportion of the absolutely poor declined significantly, the only sustained stretch of progress on poverty ever in independent India. In the decade-and-a-half from the late-1970s, the proportion of the population below the poverty line fell from roughly 55 per cent to about 37 per cent.[1] This success came about because of an unusual combination of factors. Rapid economic growth played some part. But far more important to reducing poverty was the unprecedented increase in government spending (at twice the rate of growth of the economy), which added an element of 'trickle-down' to a growth pattern that created very few jobs at all.[2] In fact, because a major share of these funds went to rural areas, where the bulk of the poor live, the impact on poverty was especially large. The rural rich and better-off groups cornered the overwhelming share of the government's largesse, swallowing funds and monopolizing the expanding opportunities for rural trade and business, but the transfer of finances was so vast as to trickle down to some amongst the poor. Had the poor gained more directly from both economic growth and government spending, far greater numbers would have been lifted above the absolute poverty threshold. But because the gains went disproportionately to the better-off and middle classes, the pace of decline in poverty did not even match the speed of population growth and the number of poor continued to grow through this period.

## The Congress' 'trickle-down' strategy

Despite the persistence of mass poverty, by the end of the 1970s the Congress no longer even made any pretence that it would seek to initiate radical solutions to poverty and inequality. Discussion of land reform and other redistributive means of addressing the structural causes of poverty was terminated. Ironically, this development was led by Mrs Gandhi on her return to power in 1980. This was a new, pragmatic Mrs Gandhi, not the rhetoric-spouting heroine of the past. Gone were the promises to redistribute land and to eradicate poverty through radical change, promises which anyway had hardly been translated into policy.[3] Though Mrs Gandhi continued to woo the poor, she did so now by promising them goodies from 'poverty-alleviation' programmes, which were in theory supposed to provide them with employment, skills and income-generating assets.

The poverty-alleviation programmes had actually begun during Mrs Gandhi's *Garibi Hatao* phase, with the launching of several rural development and short-term employment schemes for the rural poor. The most important of these was a Food for Work programme (labourers were paid with the surplus food-grains garnered from the Green Revolution), another rural employment scheme for developing local infrastructure, and a scheme for providing technical assistance and subsidized loans to small farmers and agricultural labourers.[4] None of these programmes performed well nor made any significant impact on poverty. This outcome was not surprising as the programmes were premised on the assumption that the spending of money would by itself be sufficient to reduce poverty.[5] Nevertheless, on Mrs Gandhi's return to power, the poverty-alleviation programmes were immeasurably expanded. Her decision to expand them, despite their evident failure, spoke volumes about Mrs Gandhi's true political interests. These were that she preserve the fiction of being pro-poor, a task accomplished by this array of schemes; and equally important, that the status quo of wealth and power be left undisturbed. It mattered not one whit to Mrs Gandhi or to other Congress leaders that the poverty-alleviation programmes were patently incapable of having more than a marginal impact on poverty: the Congress had abandoned any effort to aid the poor.[6]

The central government's outlay on such schemes – they were overwhelmingly initiated and funded by the centre – nearly trebled in the next five years. By the time of Mrs Gandhi's assassination in late 1984, they were a principal part of public policy.[7] Indian planning documents have since been decorated with an ever-multiplying number of unintelligible acronyms – IRDP, NREP, RLEGP, TRYSEM, JRY – all to do with these rural development schemes.

The programmes reached their acme under Rajiv Gandhi, who had succeeded his mother as prime minister. Rajiv Gandhi made little effort to hide his lack of interest in equity concerns, and the palliative schemes fitted in with his emphasis on boosting economic growth to the disregard of redistribution. The top-down, centralized programmes also complemented his technocratic approach to India's development, which was in essence that the country's many problems would be remedied if every Indian simply heeded the advice of Gandhi's cohort of whizkids.[8] Moreover, emulating Mrs Gandhi, Rajiv Gandhi exploited the vast resources for patronage offered by the schemes to mobilize electoral support from the poor. A third and crucial factor was that the centrally funded schemes aided his effort – a process begun by his mother – to concentrate power in the central government and to bypass the political structure in the provinces and districts. Under Rajiv Gandhi and his successors, expansion was so rapid that by 1997 there were about 95 central poverty-alleviation schemes, with a total budget of Rs 7,000 crore[9] (70 billion).

Provincial politicians, surprisingly, have not noticeably complained about the central government encroaching on their turf. Their acquiescence stems from a whole range of reasons. In part, most of India's major parties, whether in the provinces or at the centre, share a consensus that they should no longer vie against each other with offers of redistributive reforms; moreover, like the Congress' leaders, they care little about impact. Again, as the majority of funds go through the provincial government and have to be disbursed by their administrative officers, the provincial government garners some of the goodwill accruing from the programmes. But arguably the most important cause for the provincial politicians' silence is that they siphon off the enormous funds for the poverty-alleviation programmes to enrich themselves as well as to lubricate their political machines. With their blessing, district politicians, administrative officials, the former landlords, and a host of other intermediaries who have sprung up between the poor and the government, get a cut of this money.[10] At the village level, the primary beneficiaries of these programmes are the upper-caste ex-landlords and middle farmers, as they control the *panchayats* and are typically related to officials and politicians. (The increasing government control of the economy begun under Mrs Gandhi – for instance, in the allocation of licences to trade in essential commodities or for setting up rural industries – has for the same reasons also benefited these elites, further widening the gap between the rural rich and poor.) As a result, almost to the last paisa, the funds for the poverty-alleviation programmes go to the well-off, those who are part of the flourishing network of corruption.

Shrinath says: *The money is eaten up on the way from the MP to the MLA* [member of the provincial assembly] *to the* pradhan. *Someone takes a bit, someone else a little more, and all that is spent is Rs 5,000 while Rs 50,000 is pocketed. But on paper it is shown that all the money is spent and that development takes place!*

*Only a tiny bit of the government's schemes for villages are implemented. The administration, by the time it gets things to the villages, doesn't deliver any service, anything for progress. Even the gram-sevak* [the village-level development worker; *'sevak'* means 'a person who serves'] *is now called a gram-officer, and hence is not interested in speaking to any of us! He should tell us how to cultivate according to modern techniques and why we should give up old ways, but he doesn't tell us anything.*

Ram Dass says: *The government keeps making these announcements about reducing poverty, but the poor never get anything. We hear from the radio that the government has released so much money for the poor. But half or three-quarters of it is eaten, and here us labourers don't even get the wages we are supposed to for the work! The policy is announced, and then at this level the lower officials send back reports saying that everything has been done, but in reality nothing has taken place. And if we protest in writing officially, these officials make sure that the complaints don't go to the senior officers. There's no solution to this because everyone is corrupt from the top to the bottom. And when nothing happens from the top, people just give up. And even when there are concessions for the poor and the scheduled castes, the officials take half of it! For instance, the scheduled castes get about 50 per cent off loans from the government. From that, one official wants 10 per cent as a bribe, and then another official says he also wants something. And on top of that we have to pay interest to the government! So nothing really changes. That's why none of us ever goes to the bank for loans.*

Durbhe, a young relative of theirs, says: *There are all these schemes but nothing happens. For instance, Rajiv Gandhi had ordered that potable water be made available to all villages in Amethi* [Gandhi's electoral constituency, which borders Baba ka Gaon] *but when he came for inspection he found a handpump there but also that one old woman was still drawing water from the well. So he asked her, 'Why are you drawing water from the well and not from the handpump?' She said, 'Sahib, just one hour before you came they dug this handpump here, but believe me no water will ever flow from it.'*

Decrying this corruption, in 1989 Rajiv Gandhi's government decided to channel funds for the Jawahar Rozgar Yojana, an enormous employment programme, calculatedly named after his grandfather, Jawaharlal Nehru, directly to village *panchayats*, bypassing the provincial governments. In two public speeches that caused a furore (Indian prime ministers are not expected to reveal such things), he declared that 70 per cent of the resources earmarked for anti-poverty programmes were consumed by the administration, and that over 85 per cent of the funds allocated for development programmes never reached the people they were intended to assist.[11]

But Gandhi's assertion that the benefits of the programmes would flow to the poor now that the funds were going directly to the *panchayats* was political chicanery. In UP, particularly in Awadh and the eastern areas, as a consequence of land reform never having been seriously undertaken, the upper-caste former village landlords dominated the *panchayats* much as they continued to dominate village politics. In Baba ka Gaon, the same *Thakur* held the crucial post of *pradhan* from the first *panchayat* elections in the early 1950s until 1995. Because the former village landlords as well as the land barons had since the mid-1950s become the Congress' most influential supporters in UP, Rajiv Gandhi made no attempt at all to prevent them from consuming the funds coming to the *panchayat*. In a travesty of what he had promised, the *panchayats*' expanding budgets simply made the upper castes more wealthy and bolstered their ability to oppress the poor.

Shrinath says: *The* pradhans *are all from the upper castes and whatever comes from the government they eat up. A lot of money is allocated but no facilities are ever developed. There is no drainage system in the village and in the monsoon it gets totally flooded. These people just get together and eat the money; they don't spend it on the village. If somebody really wants to do work, there is so much money given by the government that you could build roads through the village!*

Ram Dass says: *I've been a* panchayat *member for the last six years. The* pradhan *is supposed to call a meeting every month. But in all these years we must have met just once! He and the other upper-caste members put false thumb-prints on the papers, saying that we agreed to this and this and this.* (Ram Dass was elected to the *panchayat* on a seat reserved for the scheduled castes.)

Durbhe, their young relative, says: *The* Thakurs *always had enough land and enough money. And now their bank balances have become huge by eating this money! This has been going on for years. About Rs 2.5 lakhs [250,000] comes for development work from the state government. Then more money comes for the Jawahar Rozgar Yojana from the central government. Altogether about Rs 300,000–400,000 comes for the village. Of this only about Rs 50,000 is spent each year on work, the rest is eaten up by the* Thakurs.

Shrinath says: *There is always corruption within the* panchayat. *Especially when distribution of land is involved, there is corruption. Bribes are given. And if there is a scheduled-caste man who has been allotted land, an upper or middle-caste person can always give money and somehow get the land!*

## The failure in Amethi

The inability of the trickle-down approach, even when complemented by munificent poverty-alleviation programmes, to make an appreciable dent in poverty is nakedly evident in Amethi, the electoral constituency first of Sanjay Gandhi and then of Rajiv Gandhi. Directly across the district border from Baba ka Gaon (it is part of the adjacent Sultanpur district), Amethi is where Ram Dass's father originally came from. Though under Rajiv Gandhi and now under Congress politicians handpicked by Rajiv Gandhi's widow, Sonia, millions upon millions of rupees have poured into the constituency, poverty is as intense and prevalent there as in Baba ka Gaon, across Pratapgarh or in other parts of Sultanpur. Amethi does have far smoother roads and finer government guest-houses, a plethora of industries, incomparably better telephone connections, and many more schools and hospitals, but by each and every indicator relevant to the poor it performs no better than areas not favoured by political largesse. The inequity in land ownership is as great, wage rates for labourers no higher, and oppression by the upper castes as intense as elsewhere in the region. The enormous funds pumped into the Amethi constituency have been swallowed whole by a thick network comprising the former land barons and village landlord, who form the core of the Congress political machine in the area. Opportunities for the poor to emancipate themselves have not expanded one whit more than in Pratapgarh.

Ram Dass's father was from the village of Ranipur, earlier part of the large Amethi estate. The village is 8 km from Amethi town, and roughly 25 km from Baba ka Gaon. Somewhat larger than Baba ka Gaon, Ranipur is a pretty village, surrounded by thick groves, but like Baba ka Gaon, it is approached by a dirt road. Its homes are no better than those of Baba ka Gaon.

Ram Dass's closest relative in Ranipur is Babu Lal, his father's first cousin. Though 80 years old and physically frail, Babu Lal's memory and mind are sharp. He is now hard of hearing, and consequently tends to shout when speaking. The two huts that he and his extended family live in are poorer than Ram Dass's hut in Baba ka Gaon. Babu Lal says that of Ranipur's roughly 150 families, about six have no land at all. Another six own less than half an acre. Of the remaining families, about 70 have just over an acre each. Babu Lal's extended family of 11 adults and several children owns one-and-a-half acres. With the other two dozen scheduled-caste families, they are amongst the poorest people in Ranipur. The richest are the 13 Brahmin families, descendants of the former village landlords, who each now own between 10 and 15 acres.

Two thin men, their stick-like legs and tattered *dhotis* caked with mud, sit down to talk. They are both of the Koeri caste, another scheduled caste. They are even visibly poorer than Babu Lal's family. Ram Salawan is the younger of the two, probably no more than 25 years old, with sparkling eyes illuminating an emaciated face. His vest is torn, showing his thin chest. He owns one-sixth of an acre, which he inherited from his grandfather, who received it under Mrs Gandhi's land reform programme. He has title to another one-sixth of an acre, also from the land reform programme, but this is under a legal battle as one of the

Brahmin landlord families has refused to relinquish it. In the six years since he was formally given title to the field, Ram Salawan has never been able to cultivate it, first because the landlord threatened to kill him. Three years ago Ram Salawan tried to start working the field but at this point the landlord began a court case in the district court, which passed a stay order under which the landlord is allowed to continue cultivating the field until the case is decided. Ram Salawan says that he has spent about Rs 2,500 on legal and transport costs in these three years. He has to travel on average once a month to the court in Sultanpur, about two hours away by bus, which costs him Rs 10 each way. The lawyer charges Rs 23 per hearing. Ram Salawan says there is no legal aid for the poor or the scheduled castes. The land is worth Rs 5–7,000, as it is only of average quality.

*The Brahmin has about ten acres, with about six persons in the family. And here I am with seven people living on less than one-sixth of an acre.* Ram Salawan and his wife have five young children, four sons and a daughter. *This is how poor people damn themselves. It's our lack of knowledge that kills us.* Ram Salawan says he could only study up to the fourth grade because his parents were as poor as he is now.

The one-sixth of an acre that he owns produces roughly 200 kilograms of grain each year, about two-thirds of the minimum nutritional requirement for two adults.[12] He and his wife also work as labourers, but each can find only about three months' work over the year. Ram Salawan earns about Rs 20 a day if he works at building or repairing homes. For field work, he and his wife earn Rs 12–15 per day. With these meagre earnings and small quantity of food-grain, Ram Salawan and his family are far below the absolute poverty line that marks the inability to ensure a survival-level diet. Their destitution is compounded by the expense of fighting the legal case.

Ram Lal, the second man, who is related to Ram Salawan, owns one-third of an acre. He is in his fifties. *Our village* pradhan, *the Brahmin, keeps telling us to get sterilized. But I have three daughters, they will get married off and live elsewhere, and there won't be a single person to give my wife and me a mug of water! So I told the* pradhan *that if you give me in writing that someone will look after me when I'm old, I'll get sterilized right away! But luckily our fourth child was a boy. He was born just a year ago.*

Babu Lal, Ram Dass's old relative, chuckles and says that, during the Emergency, officials caught him and a teenage relative of his and dragged them away for sterilization. They succeeded in escaping but had to hide in the fields for 15 days. *But I was already sterilized in reality by then, because I was so old!*

Shrinath says: *All the mills and industries in Amethi, not one of them gives employment to a single local person. Even the labour comes from outside. The private steel plant on the Lucknow road has employed all its labourers from Delhi or Haryana. There was one person from our village working in the cycle factory, but he got selected from Delhi. People from here try to get work in the factories, but one needs a lot of connections to get jobs. So it has not helped us at all. The only benefit has been that during the construction of the plants some of the young boys got to be employed there as construction labourers.*

## Shrinath – the 1990s

Shrinath and his wife, Draupadi, have five children. Hansraj, Shrinath's eldest son, aged 27, was the first scheduled-caste person in Baba ka Gaon to earn the Bachelor's degree. He lives currently in Allahabad where he is unemployed. He was married in 1987 and has three young children, all of whom live with his parents in Baba ka Gaon.

Bansraj, the second son, is four or five years younger than Hansraj. He is married, lives with his parents, and has one child. Vidyawati, Shrinath's eldest daughter, was the first scheduled-caste girl in the village to complete the eighth grade. She was married in early 1996, at the age of eighteen. Rakesh Kumar, the youngest son, is 16 and completing secondary school. Sarita, his youngest child, is a year younger and is in the seventh grade.

While Ram Dass, his wife and Jhoku's wife and three children live in the small hut that has been their family's home for many decades, Shrinath lives at some distance from them, at another corner of the village, in a two-roomed brick house. *Ours is a combined family, but there's a problem of space in our old home, so as there was some empty land left on this side of the village I thought 'let me build a house here because later there may not be any land left here'. Everyone from the scheduled castes was also building here. The land was given as part of the land redistribution programme. We were each given a patch of land to build homes on. It was given to those families who had two or more adult sons. The logic was that one son can stay in the parental home, but the other needs a place to live. The identification of families and the giving of land was done by the* panchayat. *At least this was done honestly!*

The house is small, single-storey, built of unpainted brick and mortar. It is entered by a small verandah. The verandah is just large enough to keep a *charpai* and some chairs. In a cage hanging at one end is a young green parakeet, who clambers around, clowning for visitors. The house cost about Rs 50,000 to build. This is about triple the cost of building a *kucha* mud and thatch hut. Kucha *houses are much cooler in summer and also warmer in winter*, says Shrinath, somewhat wistfully.

By the mid-1990s, Ram Dass and Shrinath had bought more land. Added to the patch of land Ram Dass had bought in the 1960s, the other patch from the land-ceiling programme and their first purchase in the 1980s, they now own 2.5 acres, which would place them amongst UP's marginal farmers. In part because there are currently many able-bodied people in the family, they also sharecrop more land, generally another 2.5 acres. The unfavourable terms of sharecropping have not changed: they give half the produce to the owner, beyond providing the labour and most inputs, ranging from water and seeds to half the fertilizer.

The fields produce enough for the family's annual requirements for grains. There is rarely anything left to sell. Consequently, the extended family depends on Shrinath's salary for cash. By the standards of the many poorer families in Baba ka Gaon, Shrinath's current salary of roughly Rs 4,000 per month is enviable. But when divided between a family of ten adults, three teenagers and four young children, it is barely sufficient to meet all their basic needs for clothes, medicines and education. Thus, though they are no longer impoverished or below the absolute poverty threshold, they are still poor and continue to be substantially in debt.

Shrinath says: *Money is a kind of obsession. And one's desires are endless, however much one gets. But I do have a lot of problems. My eldest son, Hansraj, has been living in Allahabad for four years, but hasn't been able to find a job. It was easier when he lived here because I now send him about Rs 500 a month. Then my youngest son is in high school and I want to send him outside as well. Because of that there will be even greater problems in my financial situation. And then there*

*are my brother's three children. Another of my daughters is studying
here. I have just given one daughter in marriage and this was a very
expensive process. Then I will have to get my daughter and my brother's
daughter married in two or three years from now. My younger brother
Jhoku only rarely sends money for his children. I have to find some
balance between these expenses and the amount I earn.*

*These days I am Rs 30,000 in debt. Ten thousand I had taken from
a bank to start some business for Hansraj. But my wife became very
sick and we had to spend all this money on her treatment. And then
I just borrowed more money to pay for my daughter's wedding. I took
this debt against the money in my government pension fund. I'm
desperately thinking of ways of adjusting so that we don't face worse
problems ahead. This is the situation.*

*When I was young, I never used to think about what would happen
in the future. But as a father I have to think about my children's future.
I have tried as much as possible to fulfil my duties to them. I've tried
to ensure that the children develop as much as they can. Their future
should be better than what I have lived.*

*But unemployment is increasing all across India. That's why I'm
sceptical that everyone will find jobs in the future. I did manage to find
a job. But for our children things are going to be difficult. My eldest
son has been applying for government jobs for four years, but even
though he studies hard for the exams he has not even been called for
one interview! There are still reservations for the scheduled castes in
government jobs, but now there are many more scheduled-caste people
applying for jobs. There is also a lot of corruption. You have to pay
Rs 50,000–100,000 as a bribe! And then many people pay bribes to get
certificates that show that they are scheduled-caste when they are not.*

## India's costly failure in literacy

Shrinath has taught at the primary school in Kusauli, a small village some
15 km from Baba ka Gaon, since 1978. He now bicycles there, six days
a week, and works from 10 a.m. to 4 p.m. Normally, he puts in an hour
in the fields before school and several hours more when he returns.

The school in Kusauli opened the year before Shrinath joined. It
is reached by a winding, tree-lined brick road that passes through one

section of the village. When Shrinath first joined, there was no building, and classes for the 70 students were held in the shade of a large banyan tree. The school is now housed in a two-room brick building. The building is dilapidated; thick cobwebs cloak the ceiling, and the creamish paint has peeled in enormous swathes. Like the vast majority of rural Indian schools, this one does not have electricity nor a bathroom. But at least there is a hand-pump for water nearby, a facility missing at many rural schools.[13] The number of students has swelled to one hundred and fifty. The children join when they are about 6 years of age. Many of the older children bring younger siblings with them as they need to be cared for while their parents work in the fields.

Apart from Shrinath, the Kusauli school has two other teachers. The principal is a *Thakur* some years older than Shrinath, while the other teacher is from a middle caste. In large part because of the affirmative-action requirement, today roughly one-tenth of the teachers in Pratapgarh district are from the scheduled castes, says Shrinath. The number of middle-caste teachers has also grown to about one-fifth, though there is no affirmative-action programme for these castes. The increase in the number of scheduled-caste teachers has come despite the hostility of the upper castes. *For a long time the head of the Pratapgarh district council was a Brahmin, who would try to appoint only other Brahmins to the teaching posts. But because us scheduled-caste people began to be educated and because of the reservations policy, they had to appoint teachers from the scheduled castes. The predominance of the upper castes persists because it is only when they retire that their posts can be filled by other castes. But slowly and gradually, the numbers of the scheduled and middle castes are increasing.*

The three teachers take turns teaching different grades, which in Indian primary schools are from grades one to five. Grades one and two are taught together on the verandah; three and four in the classrooms; and grade five outside. One group of kids is under a young banyan tree, most sitting on old gunny sacks, a large blackboard placed on a tripod. Another group sits in the sun, counting. Up to grade two, the children use slates and chalk. Older students use paper and ink pens.

As there are just three teachers to teach five grades, two grades at a time must work on their own. In practice this means that the unattended students do no work at all. But the Kusauli school is in fact better off than many other Indian government-run primary schools. One-third of them have just one teacher, saddled with the extraordinary charge of teaching five grades simultaneously.[14] On average, there are nearly 60 students for every primary school teacher in India. The low teacher–student ratio is a central cause of the abysmal quality of education.

Most of the children in the school are from the upper castes. Until 1985 or so, says Shrinath, there were even fewer lower-caste children. In comparison to the prejudice he faced in school, overt caste discrimination is now rare. *Things are so much better now than when I was a child. Now scheduled-caste children even play with upper-caste children!* Children from the lower castes are virtually all worse dressed than upper-caste children. Most younger ones are dusty and unwashed, hair caked with filth, their bodies and clothes stained by mud, slate, chalk and food. The older children tend to look somewhat tidier and cleaner, presumably because they can care for themselves. Virtually all these children wear torn clothes – some are just rags without buttons – which are so beaten into the dust that it is difficult to say what material or colour they were originally. Most of these children are barefoot; a few wear rubber slippers.

Without exception, all the lower-caste children are bone-thin. While superficially most look healthy and are voluble and active, the vast majority are much shorter and thinner than the upper-caste children, an indication that they are stunted from chronic malnourishment and frequent illnesses. Shrinath says that many children from poorer families are often too sick to study because of fevers or infections, but that virtually none comes to school hungry. *All the children get enough to eat. They may not get milk or fruits but they get enough other food. I know that in rich homes unless the child gets milk they consider the kid not to have eaten. But here it's enough that they get something to eat, whatever this might be.* The conditions at Shrinath's school reflect UP's dismal performance in literacy in the decades since Independence. Nearly 60 per cent of the province's population is illiterate. Of the population over the age of 7 years, eight of every ten females and every second male is illiterate.[15]

Though UP is amongst the worst-performing Indian provinces in terms of literacy – as it is on almost every other index of human welfare – even India's overall performance is shockingly poor in comparison to that of China and other Asian nations. In rural India, amongst those aged 10–14 years (a measure of recent performance), every second girl and every fourth boy is illiterate, incapable of writing or reading a simple letter in any Indian language. In contrast, in rural China far fewer than one in ten girls and one in twenty boys is illiterate. And although literacy has gone up moderately in India, from roughly one-fifth of the population in 1951 to just over one-half in 1991, it has lagged far behind population growth. Consequently, between 1951 and 1991, the number of illiterates increased from 300 million to 450 million.[16] Ironically, at Independence, India's Constitution had set a goal that by 1960 every Indian would have eight years of free schooling.[17]

The failure to provide even basic education has had tremendous costs in human suffering and in the perpetuation of mass poverty. Illiteracy is a major factor in keeping poor people impoverished and hence in preventing economic mobility. The illiterate are hampered in their efforts to progress as all but very low-paid, labouring jobs depend on primary education. Their prospects are further prejudiced as the inability to read and write is strongly linked to undernourishment, ill health and the early death of children.[18]

UP's dismal performance in education is rooted in its comprehensive neglect of public services. In contrast, Kerala and other provinces which have succeeded admirably in raising literacy have done so because of government commitment to the provision of primary education and other public services. Given the extent of poverty in rural India, which means that most families cannot afford the substantial fees levied by private schools, there is no plausible substitute for an efficient system of public education. Reflecting the neglect of public education, UP has the second-lowest level of average expenditure on education of India's 26 provinces. The difficulties posed by inadequate budgetary allocations are compounded because even these funds are misallocated. Thus, comments Shrinath, rather than training and recruiting more primary school teachers, the government presses ahead with spending its money on constructing schools for which it has no teachers. Matters are further worsened because the government's indifference to public services means that there is little supervision or accountability in the school system. Teachers have little incentive to take their job seriously, as their salaries do not depend on performance. The risks of being sacked are slight because they are technically hired on a permanent basis. The rare government inspector can always be bribed or dissuaded from taking any action because most teachers are upper-caste and hence well-connected.

Without an institutionalized means of accountability, parents are not in a position to pressure the teachers, particularly as most teachers are from families with considerable local influence. Ram Dass says: *The teachers in government schools often don't come or just give a holiday to the children. They instead sit in the town on the* charpai *and talk. We can't say anything to them because they all have influence, and are related to somebody or the other amongst the higher-ups. Even if you complain, because of their connections to officials nothing will happen.* At the school that his grandson Umesh attends, often not one of the four teachers will show up.

At Shrinath's own school, the upper-caste principal rarely attends. Shrinath comments: *The upper castes are predominant in everything, and naturally in education. But even when they are teachers they are only interested in politics, in chasing after politicians. Our headmaster is from a landlord family and this is all he does. He comes to school on one day, but then won't come for the rest of the week. In all the schools there are lots of people like this, who sometimes come to the school and sometimes don't come. They are not really interested in the school or in teaching.*

*Because the teachers never attend, the quality of our primary and secondary education is of course very low. Unless the teacher really wishes to teach, how will the children get educated? No one is born educated from the womb! It's only people like us, who either out of their own moral values or out of fear of the village people, come on time and teach properly.*

The persistent absenteeism by teachers and the poor quality of education means that most parents see little benefit in keeping their children in school. In UP's rural schools, for every 100 children who enrol in grade one in any year, only around two children enter grade twelve.[19] As it is, for poor rural families the cost of sending children to school is very high. Shrinath says: *Here many people find it difficult to pay the monthly fee of Rs 10, which is equal to the wages for a day's work.* In theory, education is free in government schools up to class eight, but in practice tuition and a range of other fees are charged, often adding up to a considerable sum.[20] The actual costs to parents are in fact much higher, because when children attend school they forgo a variety of crucial tasks: caring for younger siblings, helping with agriculture, looking after farm animals, and often even working for wages.

Nor does UP's cash-strapped, ill-run public educational system provide the incentives which have helped raise primary-school attendance levels in other provinces. Barely two per cent of rural primary school children receive scholarships from the government, and even they are barely helped because the scholarships give only Rs 144 for the year. And though a small percentage of UP's rural primary schools now provide meals to students during school-hours, the programme is so vitiated by corruption as not to function at all. Says Shrinath: *I wish that children would get more facilities, like meals at school. This would definitely increase the number of children coming to school. Some schools have this feeding programme already, it's called Balahari Yojana. But the food and money get eaten up because of corruption. The teachers just keep half the food in their houses!*

The dismal state of India's public educational system limits particularly the chances of the scheduled castes to acquire basic literacy, let alone education. Across India, only one-fifth of the scheduled castes are literate – half that of the rest of the population. The odds of being educated are even more adverse for scheduled-caste females: only one-tenth are literate, three times fewer than other females.[21] In Baba ka Gaon, very few of the three dozen scheduled-caste families have, like Ram Dass and Shrinath, educated their children. Of the dozen scheduled-caste men in their mid-20s, only three have passed the Bachelor's degree – including Shrinath's son, Hansraj – while none of the others has even graduated from secondary school. And Shrinath's and Jhoku's daughters were the first scheduled-caste girls to attend school. Following their example, a majority of the scheduled-caste families are finally sending their daughters to primary school. But none of the scheduled-caste women who have married into the village is educated. Says Shrinath: *It's like this in all of UP and that's why our children are absolutely worthless. Unless the base is strong how can they be good as adults?*

The persistently low levels of literacy amongst the scheduled castes reflects a welter of adverse factors. In the overwhelming majority of scheduled-caste families who are poor, children are essential to performing household and agricultural chores, making it difficult for their parents to spare them for school. As important, because many scheduled-caste parents see little room for economic mobility and continue to regard unskilled casual labour as their hereditary occupation, they see little point in education for their children. And scheduled-caste children are particularly handicapped by the low quality of teaching in public primary schools, as they can rarely turn for help to their parents or elders, almost all of whom are illiterate.

Because of their illiteracy, the overwhelming majority of young scheduled-caste men and women are fated to remain impoverished. Their families lack land or other productive assets. Their illiteracy means that they will not be able to acquire remunerative non-agricultural work, which now anyway requires much more than basic education. Shrinath comments: *It is not enough to study only through the primary level, which is what most scheduled-caste people do because of their poverty. To progress these days, an individual increasingly requires higher levels of education – at least college graduate. Even high school, which is what I completed, is now not sufficient.*

# 9

# Hansraj

THE eldest of Shrinath's five children, Hansraj was born in Baba ka
Gaon in 1970. Since 1993, he has lived in Allahabad, some 80 km from
the village.

*When my father was a child, my family's poverty was much worse.
They used to survive by working as labourers for the* Thakurs. *When my
father was studying, his family never had enough money to buy oil for
the lantern so he would go and study in another person's house. They
didn't have enough clothes. Of course there were no shoes at all. When
my father would go for examinations, he would borrow someone else's
clothes. They faced every kind of hardship. What I've seen is nothing
compared to their difficulties because when I was young we had at least
some land, even if it was just a little patch.*

*As a child, I used to go to school in an old vest and shorts. Just for
food there was a problem for many years, even after my father got his
job, which was when I was about 10 years old. In the afternoon, at some
time, one got to eat a potato or have some rice water. In the evening,
somehow we used to eat a full meal. Rakesh, my younger brother, who
is now 15, does not face those difficulties.*

*I also used to labour for those who owned land, if anybody had work,
from the time I was 13 or fourteen. I'd do any work that I got. Plough*

**Hansraj**

*or hoe the fields, irrigate with the dugla* [a large animal skin that is used like a bucket]. *I used to get 1.5 kg of grain for a day's work.*

*Some days, I would not go to school. Sometimes, my family did not have money for the fees, even though the fees were very little. When father got a job, his salary was Rs 300, which was not so much, even then. It was only about eight years after he got his job that our condition improved substantially. Then each of us kids at least had one set of striped cotton pyjamas and* kurta.

*I went to the school in Kataria. Some teachers used to discriminate against us scheduled castes; they would beat us hard; they would tell us to go and plough the fields; they would say: 'What will you do with education?' We were not allowed to touch the bucket in which water was kept. We'd have to get an upper-caste student to pour the water into our hands. We were not allowed to sit on the mats provided in the school. We'd take our own mats with us from home. And we would be told to sit at the back, to let the upper-caste students sit in front. But when father became a teacher, their attitude began to change.*

*In the first grades, I was the only scheduled-caste student. When I went to the secondary school, there were five of us in a class of 50 or sixty. Now I hear there are more scheduled-caste students attending the junior classes.*

*What with having to work as a labourer, my studies were very irregular. Somehow, I got a school-leaving degree from Bapu Inter-College in 1986. The day after I finished my high school exams, my wife came to live in the village. I was 17 or eighteen. I tried to stop my father but he said, 'What can we do, keeping the girl at her home is not fair on their family.' We had been married when I was thirteen.*

*I also don't think my brother Rakesh, who is 15, should get married soon, at least not until he gets a job, but that decision my father will make. I cannot say anything to my mother and father. They would laugh at me and say that a child born just yesterday is telling us what to do. The girl Rakesh is betrothed to is studying in the fifth or sixth class.*

*My wife hasn't been to school. I can't teach her because I'm never in the village. My father would teach her but he's away from the morning until the evening and then when he comes back he always has some work to do, to cut the fodder for the animals or to look after something in the field.*

*I have three children. They are all very small. Two are boys –*
*Akhilesh and Karunesh – and the youngest, who was born in 1995, is*
*a daughter. We've named her Manjusha. I don't want any more children.*
*I'm thinking of getting an operation done, so that I can look after the*
*children, my wife, my parents.*

*I did my BA degree in 1991 from the college in Amethi. I was the*
*first person of the scheduled castes in Baba ka Gaon to get the BA. Now*
*two other scheduled-caste boys from the village have their BA, but they*
*are all at least four or five years younger than me. I studied education*
*and military science. In the military science course you learn about*
*defence and offensives in war, which wars took place and with whom,*
*how they were fought, did it involve the army or navy or planes. I chose*
*this subject because I had heard that one could easily earn high marks*
*in this field. Its important to get high marks, even if one does one's degree*
*in a subject that is not useful for employment, because your division*
*shows up higher. I got a third division, missing a second by one per cent.*
*I enjoyed studying for the BA, and used to think that if I had had the*
*chance to study hard as a child, I could have achieved something.*

Shrinath's secondary school education had been the avenue by which
Ram Dass's family was freed from severe poverty. Hansraj's undergraduate
degree was meant to be a guarantee of continued upward economic and
social mobility for them. The hope proved to be illusory. Hansraj says:
*After I graduated, I just wasted two years at home, working in the fields.*
*Then I went to Allahabad in 1993. I've been preparing for entrance*
*exams for government jobs since then, for nearly four years. It is very*
*difficult. The application fees for the exams become more and more*
*expensive every year. This year I will sit for the Provincial Civil Service*
*exam for UP. I'm also preparing for the Lower Division Service, which*
*has posts for assistants and clerks in the government. One exam is in*
*March, and the other in February. Last year I gave exams for the*
*provincial service in Bihar and in Madhya Pradesh. I didn't get into*
*either. One doesn't get in on the first try. One has to improve oneself*
*by taking the exam many times. For each of the exams, one has to give*
*several papers.*

*I haven't tried to get a job with a private office because I don't have*
*any free time from studying to search for jobs. I want to try as much*

*as I can, to work as hard as I can, to get a government job. If I don't get a government job then I don't know what I will do. I guess I will just have to go back home and work the fields, or take up some other work. I just don't know what to do; I feel desperate all the time.*

*My father is the only one earning in the family, and there are too many of us dependent on him. There are eight or nine of us studying; there are two families to feed. Because of all these pressures my father has many debts. But even then he somehow manages to save something to send to me. In Allahabad I need about Rs 500 or more every month just to survive. This is after I take wheat and rice from home for my rations. I wish all the time that I could find some work. I have a wife and three children. But I can't look after them, let alone look after my parents and the rest of my family.*

Hansraj is dark, thin and short – no more than 5' 3" – with his family's large, slightly slanted eyes. At first glance he seems distant or painfully shy, but this is a facade to cover tension and worry. Sometimes by the end of a conversation about his life and family's circumstances, Hansraj is unable to prevent himself from sobbing.

He is always neatly dressed, though he possesses only two sets of clothes. He alternates between a pair of grey pants and a white shirt, and a grey safari suit. In addition he owns a single sweater. Hansraj shares a box-like room in a slum in Allahabad with three other young men, whom he knows from home and are of his caste. The room, no bigger than 10' by 10', is in the rear of a dirty, single-storey house at the end of the street. The room is itself clean and tidy, and there is a burlap sack at the door to wipe one's feet on; shoes are not worn inside. The room is furnished with a single metal bed covered by a ragged greenish bedspread, two tables piled high with books, two chairs, and an electric stove with a single burner. A few clothes are hung on nails around the room. A recessed shelf runs along one entire wall, and is used to store nylon bags of grain and a few cooking utensils. The room has a single window. The bathroom is outside, in a corner of the courtyard of the house.

The neighbourhood is poor – an open drain runs past the houses and pigs rootle in the sewage – but because it is located at the very outskirts of the town and most of the small houses are newly built, it is worlds better than most of India's slums. Just a few dozen yards from Hansraj's house, the area opens on to the fertile flood plains of the Ganges and Yamuna rivers, which have their confluence in Allahabad.

*I only study in Allahabad. Nothing else. I don't go roaming about or take any interest in politics. After two or three months just studying and studying here, I get very upset but there's nothing to do, it's my circumstance. I feel guilty all the time that I'm wasting my family's money. One can't study at all in the village. I was there recently for ten days and did not have one minute to study. There I have to work all the time, ploughing the fields or sowing something or cutting fodder! And then as I work the whole day, I'm so tired at night that I fall asleep while reading.*

*Here, we usually study late at night, from about midnight to about eight in the morning, because that's the quietest time. We take turns sleeping – two of us share the bed and two of us study. It's not possible to study during the day because we get disturbed all the time. There are so many of us sharing the room. And then we have to clean, and cook food and wash our clothes, all the things that we don't have to do ourselves in the village. I do most of the cooking but the others also help by cutting the vegetables or doing other things. We eat twice a day, once at about nine or ten in the morning and then in the evening. Our meals are vegetables and roti and rice in the morning and dal and roti at night. We have vegetables only once a day.*

*None of us ever goes for movies because we can't afford the tickets. But sometimes someone in the neighbourhood will let us watch television. In the summer, most of us go back to our villages because the electricity fails and so there's no water. And the electricity fails all the time in Allahabad!*

Hansraj's bleak reality – of being unemployed for years, of trying vainly for the right job, and then of eventually resigning himself to manual or other low-paid work that he considers below his aspirations – is shared by many millions of 'educated-unemployed' Indians. A large share are, like Hansraj, the first in their families to acquire a college degree, an achievement secured through incurring large expenses and forgoing years of wages. But the degree that was meant to be a surety of better things, perhaps some kind of clerical or white-collar job, proved to be nothing of the kind; instead, in a harsh turn, most find that they remain as impoverished as those of their peers who never completed secondary school, let alone college.

Their straitened situation, in part, reflects the failures of India's higher education system. Despite growing phenomenally since Independence, the higher education system has failed to provide its graduates with a decent education – though standards are better than in the abysmal public primary and secondary school system – or with employable skills. Hansraj says: *Our education in rural areas has trained us to be nothing but clerks. And not very good clerks either, fit only for government employment! It's better than having no education, but not very much better. It is true that there are no factories in rural areas, but even if there were they wouldn't employ us as none of us is trained to do anything.*

Despite the poor quality of education and the enormous number of 'educated-unemployed' – one-fifth of the people on the unemployment registers in 1990 had an undergraduate or postgraduate degree – India's higher education system continues to grow inexorably and to churn out graduates who cannot find remunerative work. Between 1950 and 1990, the system expanded from 175,000 students and about 700 colleges and universities to more than four million students and some 7,500 colleges and universities; ten times the number of institutions and 22 times the number of students! The overwhelming majority of colleges and universities depend for the greater share of their budgets on government funding.[1]

This extraordinary rate of growth continues, in great part, because despite high unemployment rates a formal college degree – rather than, say, training in a polytechnic – is still considered the only means of securing a clerical or professional job, and still carries social recognition. The system's juggernaut-like growth has come at the expense of both quality of education and relevance to India's development needs. Forced to educate incredibly large numbers, the colleges provide a sub-standard education bereft of training in job skills or self-employment-oriented courses. And because both the government and owners of colleges have taken recourse to expanding admissions to the arts and theoretical science courses, which have low overhead costs, the glut of liberal arts and 'science' students is juxtaposed against a dearth of doctors, engineers or veterinarians, as well as a shortage of skilled workers for modern agriculture, horticulture, fisheries, food processing and other business and industrial areas.

But the failures of the higher education system are only part of the reason why Hansraj and millions of other educated persons find themselves unemployed. More important, India's industrial and service sectors have failed to generate a sufficient number of even modestly remunerative jobs. Thus, total employment in India's 'organized sector' – which encompasses all offices, manufacturing units, plantations, mines and organized agricultural concerns employing more than ten persons – currently stands at just 25 million, out of a national labour force estimated to number 350 million. Not only is this organized sector tiny in comparison to the labour force, but it is even dwarfed by the number of people seeking employment on the 'live registers', which in 1990 totalled 36 million people![2]

The paucity of jobs reflects the failure of India's industrial sector, despite its size and diversity, to grow fast enough and to be sufficiently labour-absorbing in relation to the huge amounts of capital invested.[3] And because the private sector has lagged behind the public sector and government itself in employment opportunities, 70 per cent of organized sector jobs are today in government or quasi-government organizations. The private sector's share of total organized employment shrank from 40 per cent in 1961 to 28 per cent in 1990. Additional employment in the organized sector is being created at the rate of about 400,000 jobs per year, just about one-third of the number of fresh college graduates.[4] Hence each year several hundred thousand graduates are condemned to join the enormous backlog of the 'educated-unemployed'.

Given the pressure of numbers, the competition for organized-sector jobs is ferocious, more so for government jobs, as these offer job security. By the 1990s, there were often several thousand applicants for a single government post. And though the scheduled castes are constitutionally reserved 18 per cent of government and public-sector posts, a legacy of Ambedkar's efforts, competition for these posts is now bitter. One reason, of course, is that there are simply not enough government jobs for all the scheduled castes. A second reason is that a majority of the middle- and higher-grade government posts reserved for the scheduled castes are routinely allowed to lapse – they are then open to all applicants – on the grounds that there are 'no qualified candidates'.[5] In effect, this shrinks the number of posts available for scheduled-caste candidates.

Hansraj says: *The upper castes used to grab everything. Now, with reservation, others too are getting a chance. That is why the upper castes are angered by our having reservations* (affirmative action). *In my view, the biggest change that has come since Independence is that the traditional elite, the Brahmins and Thakurs, are fearful that they will be removed from their high place. And the person from the lowest caste thinks: 'I have always been working hard, and still have to work hard, but have not got to the place that I should have.' All this fighting over reservations is because of this: that the upper castes know that through reservations these low-caste people will snatch away the chair, their power. And we think these people have been the elite for quite a long time, now we should also get a chance. This is the battle today, in both the city and the village.*

Unsurprisingly, given these pressures, the application process for government jobs is dominated by corruption. *Today one can't get government jobs on merit, without corruption, as was possible in my father's time. Just to pass the Primary Teacher's Certificate one has to bribe, just like for other government service jobs. Bribing is the only way to pass the exam and to get a job, there's no attention to merit. To get a good grade in the exam you have to give Rs 50,000 to someone, or Rs 75,000, or even Rs 100,000. Even if you pass the exam on your own, you still have to bribe to get a post, otherwise you just remain at the end of the line however well you might have done. But where will I get Rs 100,000 from, when my family is barely surviving?*

In Baba ka Gaon, in the early years after Independence, reservations enabled several scheduled-caste families to get jobs with public-sector organizations, especially the railways. Though all these jobs have been either labouring or at best semi-skilled, they have boosted the living standards and self-esteem of the village's scheduled-caste families. But opportunities to secure even these jobs are drying up because the number of applicants has long outstripped the number of jobs.

In contrast, until today it is only the upper castes, and a small minority of the higher middle castes, who secure white-collar government or public-sector jobs. They have the advantages of having relations in the government, of being able to study at better colleges, and being able to afford bribes. *Of the scheduled-caste people of my age from Baba ka Gaon, most are in the cities working as labourers in brick kilns, small factories or shops. Some don't have any work. Only the children of the upper castes have got government service. Many are clerks. And the son of the* Thakur *Tilakdhari Singh is in the military. One of my fellow caste people is in the air force, but he is a labourer, loading and unloading cargo in the airplanes.*

The problem of the 'educated-unemployed' and the failure to create jobs in the organized sector mirror a failure of even greater magnitude: that India's economic development has not generated even modestly-remunerative jobs for the burgeoning labour force, whether in industry, services or agriculture. The capital-intensive industrial strategy chosen by Nehru in the 1950s is partly to blame. The strategy brought few direct gains to the poor, as it generated only a small number of unskilled jobs, the only employment opportunities open to the illiterate and unskilled.[6]

But the much greater share of blame has to be apportioned to the government's strategy for the rural economy, where, since Independence, the government has failed to foster the conditions for the kind of growth that would provide jobs, both in agriculture and in non-farm activities. The rural economy is crucial to providing employment for India's labour force, and so to reducing poverty.[7] Three-quarters of India's people (and the same proportion of the absolutely poor) live in rural areas. Moreover, though greater job opportunities in industry and services will ease the pressure on agriculture, it is impossible for industry to expand fast enough to absorb the annual additions to the urban work-force, let alone the backlog of the unemployed and 'underemployed', or, even more, the huge increases in the rural population. Assuming that industry continues to absorb labour at the same rate as it has done so far in India, industry would have to grow by an impossible 27 per cent each year to absorb just the current increments to the urban population.[8] Yet the overwhelming majority of Indian politicians and planners persist with the Nehru-age belief that industrial growth holds the key to all India's development problems, including poverty and unemployment.[9]

Not only has rural economic growth been central to poverty-reduction in the past half-century, but despite the increasing population pressure on agriculture there is still scope to raise rural employment and agricultural productivity in India. Thus, India's agricultural employment density of 35 persons per 100 hectares is still much lower than that of other Asian countries.[10] Yields could also be far higher. Despite this vast potential, job- and output-producing investments needed in agriculture and rural public works – such as better irrigation, livestock farming, and multi-cropping – continue to be under-exploited. A major reason for the failure to exploit this potential is the inequity in ownership of cultivable land. Because small farms are worked more intensively than larger ones, greater equity in land ownership would significantly boost rural employment opportunities as well as yields. In addition, without land as collateral it is almost impossible to get credit from formal banking institutions, circumscribing opportunities for setting up non-farm businesses. In effect, land ownership brings with it other assets, and if the poor owned more land they would be in a position to generate employment for themselves.[11]

Hansraj says: *There are very few options for work in the village. If work was available in the village, I would never have left. If I could have earned a livelihood there, I would not have come here. But there is no work and poor people don't have enough land. My family is better off today than many, but even then we have at most 2.5 acres, and that has to be shared between my father and his brother, even though he doesn't live in the village. And then there are three of us brothers to divide my father's share!*

Shrinath says: *The problem with my children trying to stay in the village is that you need land and we can't afford to buy enough land. Agricultural land is expensive. For just one acre one needs Rs 45,000 or more. This is why every poor person from the village runs away to the cities. And suppose we were to try to start a business here: that needs capital. But right now, I'm not able to save anything because of spending money on trying to educate the children. Only those who can save can think of such things as businesses. I think only about making ends meet.*

*I fear that there is nothing for my sons to do here. If they can get work in the cities, so much the better. If not, then we'll have to think of setting up a small business. There are three of them, and let's see who settles down where.*

Of the 22 scheduled-caste and middle-caste men of Hansraj's age in Baba ka Gaon, only four have not left the village to find work in urban areas. Poverty is the reason they leave: they are too poor to buy enough agricultural land or to raise the capital needed adequately to irrigate or produce higher yields from the patches they own. In contrast, from amongst the *Thakurs* of Hansraj's age, five out of twelve have stayed in the village as their families own sufficient land for them to work at a profit.

Hansraj says: *I feel anger sometimes when I see how many of us are so poor and others so rich. A person wants respect, dignity. One wants to be able to fill one's stomach, feed one's family well. Nobody should die of hunger, like my family has for so long.*

**Prayaga Devi**

# 10

# Prayaga Devi

PRAYAGA Devi, Ram Dass's wife, is from the village of Sarme, some 40 km from Baba ka Gaon in the adjoining district of Sultanpur. Sarme is a bigger village than Baba ka Gaon, with a population that has remained about five times as large. Till the abolition of *zamindari*, the village was part of the grand Tiloi estate.

*In the time of my mother and father we were slightly better off than my husband's family, because his family had no fields of their own to work. My father had been given one acre free of rent by the Tiloi raja. So we didn't have to earn our survival through working as labourers for others. But in return for the land we had to do all the Raja's agricultural labour for free. This was a lot of work and so our poverty was only slightly less than that of my husband's family.*

*I was about 6 or 7 years old when I was married and my husband was about ten. The wedding was in Baba ka Gaon. But I was given away in gauna* [when the bride actually moves to her husband's home] *quite late, when my husband was about twenty. It was at the time of India's Independence.*

In arranging their marriage, Prayaga Devi's and Ram Dass's parents searched only within families belonging to the same sub-caste of the Pasis, the Kaswen Pasis. When Ram Dass's father and some other male relatives first came to see Prayaga Devi, they carried a staff on which Ram Dass's height had been notched and against which they measured her; this was an effort to ensure that Prayaga Devi would not be taller than Ram Dass as an adult.

*I came here by bullock cart. He didn't come to fetch me, as it wasn't the custom for husbands to do this then. Now the husbands also go in the marriage procession to bring their wives.*

*I wept all the way here. I was very unhappy to leave my home. But every few months I would go home to my parents. I would go on foot with some relative, taking the children with me. It would take us the whole day! And I would stay there for one to two months. After my parents died about 20 years ago, I began to go only every six months. I have a brother and an uncle who still live in the village.*

*When I came here, in front of the men I used to keep my head and face covered. But when we were working in the fields, if there was no man nearby we would lift the* pallu *and only put it back if we saw someone coming. If we kept our* pallu *as low as the upper-caste women we would not be able to work, we would keep cutting our hands or feet!*

While only upper-caste women in relatively wealthy families have historically been fully secluded – the practice known as *purdah* – even amongst lower-caste women a semblance of seclusion is maintained by keeping the saree or a headcloth pulled over the face, whether at home or while working. Typically, younger women maintain the symbolic form of seclusion much more strictly than older women.

In Baba ka Gaon, most younger people from the scheduled castes address Prayaga Devi as either *Mausi* or *Chachi* – maternal or paternal aunt – as it is a taboo in most parts of rural India to address women by name. Few if any of them know her real name.

Prayaga Devi is a thin, erect woman, nearly as tall as her husband. She wears printed cotton sarees, most so faded that their colours are barely discernible. Her head is always covered with the saree's *pallu,* but unlike young women she does not pull it down to cover her face. She wears green glass bangles, a gold-coloured stud in one nostril and thin silver anklets.

At the age of 60 or so, she is frail to the point of being emaciated, a consequence of decades of deprivation, physical labour and childbearing. But she continues to work long hours every day in the fields and then at home. Like her children, Prayaga Devi is striking in appearance. Even though her skin is now webbed by wrinkles and crow-feet, the craggy nose and dark grey eyes make her commanding and attractive. Since her birth, the irises of her eyes have been clouded, as if by spreading cataract. This has not affected her eyesight, but gives her a distant look, totally at variance with the warmth of her personality.

She holds her own when she is teased by the young men in the village, which they are traditionally allowed to do with much older women as long as they show no disrespect. She says sternly that they are terrible boys and should be beaten; her look is so serious that those who do not know her would think that she is truly angry.

Where Ram Dass is nearly garrulous, Prayaga Devi is quiet, most often sitting silently. She says that Ram Dass talks too much, and that she neither pays much attention to what he says nor understands much of it. They have a visibly warm, mutually dependent relationship, marked by camaraderie. She calls her husband '*Buddhau*', literally, old man. Ram Dass says that a doctor in Amethi told him years ago that his wife suffers from blood pressure. *I took her to the doctor because she would faint from anger if she saw someone beating anyone else, or from sorrow if she saw someone hurt or sick.*

Prayaga Devi says: *All my children were born in Baba ka Gaon. The ones who died also died here. There were nine more sons apart from Shrinath and Jhoku, and one daughter. They died usually after the age of five. They would die of diseases for which we had no cure. There were no crippled children then in the village as there are these days because sick children would all die. There were no injections or medicine or doctors, so they died of any illness they contracted. There were no religious rituals for children who died. They were buried in the cemetery outside the village. I was always sad, but what could I do?*

*When my husband and I were young we never used to have enough to eat. But we managed somehow or other. We used to work at whatever labouring jobs we could get because we didn't have our own fields. But even if you were ready to work, you couldn't find many days work in a month. The poverty was worst until my husband went to Bombay for the second time and started sending more money. Before that, we would all only get one proper meal. This was at night and we would have some chickpeas and coarse cereals, from which we would make rotis. There was no rice or wheat. During the day, we would boil potatoes or chickpeas, but we would only eat a little bit of these as there wasn't enough for all of us. Sometimes when things were bad we would get even less to eat. But after he got his job at the mill no one went hungry. We could eat twice a day. But I had only one saree even after he went to Bombay, and he had one* dhoti. *If the saree or* dhoti *tore it was handed down to the children as they could make do with a smaller piece of cloth.*

*My husband used to send money through a money order. The postman would take a little cut of the money but at least we would get most of it. We would use the money to pay off the debts that we had taken from the* zamindars. *It took us many years to pay off the debts! We had taken money from them to buy food. Every six months the size of the debt would become one-and-a-half times as large.*

*After my husband came back from Bombay he worked as a labourer for a short time. I also used to work. But then he and I started working on a field that we were buying from the* Thakur, *with the money my husband had earned in Bombay. The* Thakur *was supposed to put the land in my husband's name but didn't – he just took the money. So we had to buy another smaller piece of land. And then we worked on that land as well as working as labourers for the* Thakur *and for other people. Now we weren't as poor as we were at the worst times. But it's been only 10 or 15 years since we've been much better off. First Shrinath got his teaching job and then we got some more land. Some of the land was from patta* [land redistribution] *and some we bought.*

*Things are better now for most of us people in the village. Now no one will die of hunger. No one goes hungry, we all eat twice a day. We eat vegetables at one meal and lentils at the other meal. People have stocks of grain. But there are still many, many people who don't have clothes, or blankets for the cold, or money for medicines or for school. But they manage somehow or the other. But since* zamindari *finished, things have improved slowly. Earlier, it was the* Thakurs' zamindari *and they treated us like animals. At that time they could hit and abuse us and do what they wanted.*

*The upper-caste women still discriminate against us. They won't touch us. Earlier, we couldn't even go near them! We couldn't use their wells. All this happens till today, but who cares, we now don't have any reason to go to them! Earlier when there was a new wife amongst the lower castes they would have to go and pay their respects to each of the* Thakur *families. We would go to meet their wives. But their wives would not come to meet us! None of the* Thakur *men would work. Even after* zamindari *ended they would not work in the fields. They would make us work, do everything, the ploughing, the sowing, harvesting, everything! They started working only about ten years ago because most of us scheduled-caste people stopped working for them. That was when we got possession of the land to which we had had title* [from the government's redistribution programme] *about five years earlier. Earlier all us lower-caste people, including the women, would have to stand up when the* Thakurs *passed. But now I keep sitting and don't care whether they are passing by! I never feel fear any more. Earlier of course we were all afraid, but no longer.*

*Many of us lower-caste women have been beaten by the* Thakurs! *I was also beaten by them. It was when my husband was in Bombay. I had harvested lentils and stacked it and the* Thakur *came with his men and started threshing it, and so I went to stop them and shouted at them and they started beating me. They beat me with the leather shoes they were wearing and I fell down. When I was being beaten there were others of my caste close by but no one had the courage to come to help. Later someone came and picked me up. I was defenceless as my husband was not there and his father was too old to say anything. Now I can hit them! I can pick up a staff and hit them! During that fight* [during local elections in 1995, the scheduled-caste families for the first time physically fought back against the *Thakurs*], *I took a staff and went to hit them. I was the only woman who went there to hit them.*

Such autonomy of action on the part of the average rural woman is in northern India generally restricted to women of tribal or scheduled- and other lower-caste families. Traditionally, they have exercised far greater independence and possessed substantially more rights than upper-caste women, who have borne the full weight of Hinduism's overtly patriarchal society. *The* Thakur *and Brahmin women have never worked in the fields. They do some work at home, but most often they just cook and eat! They keep their* pallu *down and they can't remarry. None of them has been to school, even though the upper-caste men are educated. They can't even leave their houses and don't even know where their fields are! But in my family, if I don't do the work in the fields, no one will do it. I take the lead and then everyone follows me.*

In orthodox Hinduism, greater constraints on women are as essential a part of ritual purity and high-caste status as vegetarianism, teetotalism and the prohibition on performing manual labour. Consequently, castes that wish to improve their ranking impose greater restrictions on women as part of their attempt to prove that they follow upper-caste practices and deserve higher status. This thinking is the basis for the web of discriminatory and inimical customs that bind upper-caste women in rural northern India.

Extreme physical and social controls are exercised over women's sexuality and autonomy, through such customs as arranged and child marriage, the prohibition of divorce and widow remarriage, *purdah*, and, at the extreme, the enforcement of *sati*, by which widows in aristocratic households were required to immolate themselves on their husbands' funeral pyres.[1] Upper-caste women are prohibited from working outside the house, as a consequence of which they are not credited with making an independent contribution to the family's finances. And because the upper-caste custom of dowry depletes the parental family's wealth, female children are considered a burden; in contrast, the male child is an asset as he will eventually augment the family wealth by gaining a dowry from his in-laws. On marriage, moreover, women are irrevocably alienated from their parental families. The woman shifts to her new home and literally becomes the property of her in-laws' family. Because she possesses few if any rights of shelter and inheritance in her parental home, she is virtually captive and open to any kind of exploitation by her in-laws' family. She is made even more defenceless because of the orthodox prohibition of divorce or of widow remarriage.[2]

Particularly inimical to women's welfare is that their traditional inheritance rights, in all but the lowest castes and tribal groups, are so circumscribed that they lack any form of inheritance comparable to the absolute inheritance rights of men. Women cannot consider their dowry as a form of economic security as it is transferred to the bridegroom's parents and controlled by them. In theory a woman's jewellery is her personal property, a category of *stridhana* or female wealth, yet in practice it is also treated as the family's common property.[3] And though women's inheritance rights to agricultural land – the most valuable asset in rural India – have been expanded as a result of legislation since Independence, the ground realities have barely changed. Thus, though modern law gives daughters and sons equal shares, in practice the land is divided solely between sons. Widows have only slightly more extensive traditional rights on land and other immovable property. If the widow leaves the village, she forfeits her rights and so do her children. If she has sons, she does not inherit her deceased husband's land, which goes directly to the sons. She is considered the temporary owner, as guardian, if the sons are young.[4]

The bias against women, particularly in the north and amongst the upper castes, is also apparent in the neglect and diverse kinds of discrimination they suffer within both their parental and in-law families. The outcome of this anti-female bias and strong male preference is that by every measure of deprivation, whether sickness, hunger, illiteracy or higher mortality, Indian women are far worse off than men, suffering greater hardships solely as a consequence of their gender. Female children are breast-fed less and weaned earlier than males; as a result, a majority of malnourished children are girls. As girls are given health care more infrequently than boys, large numbers die. Those who survive frequently fail to achieve their full growth potential. Yet girls generally work longer hours than boys, as they are expected to perform both domestic and agricultural work.[5] And despite women's higher mortality and the especially high risks of death associated with childbirth, far fewer women than men use health services, which anyway rarely cater to women's reproductive health needs. Beyond matters pertaining directly to sickness and death, females face severe discrimination in terms of access to education, work and opportunities for economic betterment. Thus, illiteracy is twice as high amongst women as men, with only about one in four females literate in rural India. In over half of UP's districts, fewer than one in ten females is literate.[6]

A graphic measure of the extremely disadvantaged situation of Indian women is the fact that India is one of the very few countries where males outnumber females. Under normal circumstances, females slightly outnumber males, as they have a longer natural life expectancy; thus, in sub-Saharan Africa and in the industrialized nations, there are more females than males. But in India, serious anti-female bias in care and feeding, and, to some degree, female infanticide, has meant that mortality rates for females are far higher than for males.[7] In effect, millions upon millions of Indian women are literally 'missing'. According to one calculation, there would be 37 million additional women today in India if it had sub-Saharan Africa's favourable female-to-male sex ratio.[8] But, ironically, despite gradually improving health care coverage in India, the proportion of women continues to decline. In 1901 there were 972 women per 1,000 males, but by 1991 there were only 929.[9]

In contrast to upper-caste women, women in lower-caste and tribal families are traditionally accorded far greater rights and better treatment by both their parental and in-law families, even though their status is rarely equal to that of men. Their relatively better situation is to some degree an outcome of the fact that by working outside the house, either as wage labourers or in their family's fields, they are recognized as making an explicit contribution to the economic well-being of the family. However, as regional patterns affect the practices followed by all communities, lower-caste women in northern India share to some degree the disadvantages faced by upper-caste northern Indian women, and are consequently worse off than their lower-caste peers in southern and eastern India, where more women work and own land, and dowry, *purdah* and violence against women are less common.[10]

Amongst the *Pasis* and other lower castes, women are not required to practise *purdah*, since their labour is needed in the fields for survival. Most of these communities do not have a tradition of giving dowry, but instead require the bridegroom's family to pay a bride-price. Divorce is allowed, and amongst the *Pasis* in UP, wives can initiate divorce on virtually any grounds, including incompatibility. If the wife seeks divorce to remarry, the new husband must pay compensation to the ex-husband. If the husband seeks divorce, he must pay a fine to his wife as well as return her dowry. Widows can also remarry. Ram Dass's sister-in-law remarried on the death of Ram Tehel, his younger brother, who was about 22 when he died. On her remarriage, Ram Dass and Prayaga Devi began to look after the couple's only child, Kaalu. Prayaga Devi says: *We took Kaalu into our family as his mother had remarried outside the village. Their other children had died earlier. His mother never came to see him because we barred her from visiting us. She married someone without our consent. Otherwise it's good that women can get remarried.*

And in the crucial arena of inheritance rights, the *Pasis* and most lower-caste communities have customary practices that are more gender-equitable than those of the upper castes. For instance, *Pasi* women are allowed a share of their husband's property on being widowed. Divorcees and widows have full rights to return to their parental home, and are guaranteed subsistence there, though they do not inherit land from their parents. All these factors give lower-caste women a substantial degree of authority and autonomy. Prayaga Devi says: *The husband and wife make decisions about the children and expenses together. The man doesn't make decisions alone. He knows what I'm doing and I know what he's doing. It has been like this right from when we got married. In my children's families it is also the same; my daughters-in-law decide everything with their husbands.* Amongst the important issues that Prayaga Devi and Ram Dass jointly decide are agriculture, the children's marriages, or expenses of any kind.

One issue on which Prayaga Devi has no interest in making decisions is electoral politics, and she says that she does not care to exercise independence in how she votes. *I have voted in every election since I was very young. Whichever party my husband gives the vote to, I do so too. I don't know too much about politics and my husband doesn't discuss it too much with me. None of my daughters-in-law or my grandchildren's wives has any interest in politics.*

The authority of women increases when they and their husbands become the heads of the household. At this point, their status often approaches that of a matriarch. *My daughters-in-law don't need to assert themselves as I am the one that everyone must listen to, whether male or female. Shrinath, you know, he touches my feet every day. Rakesh* [Shrinath's youngest son] *doesn't because he's a child, but Hansraj and Bansraj do.* In addition, Prayaga Devi is accorded high status by her family in ritual and religious matters, a role generally denied to women in upper-caste families in northern India. Ram Dass's family has for several decades followed the practice that someone from the family must bathe in the Ganga every month. Prayaga Devi has usually been the one to do this, until recently walking the 60-km distance to Manikpur, where there is a temple and bathing *ghat*, along with other lower-caste people from Baba ka Gaon. She no longer walks as there is now a bus to Manikpur from the main road.

According to Prayaga Devi, in lower- and most middle-caste families men work just as hard as women. *Everyone works hard! Not just the women. In the fields, the man does the ploughing and sowing. We do the weeding and also transplant the young rice. But we both share in looking after the cattle and goats, and in turning up the earth when the crops are already planted. The men do no work in the house. This is the women's work. But the men look after the children, seeing that they don't get into mischief or trouble; they see whether they are naked or clothed and they take them to the hospital. But they don't oil their hair or feed them! They look after the children when they are outside the house.*

The situation of lower-caste women has changed in many ways since her childhood, says Prayaga Devi. *Of course there is a change because earlier there was so much poverty and suffering and difficulties – what do my sons' wives know about what we've been through! They have so much free time! Earlier if we walked around and wasted time there wouldn't have been food to eat.* Both men and women of the lower castes have more leisure time now than they did earlier, says Prayaga Devi. In part, this is because in the past 15 years or so the former landlords' power has waned somewhat and the lower castes can no longer be compelled to undertake each and every one of their tasks. In addition, this period has seen the introduction in Baba ka Gaon of machines that save time and ease physical labour. *Earlier we had to grind the flour. But since the chakki* [mill] *came to the village, we women have had more free time. Before this we had to work many times as hard, and would only sleep until four in the morning and then set about milling the grain for the next day's meals.*

*The men also have more free time. Now they don't have to draw water for the fields from the well because of the pump and the irrigation canal. And because of the fodder machine, they no longer have to chop the fodder for the animals by hand. Just this would take them several hours each evening.*

Another change is that education is now available to scheduled-caste women, a revolutionary break from the past when they were barred by Hindu orthodoxy from education on two counts – for being untouchable and female. But given this legacy of discrimination, it is not surprising that till today very few scheduled-caste females are literate, far fewer than males of their castes or females of the upper castes. Across India, just nine per cent of all scheduled-caste females are literate, less than half the national average for females. Neither Prayaga Devi, her daughters-in-law, or her grandsons' wives can read nor write. But every one of Prayaga Devi's granddaughters has been to school. The younger granddaughters are still in school; the older ones completed the eighth grade, which is typically all that girls in rural UP study because of concerns about their safety over the long distance to school. Prayaga Devi says: *Women should study as much as they can, till they get married. It is always useful to be educated. It never harms a woman to be educated.*

Shrinath adds that from his experience of teaching, most families, whatever their caste, choose to send their sons but not their daughters to school, primarily because they discriminate against female children. He says it is essential that girls be educated and trained in some skill because this empowers them in every area of life. On leaving school, Shrinath's eldest two daughters learnt sewing in a local course.

Yet another positive change is that for the last decade women in Baba ka Gaon have been paid as much as men for agricultural tasks. Earlier, women's wages were far lower than those paid to men for the same work. But because by the 1970s a very large proportion of the lower-caste men migrated for many months to urban areas to work, women were able to pressure the landowners into increasing their wages so that they were on a par with those of male workers.

But on balance, the gains that have accrued to lower-caste women in UP in the decades since Independence have been outweighed by a countervailing trend: the adoption by the lower castes of orthodox upper-caste customs, including the myriad practices which are antagonistic to the well-being of women. Thus, while neither Prayaga Devi nor her sons' brides brought a dowry, Shrinath gave a dowry for his daughter's marriage as well as accepted dowries when his sons were married. The trend for lower castes to adopt orthodox customs has strengthened in northern India in the past few decades because the weakening of the caste hierarchy – a result of the new-found solvency of castes that were once destined to penury – has offered the lower castes a singular opportunity to attempt to improve their caste status by emulating the upper castes. But as a consequence younger generations of lower-caste women are much more disadvantaged than older women of their communities.[11]

The deteriorating situation of lower-caste women is explicitly visible in the precipitous decline amongst the scheduled castes in the number of females to males. Earlier, the gap between male and female mortality was smaller in poorer households, which are overwhelmingly from the scheduled and other lower castes, than in more prosperous ones. Thus, in UP in 1961, the female-to-male ratio for the scheduled castes was 941 while the ratio for all females, at 909, was far lower.[12] But by 1991 the scheduled-caste female-to-male ratio had fallen to 877, even lower than the average of 879 for all females, which had also fallen in these decades.

# 11

# The Poorest Families

THE gains made in the 1980s in reducing poverty proved to be impermanent. By the close of that decade India's economy was in crisis, in large part because of the government's unsustainable spending spree. With the economy stagnating and severe cuts made in government spending, the decline in poverty slowed and by the beginning of the 1990s had reversed.

Despite this reversal, many amongst India's middle and upper classes, as well as observers abroad, began to believe that poverty was no longer a significant problem in India, that there were simply no longer any hungry, sick, illiterate or otherwise deprived people. This peculiar misconception stemmed partly from the previous decade's boom and the continued prosperity of India's upper and middle classes, who did well despite the government's austerity measures. Hence, they assumed that India's masses too were doing well. The fallacy was also encouraged by the food-grain 'surpluses' overflowing in government warehouses, which were taken to mean that everyone was well fed.

But the most important reason was the deliberate campaign of falsifying official estimates of poverty, begun at the close of the 1980s by the Congress government of Rajiv Gandhi, which was then continued by his successor, P.V. Narasimha Rao. The campaign's aim was to create the impression that their efforts to liberalize the Indian economy and to slash government expenditure was benefiting the poor. Thus, the Planning Commission asserted that in the half-decade from 1983, the proportion of the population below the poverty line shrank from over 37 per cent to about 30 per cent, reducing the number of the poor by over 30 million. It reported even greater progress between 1987 and 1994, claiming that poverty had fallen further to under 19 per cent, shrinking the numbers of the absolutely poor by nearly 70 million, so that about 170 million people were left below the poverty line – half the level of the mid-1980s!

These estimates were invention. Worse, the government was actively suppressing the findings of an official expert committee whose report contradicted these claims. The expert committee's estimates both began and ended with far higher proportions and numbers of people below the poverty line. For instance, its estimate for 1987 was 75 million greater than the government's. Even more damaging to the government's propaganda effort, the committee concluded that poverty had sharply worsened after the initiation of economic reforms in 1991, with rural poverty rising in the following 18 months by about 10 percentage points, to 44 per cent in 1992, the numbers of the absolutely poor rising by about 60 million. For 1993, the last year for which data is available, estimates based on the expert committee's methodology showed that 40 per cent of the population was below the poverty line, more than double the figure asserted by the government, and greater than the national population at Independence.[1]

In December 1996, with the Congress out of power, the United Front government of Prime Minister H.D. Deve Gowda accepted the expert committee's methodology for estimating poverty. Overnight, in government records, the number of people below the poverty line swelled by about 180 million to total once again more than 350 million.[2]

Though Ram Dass's family was once amongst the very poorest in Baba ka Gaon, since the mid-1980s their poverty has lessened to the extent that they are at least able to meet their basic needs. From the perspective of the many families in the village who are still impoverished, this puts Ram Dass's family in a higher bracket of well-being – despite their crippling debt and difficult circumstances. The consensus among the poorer families is that about 10 of the village's 100-odd families come in this loose 'middle' group, ranging from those who are just above the threshold of absolute poverty to a few who have relatively ample incomes, sufficient land to feed themselves and just the right number of able-bodied adults. This small group comprises a large number from the middle castes and the best-off scheduled-caste families.

The 'middle' families in Baba ka Gaon typically own between 1.25 and 3 acres. Ram Dass's extended family of 13 adults and four children today share about 2.5 acres, but their finances are bolstered by Shrinath's salary of roughly Rs 4,000 per month. The poverty line per adult per month is at this time roughly Rs 250.[3] Durbhe, the impoverished 24-year-old relative of Ram Dass's, says: *My uncle's family became better off only because of Shrinath Masterji's employment, as this gave them an income that they can invest in renting land and in farming. They were absolutely poor before this. It takes just one person's good employment to become better off.*

*For a family of five, for example, of which three are children, you need about Rs 1,000 per month to survive. Rice costs Rs 6 per kg, lentils Rs 30, wheat Rs 4 per Kg. Each man will often eat about one kilo in a day! What children eat in three meals we eat at one meal. School fees are Rs 5 per month. And then clothes, oil, soap, slippers . . . and clothes are very expensive. A half-sleeved sweater costs two hundred rupees. You can get cheaper ones for Rs 90–100 but then they don't protect you from the cold at all. So what is a poor person to do? Should they eat or feed their children? Anyway, where does one find a job to earn even Rs 1,000 per month?*

Above the handful of middle-ranking families are about 30 comparatively well-off families. This group essentially comprises 20 *Thakur* families, the 3 Brahmins, and about 5 of the higher middle-caste families.

But roughly two-thirds of Baba ka Gaon's families are still deeply impoverished. At least 50 are so poor that they probably fall below the threshold of absolute poverty, with the poorest 5–10 of these families destitute. Whether destitute or close to the absolute poverty threshold, this huge group shares many commonalities. About half are from the scheduled castes, with a slightly smaller number from the lower ranks of the middle castes, and seven from the scheduled tribes. (The proportion of impoverished people within these groups is highest among the scheduled tribes, next amongst the scheduled castes, and then among the numerous but diverse middle castes.) They all own little land. The poorest 50 families own no more than two-thirds of an acre each, almost always infertile. Of these, five families own just one-sixth of an acre each. Three have no land at all. According to Ram Dass and others in the village, a family of five would need about 1.25 acres of good land – and very hard work – to be able to meet the essential needs of life.

Ram Dass says: *Nearly everyone in the village has very little land. All the people who got land from land reform got very little land. Some have one-third of an acre, others have two-thirds. Very few got more than two-thirds of an acre from the land reform, even though the government had said they would be given three acres each. But they just gave these little bits of land, not what they had promised. And the land given to most families was so bad that it is of no use to them.*

Because they own so little land, virtually all the members of these families earn all or a major part of their income from working as wage labourers for others. In many families, men work most of the year in urban areas, almost always as unskilled labourers. Most men over the age of 30 or so and most women over the age of 20 are illiterate. Many of these families have a large number of dependents, including young children, the disabled and the old. A sizeable number are headed by widows.

Their lack of productive assets and savings, as well as precarious earnings, makes all these families vulnerable to the threat that any large expense or catastrophic event will intensify their poverty. Those above the poverty line will sink below it, the impoverished will become destitute, the destitute pushed to the brink of death. And though there is some upward mobility within this group, including the experience of families like Ram Dass's, who have moved onto a more secure financial level, this large group of families comprises the core of the poor in Baba ka Gaon. They have been poor for endless decades and continue to face equally bleak prospects.[4]

## The widows

Sathan's widow, which is how she is referred to – in the third person – in the village, looks immeasurably old, but is about sixty. She is tiny, reed-thin. Under the saree's *pallu*, the dark, emaciated face is gentle, but almost broken in expression. She shakes constantly from some kind of palsy. *I have about one-fifth of an acre of land. I was left this by my husband and his two brothers. They each had one-sixteenth of an acre of land. I also have two-thirds of an acre of land that was given to my family from the land reform but it is completely infertile. No one will rent or buy it.*

*My husband was a labourer. He never worked in the cities. He was crippled by illness for many years. He could only work slowly, doing a day's work in four days. Apart from the little land he owned, he would take land as a sharecropper. He also had two small bullocks and would hire these out. We could manage somehow when he was alive. Now I can't.*

*I have given the land away on sharecropping and now work as a labourer. I get about 40–50 kg of grain each year for the land, as it's good and near the irrigation canal. A man in the next village has rented it. He is not of my caste; I am a Chamar* [a scheduled caste] *and he is a* Pasi.

*I work as a labourer. Wherever I'm offered work I go running. But I get very little employment as I can't do the heavy work. I get paid about 3 or 4 kg [Rs 10–15] for a full day's work.*

*My child is too small to work. He can just about walk now. He is not really my child, but the son of my younger brother-in-law. My brother-in-law died about the same time as my husband, a year ago. His wife ran away.*

*My parents were very poor, like I am now. My life improved a bit when I was married here, because there were men to work in the fields and some land and no problems, but now life is bad again. Some years ago my father-in-law died and then the older brother-in-law. And then my husband and his younger brother.*

*Sometimes I eat dal and roti, but sometimes just roti. Vegetables – I can only rarely afford them.*

*My brother helps me a bit by sending me some food. He has one acre in the village that I am from. He gives me clothes sometimes. This saree was given by him.*

*I got the widow's pension from the government once. It was 100 rupees. But since then I have got nothing. I filled the form again, but nothing can be done without bribes. From the bottom to the top you have to pay people. The* lekhpal [village land records keeper] *took Rs 20 from me, but he still hasn't done anything. That was all the money I had. I've been to him twice but he keeps putting me off.*

*The postman* [a Brahmin] *also took Rs 10 of the widow's pension from me, saying 'You're getting this money for free from the government so why shouldn't I keep it?' I cannot say anything to him.*

There are seven other lower-caste widows in Baba ka Gaon. Two of them are as destitute as Sathan's widow. The other five receive some support from their adult sons, but are also impoverished.

Widows form a large core of the very poor throughout India. According to the 1981 census, there were more than 25 million widows, comparable in number to the total of male agricultural labourers, another particularly impoverished group.[5] The number of widows is larger than that of widowers, even though males outnumber females in the total population. Rural Indian women have lower mortality in the older age groups (after emerging from the peak reproductive years) than men, and are generally substantially younger than their husbands, and far fewer women than men remarry. Hence, most women are highly exposed to the risk of widowhood and the perils that generally result.

A very large proportion of widows are impoverished. The loss of the husband – generally a major earning member – cuts into the economic well-being of the family. Because upper-caste widows are subjected to myriad forms of discrimination by their in-laws, including being disinherited from their husband's property, even widows within well-off families may be impoverished. And though scheduled-caste women face less discrimination than those higher in the caste hierarchy – generally possessing greater inheritance rights, the right freely to remarry, and to be employed outside the house – they almost always face enormous economic difficulties. Most of their families are poor to begin with. Even where they own some land or possess other productive assets, there are enormous hurdles to their remaining solvent. They are often unfamiliar with modern cultivation practices, are denied credit from banks and other institutions, and are ill-equipped to cope with the male-dominated culture of rural north India, for instance in dealing with male creditors. Because most are illiterate and lack general skills, they are unable to find remunerative non-agricultural work. None of the lower-caste widows in Baba ka Gaon is literate. And because the majority of rural widows are over the age of 60, most are too infirm to undertake the gruelling labour that agriculture entails. Consequently, they and their families slip into destitution.

Despite the large numbers of widows and their intense poverty, the government has done little to aid them. Like most Indian states, UP in principle has a pension scheme for widows, in theory to provide a base income of Rs 100 each month to widows who lack adult supporters. But the pension scheme has had virtually no impact. The budgetary allocation is too small to cover even this destitute subset of widows, and complex application procedures and widespread corruption have further gutted the scheme.

Ram Dass says: *Not each and every widow without people to support her gets the pension! The government said they would give pensions to no more than 100 widows in a block* [group of villages], *but in our block there are 104 villages and so in some villages not even one widow gets the pension. In our village there are three or four who don't have people to support them, but just one gets the pension.*

*And anyway, what can you do with 100 rupees? It's not enough even for a single old woman. A single person requires about Rs 300 or Rs 400 every month to get enough to eat and to survive. In this expensive time to buy dal, rice, wheat and vegetables one needs this much. And you also need something for clothes.*

## The orphan

Durbhe was orphaned when he was twelve. His father was Ram Dass's first cousin. *When my mother got sick and died, I was in the eighth class. My younger sister was nine. My mother had liver cancer. We took her to hospitals in Ludhiana and then to Lucknow.*

*She had four daughters and me. Three of my sisters were older, and these three were all married by the time of my mother's death. The youngest of my older sisters was seven years older than me.*

Durbhe's mother died in 1985, in her late 40s. His father had died in 1977, from an occupation-related injury at his job as a crane driver with the Western Railways in Bombay. Durbhe's mother was left a small pension of Rs 106 per month, roughly the equivalent of Rs 350 today. With this income, by labouring for the Thakurs, and through hard effort in cultivating the acre of land she owned jointly with her brother-in-law, she managed to keep her family solvent. She sent Durbhe and his four sisters to school, forsaking their help in cultivating the field.

But on his mother's death, this relative economic security shattered. Durbhe and his younger sister were plunged into poverty. The primary factor behind this rapid descent was that the two young orphans were left to fend for themselves, with relatives and caste-people in Baba ka Gaon providing very little support. *No one helps anyone in the village. When problems come you have to face them yourselves, you have to act yourself, and no one is going to become your crutch. We lived in our parents' hut and we looked after the field. We first didn't know any agricultural work because my mother had never let us work with her. At least we knew how to cook our food! But you learn everything by watching people. When faced with adversity, you learn quickly.*

*No one would give us food or money even when we were very hungry. But if someone had tried to steal our land or trouble my sister then Ram Dass Chacha [uncle] and the rest of our* Pasi *community would have supported us.*

*My elder sisters would come occasionally, sometimes every 15 days, sometimes every few months. My eldest sister used to come the most often. They tried to reassure us and to give us emotional support. They would say, 'If you need anything, tell us.' But who tells others what they need? One can ask one's parents for things, but one can't ask others no matter how much they love you. So somehow my younger sister and I managed to get things going on our own.*

*The rest of our relatives were in Lucknow and Bombay. My father's brother in Bombay never came.*

Durbhe's case is the norm for the poor in Baba ka Gaon and, with few exceptions, for rural India. Support for orphans or others who need care or are helpless, such as infirm older people, the disabled or widows, comes almost entirely from very close relatives.[6] If there are no close relatives, neither more distant relatives nor people of the same caste will provide much care at all, leaving them to fend for themselves as best as they can.

Forced to do so, Durbhe and his sister coped on their own. To try to get his father's pension from the railways transferred to his name, Durbhe, though he was just 12 years old, travelled alone to Bombay.

On reaching there, he found his way to his uncle's house in the Jogeswari area. *I wasn't scared, because if you have to do something, what's the point of being scared?* But the journey was in vain, as on one ground or another the railway's officials refused to give the pension to either Durbhe or to his uncle, who was legally his guardian.

For the next few years, Durbhe supported himself and his sister by cultivating the field that he had inherited from his mother and by working as a labourer. His uncle was in Bombay and let him cultivate his share for free. *My sister no longer went to school. But I worked and also went to school. For these four years, we managed with great difficulty. We had just one set of clothes each. This set of clothes had to last us one or one-and-a-half years.*

*I left the village in 1988 because we were in worse and worse money trouble here. I had no income. My schooling was also stopping because I didn't have money for books or for the fees. To whom could I say that I wanted books? My sister also had needs. Everyone has needs and desires.*

*I also had to earn money so that I could save to get my sister married. In our caste we have no system of giving dowry and we spend according to our means on the marriage – we only want the girl, not what she can bring with her. There were no demands from the in-laws but I gave about Rs 1,200 which was all I could afford.*

*Because of all this I went to my brother-in-law in Ludhiana. I thought I would learn some work that didn't require too much skill. I learnt how to knit sweaters. It is very difficult work; children can't do this. Most people do this when they are in their 20s, but I was about fifteen. But I had to learn. Working on the sweater machine is very difficult. When you work in the fields breaking the sod for many hours you don't sweat as much as you do in one hour with this work! Somebody over the age of 50 couldn't do this work. No women are employed because the work is so exhausting. You have to keep the machine pressed against your chest, and then you push the spindle right past you with your right hand. And you keep up this rocking motion with your body, back and forth. And with your left hand you feed the wool, test it, raise it higher, or lower it. It takes a whole month just to get your hand set. And your arm hurts so much that when I first go back to work then for at least a month my right arm aches so hard that I use my left hand to soap my body!*

*First I earned nothing, but as I worked my hand became faster. Now I make about 25 sweaters a day. We get Rs 4 per sweater, so I earn about Rs 100 per day. I spend about Rs 1,000 on living there. As I work for about 22 days a month, I have left another 1,000 rupees. All of this I send to my wife in the village. So I have zero! Sometimes I get letters from my wife that this is running short, that something else is running short, so I send her more money and oil and other stuff through friends.*

*The season lasts from early March to early December. You are assured of work in these months. The rest of the time I stay in the village. Earlier, when I used to come back I would study very hard, so I passed my Bachelor's degree in 1995. Only three of us from the scheduled castes in the village have this degree.*

*First my sister used to look after the land when I wasn't here but now my wife looks after it. I still need to work every year in the sweater factories because you can't survive on the amount of land I have if you don't have an outside income. And I can't find any other work even though I have studied so much.*

At 24, Durbhe is so thin as to appear malnourished. Just over five feet in height, he is dark, with sharp features, and intelligent, watchful eyes. His small moustache is almost unnoticeable against the darkness of his skin. His teeth are stained brown from his fondness for *paan*. He has made several efforts to get the arrears on his father's pension released, which now totals nearly Rs 50,000, a fortune for him. But the railway authorities have stalled payment on one excuse after another, waiting for him to offer a bribe.

Durbhe is heavily in debt. *You have to borrow from the* Thakurs *because they are the only ones with any money.* By 1996, he owed the *Thakurs* Rs 6,500, equal to three months' salary at the sweater factory. Five hundred rupees of this he took in 1994 because his wife was ill and he didn't have money to buy the medicines she needed. The following year, he fell sick with a severe stomach infection, for which he had to be hospitalized in Pratapgarh town. The private clinic there ran an ultra-sound test, put him on a drip, and two days later presented him with this huge bill. Durbhe pays five per cent interest each month on the loan – in contrast, banks charge 12 per cent annually – and has had to struggle so much to pay the interest that he has not been able to pay off any of the capital.

*It's true that we younger people haven't had to suffer poverty as intense as that suffered by our elders, such as my uncle Ram Dass. At least now we can eat what we produce from our work. They had to give to the* Thakurs *what they grew from their labour. And on top of that they would be beaten! We don't have to suffer this; we can fight back. But still, I saw a lot of poverty when I was young and my mother had died. And I'm still poor. We're all still poor.*

## The costs of ill-health

Though health conditions have improved significantly since Independence, India's performance in the past half-century on reducing ill-health and early mortality has been worse than that of comparable Asian countries and even below the average for all developing countries. Sickness, disability and early mortality still result in enormous suffering and economic deprivation amongst the Indian poor. The most pervasive and gut-wrenching sights of poverty in India continue to be related to disease or lack of health care.

To those of Ram Dass's generation, health conditions are today incomparably better than they were when he was a child or even a middle-aged adult. In the 1930s, mortality from famine, malnutrition and infectious diseases was so high in India that life expectancy was only 32 years, and no more than half the children born could be expected to survive to the age of twenty. At around the time of Independence, over one-third of all children died before they reached their first birthday. Though the levels of mortality for both children and adults had declined considerably by the 1960s, at that time two of Ram Dass's siblings died in their early 20s, another in her early 40s, while ten of his twelve children died from the 1950s to the mid-1960s.

Ram Dass says: *Earlier there was no polio here, now lots of children get it. Earlier the children would just die whenever they got sick. Just 30 years ago, children used to die from hunger. They used to wither away* [from marasmus, an acute form of malnutrition]. *Now they get some milk from the goats and cows and don't die like this. Cholera used to come in summer. And smallpox in April or May. There used to be cholera in everyone's family, including ours. There was no cure for it here. There were no doctors or hospitals, and we used to take home-made medicines.*

*Whenever this illness struck, there would only be four, five or ten people left in some villages, and in some families not even one person would survive. And there was a lot of smallpox. Some people used to lose their eyes, others would get such scars on their face that you could not recognize them. I still have scars all over my body from when I got smallpox. I was very young, just about 8 or 9 years old. Smallpox would get the young and the old. Two of my children died of this. There was plague too. Often whole villages would get exterminated. We used to know there was plague when the rats died. Then their insects would jump on to people. So whenever the rats died we would leave our houses and live in the fields for some weeks. But from 1950 or 1960 or so the plague has become less.*

Prayaga Devi says: *Once when Shrinath was a child the rats started dying and so we all ran away into the fields and we stayed there for 15 days. We took all our grain with us and we would cook there. No one died among those who had run away, but whoever stayed in the village died, maybe about 50 people.*

Ram Dass says: *When we were young, we didn't know what doctors were. There was a hospital in Sanghipur. And there was a compounder there who used to give you medicines in little paper packets. And if anyone had a boil or something they would apply an ointment. And it used to be free. But most people didn't go to doctors. They were afraid of them.*

*Cholera ended because there was education from the government about not eating exposed food or food that had been stored for any length of time. And smallpox ended about 20 or 30 years ago. All these diseases ended because the government made the arrangements and gave us medicine. The immunization for children started here only about 12 years ago.*

Though the first sustained improvement in health conditions in India took place in the decade 1931–40, more substantive increases occurred in the two decades between 1951 and 1971. As a consequence, life expectancy at birth increased from 32 in 1941 to 45 by 1971. By 1965, the infant mortality rate – a measure of how many children die before their first birthday – had fallen to 160 per thousand live births from 225 two decades earlier.[7] The decline in mortality came overwhelmingly from the control of the handful of infectious diseases that had caused millions of deaths earlier. The single most important cause of the decline was the control of malaria through the spraying of insecticides and other forms of mosquito control; from the early 1950s to 1965, deaths from malaria fell from over a million annually to no reported deaths at all. Mortality from tuberculosis was reduced through the expansion of curative medical services and vaccination. Deaths from cholera also fell, through modest improvements in water supply and quality of food, and increased access to medical services. Another major killer, smallpox, was wholly eradicated by 1975 through an ambitious inoculation campaign.

But the improvements in health conditions and the decline in mortality had slowed by the close of the 1960s. The stagnation – especially in states like UP, where mortality levels were still very high – was a consequence not just of inadequate budgets and the poor quality of services, but also stemmed from the government's failure to tackle the huge problems of poverty and illiteracy that lay behind the high levels of malnutrition and endemic disease. For much of the next decade, little headway was made in improving health conditions in most areas of India. As late as 1978, the infant mortality rate in UP was 172 per thousand live births, far higher than the national average and not appreciably lower than the rate at the time of Independence.[8]

Though the expansion of immunization efforts and programmes targeted at mothers and children has since led to significant reductions in mortality – even in UP – the poor in India continue to suffer from crippling communicable diseases (including diarrhoeal infections, measles, pnuemonia and tuberculosis), malnutrition, and complications of pregnancy and childbirth. Consequently, India's performance to date on improving health conditions and reducing mortality has been far worse than that of other Asian countries, such as China and Indonesia, which suffered from equally devastating health problems half a century ago. In fact, India's performance is worse than the average of all developing nations. Thus, though life expectancy at birth in India rose from 44 years in 1960 to 59 in 1990, in the same period it rose in China from 47 to 70 years, and in the developing countries overall from 46 to 62 years.

The government's neglect of health is epitomized by its paltry spending on disease prevention and health care. (In theory, the government makes available free preventive and curative health services through a network ranging from primary health centres to hospitals.) Taken together, India's federal and state governments today spend about 1.3 per cent of gross domestic product (GDP) on health, far less than other Asian countries. This level of spending, which works out to just US $2–3 per person per year, is simply inadequate to meet even rudimentary health goals. But even these funds are misallocated, with over three-quarters absorbed by wages, specialized hospitals and medical education, leaving precious little for disease prevention, rural health care, or for drugs and essential supplies. Compounding these problems, the public health network is blighted by the corruption and inefficiency that afflicts every public service in India.[9]

The government's failure to improve health conditions disproportionately affects the poor. This is because poverty and sickness are inextricably intertwined, with each synergistically multiplying the risks of the other. The poor face higher risks of malnutrition, disease, disability and mortality than do more prosperous families. As children, this endangers both their physical development and their performance at school, quite apart from their survival. (Survival is still far from a certain prospect in UP, where more than one-tenth of all children die by the age of 5.)[10] The frequent bouts of sickness and malnutrition suffered in childhood mean that as an adult he or she is likely to be shorter, weaker and more susceptible to disease than those from more prosperous backgrounds. In Baba ka Gaon, both the men and women of scheduled caste and other poor families are on average three to five inches shorter than the *Thakurs*, and significantly frailer. These handicaps reduce their earning prospects, as stronger and taller people are employed more readily and paid higher wages in labouring jobs. Moreover, illness is a major factor in pushing the poor deeper into poverty, because of the loss of daily wages as a consequence of absenteeism, from being unable to work productively (or at all, in the case of the disabled), and from the costs of medicines and care. Medicines for a simple sickness can cost more than two days' wages in Baba ka Gaon. In 1995, two months of ordinary, uncomplicated fever forced Shrinath to spend Rs 700 – nearly one-fifth of his monthly salary – on medicines. The expenses for more serious problems are devastatingly large. The debt of Rs 30,000 that currently Ram Dass's family owes includes Rs 10,000 that was spent on treating Shrinath's wife for a severe obstetric problem.

# 12

# The Land Still Belongs
# to the Richest Families

RAM Dass says: *Apart from the* Thakurs, *everyone was poor before*
zamindari *abolition. Some of the Banias* [traders] *did have money from*
*business. The middle castes were also poor, though not as poor as us*
Harijans. *And even up to now, the richest are the* Thakurs, *then the middle*
*castes, and the poorest are the* Harijans! *The* Thakurs *had all the*
*advantages earlier: they were rich, they were educated, they had land,*
*and they had us* Harijans *to be their slaves. So it is not surprising that*
*till today they are the lords and we are still poor.*

   Mata Prasad, a *Pasi* man in his 40s, comments: *All the* Thakur
*families in the village are much richer than the middle castes and*
*scheduled castes. Now there are 20 houses of the three* zamindars.
*Because of this their holdings have become less. But they still have more*
*land than families of other castes. They have more money. And in each*
*of their families there is someone with a job. They have government*
*jobs, one is a professor, another is in the police, someone in the army.*
*The poorest* Thakur *has 3.5 acres and quite a lot of money. He sold*
*a lot of his land. The richest, the former* pradhan, *has more than 35*
*acres, and he is alone, no brothers. Another of the richest lives near*

*Rae Bareli. He supervises the work on the land he owns here and then leaves. He is a businessman, he has a brick kiln and lots of land in other villages. He comes now and again on his motorcycle, the fat fellow, creates all the trouble and goes away.*

Until today, the most prosperous families in Baba ka Gaon are the 20 *Thakur* families. At a level of wealth equal to that of the less prosperous of the *Thakurs* are the three Brahmin families. About five of the higher middle-caste families are also relatively prosperous in terms of the amount of land they own, but still do not approach the *Thakurs* in terms of other assets, such as the size of their homes or monetary savings.

Primarily because the three original *Thakur* families have branched out into 20 smaller families, none of the *Thakurs* individually owns more than about 35 acres and about an acre of orchards. While the two largest landholders in the village would by national standards be classified in the top bracket of landowners – and also be violating UP's land ceiling laws – the remaining *Thakur* families on average own about ten acres each, which ranks them as large holders by current Indian and UP standards.

But although their individual holdings are no longer on the scale of their undivided families, the amount of land owned by Baba ka Gaon's *Thakurs* as a group has not greatly diminished since the abolition of *zamindari*. Moreover, of the land sold by them in the past 50 years, the bulk was bought by the higher-middle castes, with only a small amount purchased by the few scheduled-caste families – including Ram Dass's – which have improved their economic position. The rest of the families in Baba ka Gaon have simply been too impoverished to purchase any land.

In comparison with the impoverished and the merely poor (like Ram Dass), who comprise three-quarters of Baba ka Gaon's population, or even with the well-off among the higher-middle castes, the *Thakurs* are still an incomparably well-off elite. By national standards of income and wealth, they range from middle to upper-middle income. They own very many times more land than people of other castes in the village, and their land is of far better quality. Every one of their homes is large and built of brick. Two own the only tractors in Baba ka Gaon, and one the only jeep. Of the six pumps for irrigation, four are owned by *Thakur* families. They are also very much better off in terms of education, current jobs and future prospects. The vast majority have incomes from family members who have secure, middle-income jobs in urban areas, generally with the government, quasi-government agencies or the armed services. Their children are likely to be employed in similar jobs. Virtually no other family in Baba ka Gaon can aspire to such things.

Ram Dass says: *The British have been gone for 50 years, and India has been independent, but we are still not free of these oppressors! We have gone from one bad spot to another! On the government's papers it's all there that this has been done for the poor, this assistance, this land, for this poor person, but it all gets eaten up on the way and the poor person gets nothing. And if there's ever an enquiry, they are all in league with each other from the top to the bottom, all the way from the officials to the village* pradhan.

*Our poverty is man-made. The rich know how to extract money. If I take one rupee from them, they make two rupees profit from this. The rich become richer because they are in the business of being rich! If you have the facilities it is easier to make money. It takes me a day to reach Pratapgarh, but the rich can reach it in one hour by jeep. And those who have money can also pay for a good education, so they have the skills to prosper. And once you've made enough money you pass it on to your children. And even if you lose some you never become badly off. But if you're poor you can only progress slowly, and that only if you're not being oppressed. The big fish eat the smaller fish and that is why there is no progress for the poor. Those of the poor who manage to survive may sometimes progress, but they are the targets of the anger of the rich. The rich find means of keeping us in bondage, keeping us down. They don't want us to rise.*

*These rich people will even take our little land away from us! Bhagwan, who is of my caste, has had half his land eaten up by the Brahmin lawyer from Lalganj. The Brahmin has got the* lekhpal *to draw a boundary across part of Bhagwan's land. Bhagwan has been working this land for the last 20 years since he got it on patta* [from land reform]. *It was very poor land, sloping, but Bhagwan cut it and worked on it until it was good. Then the Brahmin paid off the* lekhpal *and got the land!*

Durbhe, Ram Dass's young relative, adds: *The* Thakurs *have also forcibly occupied the village waste land, about 35 acres of it. They are sitting over it like a cobra with its hood spread.*

In Baba ka Gaon, throughout UP, and across India, the battle over land continues. The winners in the conflict today – as in the past half-century and earlier – are almost always those with large land-holdings, not the poor. Where the large landowners have lost land, the ones to gain have been the medium, prosperous farmers just below them.

By the 1990s, a review of land-ownership data for UP and India would suggest that in the past half-century all the large landholdings had disappeared, equity had increased correspondingly, and there is no room left for meaningful redistribution of land. These conclusions are diametrically opposed to reality on the ground. True, the numerous huge estates of 10,000 or 20,000 acres owned by the princes and grand landlords no longer exist. But beyond bringing about this change, the Indian government's land reform efforts have achieved little, and even less when seen from the perspective of the impoverished.

Thus, in UP and many other parts of India, many of the former feudal lords still own several hundred acres each of land, either through exploiting the liberal exemptions granted in the land reform laws or through illegal strategems. Most also own the hugely profitable orchards that they were allowed to keep under the beneficent terms of *zamindari* abolition. In the area around Baba ka Gaon, most of the grand ex-landlords are each estimated to own between 500 and 1,000 acres of land, each adding up to a fortune of tens of millions of rupees.[1] Many have had long-running land-ceiling cases filed by the state government against them, including the ex-rajas of Kalakankar, Pratapgarh, Bhadri and Amethi.[2] If the cases have been pursued only desultorily, and never won, it has a lot to do with the fact that these ex-rajas have all been Congress worthies and held prominent political posts. A confidant of Mrs Gandhi's, Dinesh Singh of Kalakankar, was India's foreign minister in the late 1960s; on his death, his daughter was elected to Parliament. Abhay Pratap Singh of Pratapgarh has been an MP twice. Vir Bhadra Singh of Bhadri was governor of Himachal Pradesh; his son, known across Awadh as Toofan (Hurricane) Singh, has a long list of criminal charges against him, but the police or government dare not arrest him. And the infamous Sanjay Singh of Amethi, accused by a federal investigative agency of masterminding the murder of his girlfriend's husband, was a Sanjay Gandhi strongman and later MP and junior minister.

To the estates of the feudal lords have been added very many – no one knows quite how many – huge farms and orchards owned by rich businessmen, film-stars and politicians. They have purchased farms in part for the status and pleasures of possessing luxurious country retreats. An equally potent reason has been that the farms are used to launder their black money, as income from agriculture is tax-exempt. In UP's Terai region, farms of as much as 3–4,000 acres are no rarity, owned by very rich and powerful Indians, including H.P. Nanda of the Escorts industrial empire, and Akbar 'Dumpy' Ahmed, a courtier of Sanjay Gandhi and a former MP.[3]

The disregard of ceiling laws is so blatant that even on the outskirts of Delhi the very rich own huge farms. The show piece is certainly the (roughly) 180-acre spread owned by the Oberoi hoteliers, the land alone conservatively valued at Rs 200 crores ($60 million). And by the mid-1980s, farms around Delhi and other large cities were no longer used for farming, but sported (in violation of building codes) huge mansions, most boasting swimming pools, tennis courts, fleets of servants, and the other necessities of the good life. (Ironically, these multi-million-dollar mansions are typically rarely used second homes.) The government's blind eye to this visible abuse is because the owners of these farms are the very elite of India, including the Gandhis, former prime minister Chandrashekhar (once, professedly, a socialist), several ex-maharajas and rajas, every media baron including the hugely influential owners of the *India Today* magazine empire, and *arriviste* politicians who have made illegitimate fortunes in the 'get-rich-quick' spirit of 1990s India.

Because so much land is held illegally or through disguised ownership, land ownership data for UP – or India – masks the extent of the inequity.[4] But even if the data is accepted at face value, the inequity is enormous, exposing the failure of land reform since Independence. National data indicates that the top 2.4 per cent of landowners, each with 25 acres or more, own nearly one-quarter of the country's total arable land. In contrast, the bottom 57 per cent of India's landowners, each owning less than 2.5 acres, occupy a little more than one-tenth of the arable land.[5]

Given this inequity and the vast amount of land held illegally beyond the maximum allowed by current ceiling laws, the scope for further land redistribution is still gigantic and would significantly reduce poverty. A planning document in the mid-1980s estimated that roughly

20 million acres could be redistributed if existing land-ceiling legislation was enforced; this is about ten times the amount distributed under Mrs Gandhi's much-touted land-ceiling programme in the 1970s. Clearly, a stricter ceiling would free more land for redistribution.[6]

But with each year, the constituency advocating land reform weakens and the numbers of those pushing to revoke land ceilings strengthens. Especially in the period of economic liberalization begun in the late 1980s, there has been a growing consensus amongst the elite, opinion-makers and politicians that ceilings on land are inherently bad and counter-productive, and hamper the development of agri-business. There is complete disregard of concerns of equity or of the fact that landlessness, unemployment and poverty will inevitably rise if more land comes under large holdings. It is now progressive for a politician to propose easing land ceilings, though three decades ago such talk would have been condemned as heresy. Consequently, in the past decade ceilings on agricultural land (as well as restrictions on industrial use of forest land) have rapidly been eased. In 1995, the government of Madhya Pradesh leased out 10,000 acres of forest land to a private orchard business. The following year, on the grounds of the 'new environment of economic liberalization sweeping the country', the land ceiling in Karnataka province was raised fourfold under Chief Minister H.D. Deve Gowda (soon to become prime minister). Also inserted into the legislation was a remarkable clause allowing the state government to allow holdings of any size in any case where it deemed it was in the 'public interest' to do so.[7] As prime minister, Mr Gowda attempted to do away with land-ceiling laws across India. He failed – but only just – because of opposition from the Communist members of the Front government. His attempt is a premonition of the direction of change.

## The Rajapur overlords

Ram Dass says: *Land redistribution is very important. Take the zamindars. They save the land that they have by claiming it is under a temple or part of a co-operative. They are very clever. Take the Rajapur family. They lost some of it due to the ceilings as they had chunks of 400 or 500 acres. But most of it they saved. And they can always save it by planting orchards or claiming it is orchard land. Hence every large landlord has managed to save a large portion of his land. And lots of it they leave it lying fallow, and they won't even give it over to sharecropping.*

Lalit Kumar Saroj, a distant relative of Ram Dass's, who lives in the nearby village of Anni, worked for decades as a guard at the home of the Rajapur *zamindars*, the overlords of Baba ka Gaon, a job that his father had also done for decades. He left this job in the early 1990s, when he was well over 70 years old. These decades of association made him uniquely intimate with the affairs of his and Ram Dass's erstwhile overlord. (To protect their identities, the names of people interviewed here have been changed, as has the name of the village.)

Lalit Kumar says: *About five or six people still work at the Rajapur kothi* [mansion]. *When I first joined, about 40 or 50 worked there. The zamindari covered 12 villages and all the land in the villages. Today, near their home, they still have 50 acres on one side and 40 on another, between three brothers. They have more land further away, not even counting their orchards! Altogether, they have more than 125 acres apart from the orchards. They leave about 40 acres fallow. And they have about 20 acres of mango orchards, which they sell to contractors each year.*

*The zamindar is Lal Pratap Singh. One of his brothers is a lawyer in Pratapgarh. They are very educated – in Allahabad and Lucknow. The other brothers look after the land. None are in politics. They still have a lot of cash but they don't show their money. They have tractors and jeeps. They hire labour; they don't allow sharecropping. They have very recently stopped the old system where they would give half an acre or so to the labourers who work for them; there are still some left, particularly on distant areas of their land, but this is a diminishing practice. They know that even poor people now know about the tenancy law – that tenants get title to the land after ten years – and they don't want them to stake their claim.*

*I have 3.5 acres of land. My elder brother and I each had 2.5 acres that we received from our father. He was given this land by the Rajapur zamindar. Since then we have increased the amount of land we own. My brother now has 7.5 acres of agricultural land and 2 acres of orchards.*

An old man from the Nai (barber – a scheduled caste) caste says: *In our village, the scheduled castes were about 20 years ago each given about one-seventh of an acre by the government. Not only was this very little but most of the land was such that three generations could spend their lives working to improve it and it still would not produce anything! So we have land only in name because we end up spending more on the land than we get from it. If you saw the land you would understand why! And, anyway, if you do start producing something, the* Thakurs *will occupy it! There was a hillock that I had chipped away at and levelled and when it was flat the* Thakurs *occupied it!*

A young woman says: *Some don't even have this much. We have to depend on our children to send us money so that we can eat. Our small children have to go and work in roadside shops. My small son works in a shop where they repair stoves. People learn trades because they have to live.*

Lalit Kumar: *Pasis, Nais, Chamars, Yadavs, Mauryas – they all had land here as sharecroppers at the time when* zamindari *was abolished.* [The first three are scheduled castes; the other two higher-middle castes.] *The* Pasis *had taken a lot because they were numerically large. The* Thakurs *would never work on the land. They would give us a little patch to cultivate in exchange for our having to cultivate the rest of their land.*

*When* zamindari *was abolished, we sharecroppers were forced off the land. None of us poor people had any money when these reforms began. And we were all illiterate. But the rich people knew everything about the laws and paperwork. Because of this we were all fooled. We believed whatever we were told. Anyway, very often we didn't even know whose land we used to work on, we were that simple! Because of this the* Thakurs *cornered all the land during* zamindari *abolition.*

*It was only when some of us started going out that we acquired some knowledge about these things. Thus, even though the reservations for government jobs had been started since Independence, none of us knew how to take advantage of the reservations. It was only when our people rose up somewhat that we gained knowledge of these things. Some became teachers and learned about the law and our rights. Before that the* Thakur *teachers would thrash the students from the scheduled castes and purposely fail them!*

Ram Lal, a destitute *Pasi* man: says, *We are three brothers who own two-thirds of an acre between us. We support a mother and several children on this. Earlier we used to work as sharecroppers, we would* take one acre or more, but when the zamindari abolition law came the Thakurs took the land away from us. Now they give land on sharecropping only for one year.

We all get angry that the Rajapur zamindar and the other big lords have so much land lying fallow, when we are dying for land. But most of the time we are so busy trying to survive that we don't think about it.

Lalit Kumar interjects: The Thakurs would rather leave the land fallow than give it away or give it to sharecroppers. In fact, they keep hoping that one day our wages will fall because we are still poor and then they will again get us to work all their land.

Ram Lal adds: We don't revolt because the few who want to revolt are outnumbered by those who are scared of losing what little they have.

An old man says: We don't have the strength to fight because we are afraid that the little bit of wages we get, we won't even get that. Anyway, the District Magistrate and the other officers don't do anything even though they know that the zamindars have benami [illegal – literally, without name – implying that its ownership is disguised] land.

Lalit Kumar: And we are still very afraid of the Thakurs in the village, let alone the big zamindars. If they see us sitting in this group today they will abuse us and ask us what we were talking about. Earlier, of course, we could not have dared to talk like this! The Thakurs would have beaten us all up. It is because of these laws and reform that they've become a bit cautious. But even today many of them will still hit you before they bother to speak to you.

In neighbouring Rae Bareli district, once Mrs Gandhi's pampered pocket borough, the District Magistrate recounts his experience with land reform: You know, poor people are so scared of fighting for the land that they have been given title to that I often find them saying that they don't want the land. Or even more common, they will give it to us in writing that they have possession, when actually the Thakurs still have it!

During disputes I send police to see that the poor get possession of the land. At this time the Thakurs won't do anything. But the minute the police go back the situation reverts to the status quo. The Thakurs are still too powerful for any poor person to challenge them. I sometimes *feel it is almost like going against nature to take land from the rich and then to give it to the poor. It's much easier to allow the rich to grab the poor's land!*

*The resistance to land reform comes because the landowners feel that this land belongs to them and should never be given to anyone else. Even if their land is taken away and merged with the gaon sabha land* [common land vested in the village council], *they continue to act as if it is their land. In fact, they often act as if all gaon sabha land belongs to them. And anyway, there are a lot of exemptions given in the ceiling laws. For instance, take groves, which are exempt from any ceiling. Because of this a lot of landlords have converted their agricultural land into groves. They also do this because it is difficult to get the manpower needed for agriculture as the old system of* begar *is no longer available to them.*

*In Rae Bareli district, to date only 4,000 acres have been taken over as surplus land. That's really nothing at all. There are thousands and thousands of acres left with large landowners. Much of this land is left fallow, which is a waste of a national resource. The problem is not that we don't know which land or how much is* benami *land. We know all this. The problem is to act.*

# 13

# How the poor are Subjugated, and how they Fight Back

NEARLY 80 years after the Awadh revolt and 50 years after Independence, the upper-caste former landlords of Awadh – *Thakurs* and Brahmins alike – remain the most influential and powerful group in the region, though they are far from being the supreme lords of the past. Many of the former grand landlords are currently, or were earlier, members of parliament or of the legislative assembly, generally representing the Congress, the BJP (the former Jana Sangh) or the Janata Dal. They and their kin include ministers, rich businessmen, prominent lawyers and judges, senior officers in the civil service, foreign service, army and police, and even a former prime minister – the elite of independent India. And in virtually every village, the former village landlords are still the local bosses and crucial intermediaries in the political machines of the Congress and other major parties. From their ranks have come a large share of members of the legislature, district-level politicians, provincial bureaucrats, police officers and staff, lawyers, professors and teachers, and, not least, prosperous 'Green Revolution' farmers.

The persistent domination of both land ownership and positions of power by the upper castes has meant that the poor and low-caste have had little scope for emancipating themselves. Because the Congress spurned radical land reforms, the poor began at Independence with little or no land, with no other assets, and from a position of subjugation to the grand and village landlords. In their quest for land and for emancipation since then, they have had to contend not only with the hostility of the landed upper-castes to claims for redistribution but also the upper castes' domination of virtually every position of power, be it in the police, bureaucracy, legislature or judicial system. In such a system, the upper castes have used money, superior information, status, fear, violence, and their kinship ties to ensure that the poor get neither land, nor higher wages, nor freedom from their bondage. The result has been that the poor of Awadh remain poor.

In Baba ka Gaon, the descendants of the village landlords – 18 families or so – have managed to dominate the rest of the village, despite the passing of a half-century since the abolition of *zamindari*. Till about the mid-1980s or so, their hold was so strong that life for the poor seemed not to have changed since Independence. In the past decade, the momentum of change has become faster, and though their power has now visibly diminished, the *Thakurs* remain by far the most powerful group and caste in Baba ka Gaon.

Ram Dass says: *It is more peaceful in the village now than in the past. Things have improved by at least 50 per cent since when I was a youth. But true independence has not come. Independence means that the village is also independent, not just the nation; that in the village the big and powerful listen to the small and weak as much as the small listen to the big. There shouldn't be tension and this oppression. It's not enough that we have a little more to eat now than before. We should also be free of tension, we should not be oppressed. The attitude of the* Thakurs *towards us hasn't changed. They still feel that if anyone has to eat, it has to be them, if anyone wears clothes it must be them. Their desire is this: that there be rich and poor and the division between them be as great as it has always been.*

Begar *might have stopped 20 years ago but even until ten years ago the* Thakurs *would only give 1.5 kg of grain for 14 hours of work. This is not wages! A healthy man eats 1.5 kg for one meal. The* Thakurs *would ensure that you didn't die, that you had enough to survive, but that you didn't live either! They knew we would then end up taking loans from them and we would then be stuck forever in their hold. It used to happen that many who had taken loans would have to sell their land to the* Thakurs *because they couldn't pay off their debts. The only way you could have fought this is by filing a case, but how could you file a case when you didn't have enough to eat!*

*You need to organize to change things but until ten years ago we were unable to do so, we were all too poor and defenceless. The* Thakurs *would beat us up, they'd come, three or four of them, to our house and beat us. The rest of us would run away. We were fearful because they owned everything, nothing was ours, even though* zamindari *had been ended. They decided who got more, who got less, where one's cattle could graze, even where one could walk! And no one listens to the poor at the police station, even now. But over the years some of us got little bits of land, and the government road opened, so we can walk freely. And we have our own grinding-mill. It's only since all this happened that we began to slowly resist them.*

*We had to fight the* Thakurs *ten years ago to raise the wages. We fought by all of us scheduled and middle castes saying to them that we wouldn't work for such wages, even if we died of starvation. We said that anyway we can't live on what you give us, with this 1.5 kg only I can get to eat, and so what is my son to live on? At that time the government used to say that we should get Rs 18 per day, but we got nothing of the sort. So we all decided to fight for this, though of course this was not a violent fight like a* lathi[a long, heavy wooden stick used as a weapon in India]-*charge. We forced them to give us what we demanded. If someone went and worked for them for less, we put pressure on that person, saying 'Why did you do this?', and they stopped.*

*The* Thakurs *tried to scare all of us by saying that they would get an outside militia to intimidate us. Many of us would wonder what is the point of fighting because we'll just get killed. We were so used to not having land or money and being defenceless. But since by then many of us had some land, even though it was so poor, and we'd earned some money and been to the cities, we were braver than earlier. The* Thakurs *only began to do any work in their fields after this battle with them! Till then they would just stand there and order us around. Now they do some work, even if it's only running their irrigation pump or driving the tractor. And it was only at that time that we stopped the practice of getting up from the* charpai *whenever a* Thakur *came. Till this time the* Thakurs *spoke as rudely to us as they had done when I was a child. 'Go and work in our fields, do this, go there!' You can't do anything about the* Thakurs' *rudeness or cruel comments. You have to bear it. Just like earlier we used to bear it when they took off their shoes and hit us. Like they used to drink liquor and pass this way and insult our women. Earlier, we would even ignore what they said about our women. We were afraid of getting into a fight. But now we can't bear their abuse of our women.*

*In my 70 years I went to the police station for the first time during the* panchayat *elections in 1995. There has been some good from that fight* [during the *panchayat* elections, for the first time the scheduled and middle castes in Baba ka Gaon physically hit back on being attacked by the Thakurs; see next chapter], *even if we all end up going to jail for it. The* Thakurs *have been doing this in the past too, involving people who are trying to progress in false cases. They can succeed in this because they have the police and the officials on their side. The local officials and police are all upper-caste, or if they are of the middle castes they will still follow the orders of the upper-caste people here. They get two people of this family involved in one case, get the schoolchildren involved so they can't study, get those who are progressing. When the* Thakurs *see us progressing, it hurts them like they have dust in their eyes.*

*We have a saying here that if there are maggots in the wound of a domesticated animal, all one does is to take the name of seven* lekhpals *and seven darogas* [local police officials], *and you sing this mantra: the maggots will get out and crawl away because the* lekhpal *and daroga are even more parasitic and destructive than them!* [Both sets of officials have historically been of the upper castes.]

*As us poorer people have become more aware of our rights and how we are exploited, there have been more fights in the village against the upper castes. If one has no option, then one has to labour for the upper castes who own land. But now most of us have some of our own land and won't work for them. This is what makes them behave even worse towards us. Their oppression of us continues. We will have to learn to do what they do. To use money or violence. By remaining naked and helpless, you don't get your rightful share. But there is no point in getting angry that things have only changed so slowly and so little.*

*One has to be happy even for the small changes that have taken place. Earlier there was no food and now most of us have something to eat. Earlier there was no road. We never knew what electricity was. Some people grew old without even seeing a train, let alone climbing into one. We used to live like animals. After Independence came and* zamindari *was abolished, those of us who worked hard got a little. Those who didn't have land were given a patch.*

Shrinath says: *My father feels there has been a revolution because he's lived through slavery and terrible poverty. But I've lived through comparatively better times. How can one be happy in slavery? If my father had been happy, why did he run away, why did he leave his home? He tells me – I was just a young child then – that every scheduled- and low-caste man in the village used to work in the* Thakurs' *fields or in their houses. Everyone in the village was tied to them; even the people who had some land had to work for them. And the wages for working the entire day and night for them was only 1.5 kg of grain. My family would live just on this much grain! Nobody is happy in slavery. Happiness is only in freedom. What kind of happiness can there be in bondage?*

*Even in the years since my childhood the oppression in the village has lessened. We are more free. There was much more oppression when I was in school. Every scheduled-caste person still had to work as labourers for the* Thakurs. *This was in the early 1970s. Even when I became a teacher I still had to work as a labourer for the upper castes. Only when I saved some money from teaching were we able to buy some land and gradually stop working for others. But even this was just 10 or 12 years ago.*

*The upper castes have nowadays become softer and more mild in the way they treat others. They used to be the* zamindars *earlier, but now there is some kind of equality between us because we also own some land, even if it is much less than them. Earlier we were absolutely poor, we could not say anything, we were not free to leave the village. Now at least we people are educated, we know our rights and about the laws and regulations.*

*Now the upper castes don't do us harm directly, like they used to beat us earlier. They do it indirectly. For instance, if I'm going alone somewhere they'll inform their relatives outside the village that I am from a low caste and that they should beat me up. They are very experienced in this kind of thing. So they encircle you and beat you up. And their people are in big posts in the police and government, so no one bothers to listen to our complaints. In both the government and administration, 90 per cent are upper-caste people. If there was an equal balance between the upper and lower castes in both government and administration, then everyone's interests would be kept in mind. But until then, the government and administration will work only for the upper castes.*

*It is not constantly tense everywhere. From village to village, it varies depending on the proportion of upper- to lower-caste people. The battle between us has been going on for centuries, and the upper castes keep harking back to the time when they were the lords and every word they uttered was law for us! But their word is no longer law in villages where the lower castes are in large numbers, or where the lower castes have managed to get educated. But in places where the lower castes are not educated or where there are few of them, they are still very repressed because they are not able to understand or demand their rights.*

Hansraj says: *The village has changed even from when I was a teenager. One could not move around the village freely like Rakesh, my younger brother, does now, though even now none of us goes to the* Thakurs' *side of the village. Earlier, there was always tension. The* Thakurs *were always beating somebody from the lower castes. Even the children would be beaten by them. Once our bullocks went into a* Thakur's *field. I was thrashed with a staff.*

*It's only in the last seven or eight years that the oppression by the* Thakurs *has slowly become less. This happened because most of us found some alternative means of employment, of feeding our families. Some of us got a little land from the land reform, others went to the city and came back and bought some land. So some of us stopped going to the* Thakurs *for work and so stopped fearing them so much. It's only the people facing the most hardship who have no alternative but to work for them and these people are still terrorized by the* Thakurs.

*But the* Thakurs *are still very powerful and oppress all of us. There's still always tension in the village even though we are less afraid than we used to be. Now what has changed is that they don't shout at us or order us around face-to-face, like they did earlier. Only the future will tell whether the tension and oppression will get less.*

## Discrimination

Ritual discrimination by the upper castes against the former untouchables has lessened in Baba ka Gaon, but is still pervasive. Fifty years of protective legislation and other safeguards have not made an enormous dent on untouchability in rural India, where the vast majority of the scheduled castes live, though the situation has improved radically in urban areas.[1] In practice, discrimination is now muted in public arenas, such as schools or roadside hotels, but extensive in the 'private' sphere of the home.

Ram Dass says: *There were so many discriminations against the scheduled castes that it will take a long time for it to end. There are still upper-caste people in the village who believe in untouchability. If we touch something, they will sprinkle Ganga-jal* [Ganges water] *on it.*

A decade ago the scheduled-caste villagers defied the upper castes and constructed a modest, whitewashed shrine in the lower-caste area of the village. Says Ram Dass: *The temple on our side of the village was recently built by the Dom* [a scheduled caste]. *Earlier there was a pedestal there with a Devi statue. Now the upper castes let their sewage and water run past it because they say a low-caste person should not have dared to build a temple. Things like untouchability will only change when we stop going where we are not allowed to sit. When we refuse to go to the* Thakurs' *houses. We've started doing this already.*

Durbhe, says: *We now treat the* Thakurs *the way they treat us. We might have eaten at their house once or twice during their weddings or festivals. Which is fine because they are bigger than us, but how many times can we allow this if we keep offering them hospitality in return and they never accept? We are also something after all, we are humans. However weak you are at some point you are going to rebel. If you are rich you don't eat gold and silver, you only eat wheat like we do!*

Ram Dass: *One old* Thakur *woman had fallen into the well, and a man of our caste pulled her out. And on coming out of the well she had a bath, saying that the man had contaminated her by touching her when he climbed into the well to pull her out! This happened about 15 years ago, in the well near her house. And then she goes and cries to her relatives, 'Bring me water, I need to bathe,' even though she was soaked in water! When it came to saving her life then there was no question about untouchability, but when her life was saved she went back and said that she had been contaminated.*

*Everybody makes dirt. But people think that the person who cleans the dirt is a dirty and polluted person. But this is completely wrong. It is the person who makes the dirt and does not clean it who is unclean. The people who clean not only their dirt but that of others should be considered great or god-like, because they do what parents do for their children. So why is it that people who clean for others are considered dirty? Even with officials its like this. If the* patwari *is of the upper castes, if we go to him, we can't even sit on the* charpai. *We will sit like dogs on the floor. Only if there is a middle-caste* patwari *can we sit on the* charpai.

Shrinath says: *Look at all the other religions, whether it is Christianity, Sikhism or Islam – there isn't as much discrimination in them as in Hinduism. The essence of any religion is 'Roti ya beti'* [bread or daughter] *– you have to eat freely or intermarry with each other. It is important to have at least one of these relationships with another person if there is to be any equality. There might not be a relationship of marriage; that will only happen when we are equal. A poor person cannot have marital ties with a rich family because the question of status comes in. But at least you can eat together! But it's not like this in the Hindu religion where everyone is divided from the other by caste! And all these upper-caste people are the root cause of the problem.*

Ram Dass: *My father would eat meat, but I stopped at about the age of thirty-five. I got into the community of people who believed in the sanctity of life. We save ourselves from sin by not eating meat, because God is in everything. But even though I am a vegetarian, the upper castes will not take a smoke from my chillum* [clay pipe] *even though so many of them eat meat! Their sense of caste discrimination is still so strong that they still consider us unclean. But I give my chillum to people irrespective of whether they eat meat or not.*

*I am friendly towards all people, whether of high or low caste, or whether Hindu, Muslim or Buddhist. Everyone is mortal, everyone has been created by God. All people do their own work, they live in their houses, and feed themselves. We all have come the same way and will go the same way. We live together. Religion or caste is not written in our blood, nor in our appearance. If God had meant these differences to be important he would have given someone horns and someone else four hooves so you could distinguish them.*

## Terror and Violence

Across Awadh, the equation between the upper and lower castes varies enormously from village to village. Thus, even in villages neighbouring Baba ka Gaon, the power of the upper-caste landlords, and their monopoly on land, is almost as absolute as it was before the abolition of *zamindari* a half-century ago. Their hold is reflected in their being able to keep wage rates for labourers very low, in some instances three times lower than in Baba ka Gaon. Generally, these are villages where the upper castes outweigh the lower castes in number.

But despite this diversity, one constant across Awadh and most of UP is that upper-caste violence and brutality against the scheduled and lower-middle castes is unrelenting. Much of this violence is a continuation of the old pattern of subordinating the lower castes; some of it also reflects heightened assertiveness on the part of the lower castes.[2] According to Ram Dass and others in Baba ka Gaon, upper-caste violence against the scheduled castes is commonplace in the region.

To comprehend the scope of the violence, consider that on consecutive days, within a radius of 35 km from Baba ka Gaon, there were brutal attacks by the upper castes on the scheduled castes. On 1 July 1995, an adolescent scheduled-caste girl was raped by a young *Thakur*. A day earlier, a young scheduled-caste man had his forearms lopped off by a *Thakur* landlord.

The village of Pithi, some 25 km from Baba ka Gaon, is cut off from the mainstream of Pratapgarh district by the river Sai, which must be forded to reach the village, as paths from other directions are impassable most of the year. (The names of the village and people have been changed to maintain privacy.) The village seems idyllic: groves of mango and other fruit trees cascade down small hillocks to the river, and peacocks call in the dark. It is about half the size of Baba ka Gaon.

Ramesh Pasi's family lives in a rudimentary hut at the edge of the village. He and his family sit in a tight, tense knot outside, whispering. According to the report filed at the police station by Ramesh Pasi, his daughter Champa, aged 15, went at 7 a.m. to the fields to defecate. While she was pulling up her *salwar* (stringed pajamas), she was attacked by Prahlad Singh, the 25-year-old son of an important *Thakur* landlord, who 'caught hold of her hand with bad intentions', reads the text of the report. Champa's mother says, 'He was hiding somewhere and when she was pulling up her *salwar* he attacked her from behind. Then she started screaming and he covered her mouth. So she bit him and screamed again, which is when we heard her. And then he ran away. We all saw him running away.'

In fact, Champa was raped by Prahlad Singh, said Shrinath, who found this out because he is of the same caste as her family. Shrinath explained that the father did not write this in the complaint to the police – and the mother denies it in public – because it would ruin his daughter's marriage prospects. But as a result of the parents' reluctance to state that Champa had actually been raped, their complaint was classified by the police under a statute that is far less serious than rape. This makes it unlikely that Prahlad Singh will go to jail for any length of time, even if the case reaches the courts, which is itself improbable.

Champa's father says: *The case was written up right away by the police. The station officer came the next day for one hour. He did not meet the boy; he only went to the place where the incident took place, took my daughter with him, asked her a few questions and wrote something. Then he said he would come back, but it's been a month and he hasn't done so. We went a week later to see the officer, who said, 'Why are you worrying, your case is registered and we will do what is needed.'*

His wife interjects angrily: *They then went to Ram Lakhan.* [The Bahujan Samaj Party candidate for MLA; the party represents a large section of the scheduled castes.] *He took them to Lucknow to meet Mayawati at the rally. But the crowd was so great that they couldn't even get close to her. What can we do if no one listens to us?* [A scheduled-caste woman, Mayawati was UP's chief minister for a few months in mid-1995. She is a leader of the Bahujan Samaj Party.] *My husband has sent a registered copy of the FIR to the police in Lucknow, to Pratapgarh and to Allahabad.* [The head of the district police is based in Pratapgarh, the head for the region in Allahabad, and the state head in Lucknow.] *But the* Thakurs *went to see Pramod Tiwari, the Congress MLA, and perhaps gave him some money, this is what some people told us, which is why this case is not progressing.*

The father says: *The* Thakurs *are constantly threatening us now. They pulled off the thatch from our roof. And they have threatened to burn our house down. We don't work for them anymore, but we work for anyone else who will employ us. All of the* Thakurs *are allied with each other, so it's very difficult for us to find work. Our house is surrounded on all sides by fields belonging to the* Thakurs. *So they say that unless you work for us we won't let you cross our fields. We have one-and-a-half acres between my whole family, but it's near the river and gives just one crop every year. It's one kilometre from here, but it's flooded most of the time. We don't get any rice from it. We plant some things, but not much.*

*Only ten per cent of the scheduled castes and lower castes have land. Earlier none of the scheduled castes had land. Then some went out and with their earnings bought some; others got a little bit from land reform. The majority of land is with the* Thakurs. *They have at least eight acres each. One has about 30 acres, and this family also controls all the village common land, which they've taken over. This family has even taken over the village burial grounds for use as fields!*

*You get Rs 5–10 for a day's labour.* [One-third to one-half of the wage rate in Baba ka Gaon.] *The* Thakurs *are shameless, and despite these wages don't pay us even when we go to ask for it. There are so few lower castes here in the village that we can do nothing against the* Thakurs, *unless the police help us. If any action is taken on my daughter's case, the tension will increase. But the* Thakurs *will try to oppress us further if nothing happens. If on this thing we cannot get anything done, how will we ever manage to fight them again? We wish and hope that they get as severe a sentence as possible.*

The village of Kachwahan ka Purwa – literally, the hamlet of the Kachwahan *Thakurs* – is in Rae Bareli district, which was for two decades the pocket borough of Indira Gandhi. But these years of being a 'VIP constituency' and having millions of rupees poured in for 'development' has made the situation of the poor in Rae Bareli no better than in Pratapgarh. The village is 35 km or so from Baba ka Gaon.

The hovel is ragged even by the standards of the poor in Awadh, the thatch torn and the mud walls crumbling. Outside the hut is an emaciated, hunched, small male figure, the limbs skeletal, a bony neck supporting a face across which course, transparently and almost without break, waves of agony. The figure wears small shorts and a sleeveless vest, both tattered and dusty. Across the tense shoulders is a thin cotton towel, the ends just hiding the stumps of his arms, both of which end just above the elbow in dirty bandages. This figure, slack-jawed, empty-eyed, shrouded in despair, tries to prevent the towel from slipping off by touching at it with the stumps of his arms. The movement is unpractised, tentative and elicits even more anguish; the wounds are less than a fortnight old. Jerking in pain, the figure screams at the two toddlers who come out from the shack and try to approach him. Though his stick-like figure and dress make him seem just a young boy, Samar Bahadur Koeri is 18-years old, married, and the father of the two toddlers. He speaks blankly, softly, so gently that it is almost a mumble.

*My father and my uncle were not here. Some relatives had come so I decided that I would not work today. I was at home and then Om Prakash Singh came and ordered me to work, to come and chop the fodder. This is the work that I always have to do for the* Thakur. *When I told him that I couldn't work because there were relatives visiting, he abused me and said I had to come, that he would beat me up. He forced me to go; he always terrorizes me. So I started chopping fodder, and he said, 'Why are you feeding the machine so slowly?' It is a diesel fodder machine, not a hand-powered one. And I said, 'This is the best I can do.' And then Om Prakash said, 'Come, I will show you how the machine is fed,' and he caught both my arms and pushed them into the machine.*

*I screamed and then fainted. When I screamed and my hands had been cut off, Om Prakash ran away. And then two of my caste people were passing by and they came running when they heard me scream. They told me later that they were carrying sticks in their hands and they pushed this into the machine to make it stop, or otherwise even more of my arms would have been dragged in and cut off. They told me that my hands and cut portion of the arms came out from the machine like strips of fodder.*

Samar Bahadur's father, Juggu, is a visibly worn, exhausted man; short, thin, grey-haired, with eyes streaming with mucus from some infection. *I was in Ambala* [in Punjab province] *working at a brick kiln when this happened. I only came to hear about it two weeks later.*

*Because my son was alone anyone could coerce him into doing anything they wanted. When I got back and saw what had happened to my son, I went in anger to Om Prakash. He made me stand outside the door because my family is untouchable. He told me he was very worried about my son, that my son had cut his arms while using the thresher, and that he would pay for the treatment. He then said, 'If you file a case against me I will ruin you all.'*

*I saw that the boy cannot support himself; he is incapable now. So I took his wife and young daughter, and the three of us walked to the police station and filed a case. The police wrote everything down and then they came here and arrested Om Prakash on the same day. This was on 19 July. He is in jail now. The senior policeman at the Jagatpur station is a Verma, a backward [middle] caste man. He wrote down our complaint without any problem.*

Kachwahan ka Purwa is smaller than Baba ka Gaon. Of the 40 or so families, roughly a dozen are upper-caste, the rest middle- and scheduled-caste. Between them, the middle and scheduled castes own only five per cent of the agricultural land in the village, substantially less than that owned by these groups in Baba ka Gaon. Though titles to plots were given to tenants and also to the landless during the several rounds of land reform, most of these people have not been able to occupy the land they had been given titles to.

Om Prakash Singh, the *Thakur* who assaulted Samar Bahadur, is not the village's largest landowner, but he is arrogant because he served in the army, where one of his sons now is, according to Samar Bahadur's father. He used to boast that he would have anyone who dared defy him killed by the army.

Samar Bahadur's father says: *I work as a sharecropper because the* Thakurs *have not allowed us to take possession of the land that belongs to us. My father has half an acre of land near the pond but we have not got possession of it. The few times I cultivated the land the* Thakurs *prevented us from harvesting the crop. They beat us up, so we stopped trying to work it. And anyway it is useless land because it is most often inundated by water.*

*What is the point of fighting, of going to the courts? We went to the court and won the case about our land but even then the* Thakurs *bribed the court people and got the case dismissed.*

*My son has studied until the tenth class. Earlier, like me, he would work in the fields or doing whatever else we could get. We have no other work. You can get work every day if you want, but the wages are only Rs 8–10 for a 13-hour day – from 6 a.m. to 7 p.m. and sometimes you will have to work even later.* [Wage rates in Baba ka Gaon are nearly twice this.] *But even at these low wages the* Thakurs *will not pay us what we are owed! We are owed about Rs 2,000 in back wages, but the* Thakurs *have not paid us. I made that brick house over there, but they have not paid me yet. When we go to ask them they shout at us and say, 'We have no money so come back in four or five months.'*

The District Magistrate of Rae Bareli is sympathetic and intelligent. Commenting on Samar Bahadur's family being owed a huge sum by the *Thakurs*, he says: *No poor person in his right mind will go to the police to complain about this or other kinds of exploitation. They will either try to resolve it or will just forget about the money they are owed. Academics always emphasize how poor people in rural India are always in debt to rich people. But everyone overlooks how the rich owe money to the poor and never pay! This is just another way for them to keep the poor in their power.*

In great part because of the District Magistrate's conscientiousness, Samar Bahadur's family received Rs 100,000 from the state government, compensation given in cases where atrocities are committed against scheduled castes. The District Magistrate also promised Samar Bahadur that his family would be given secure title to 2.5 acres of arable land. Three months later they had received most of the land. And a contingent from the state constabulary was posted at the village to prevent the other *Thakurs* from fulfilling their threat to kill Samar Bahadur and his father because of their defiance of Om Prakash Singh. Samar Bahadur's father put the cheque from the government in a fixed deposit in a nearby bank. The interest on the amount is about Rs 1,000 per month, which the family will use to survive now that they have lost their only young, able-bodied wage earner.

Samar Bahadur's father praises the District Magistrate for his empathy, but reviles the local member of the state legislature, even though the latter is from the same scheduled caste as himself. *The MLA, who is from our caste, came and asked us to compromise with the* Thakur, *but we said we don't want to have any dealings with the* Thakurs *and so we don't want to have anything to do with you. The MLA asked us how were we managing for food and other things and we said we are managing because of our relatives. So he then asked us to come to the hospital in Rae Bareli where he would meet us, but when we went there at the appointed time he wasn't there. Look, he told us he would give us money for food but he didn't even give us a sip of tea! Then we just left and went to the District Magistrate's office and when we got the cheque, the MLA arrived and told us to keep it carefully. So we got angry and told him, 'What do you think we'll do if not keep it carefully? Do you think we will put it in the fire?' He is from among us, but now he is a big man and lives in a bungalow. He moves around in a car and has sentries with him. When the District Magistrate told us to have tea before we left the District Magistrate's office, the MLA said, 'Yes, yes, have tea before you leave,' but he himself left straight away! He had no time for us.*

Samar Bahadur is helped by his father every second day to the doctor, where the bandages are changed and his amputated arms cleaned. The roughly 10-km journey is done on a pony-cart or a tractor's buggy, as Samar Bahadur cannot bicycle or walk this distance. His father says: *This kind of violence happens here all the time. Just five days ago a Brahmin landlord beat a* Pasi *man so badly that he lost six teeth. And this is when the army was already posted here! The police have also arrested the Brahmin, but he has now been released on bail.*

# 14

# Why Political Democracy Has Not Led to Economic Democracy

RAM Dass says: *I have voted since the first election in 1952. I was in Bombay. My wife voted in the same elections, but here in the village. I felt excited, but not as much as I was when* zamindari *was abolished. That was the most important thing in my life. Having the vote is better than having rajas! With democracy you can change governments, but with rajas there is just dynasty and dictatorship. But even then we have not gained much from the vote.*

In 1956, inaugurating a seminar on parliamentary democracy, Prime Minister Jawaharlal Nehru expounded:

Democracy has been spoken of chiefly in the past, as political democracy, roughly represented by every person having a vote. But a vote itself does not represent very much to a person who is down and out, to a person, let us say, who is starving or hungry. Political democracy, by itself, is not enough except that it may be used to obtain a gradually increasing measure of economic democracy, equality and the spread of good things of life to others and removal of gross inequalities.

Nehru's words – echoed by Ram Dass – have a prophetic ring four decades later. The persistence of chronic and intense poverty, as well as the continuing oppression of the poor, is incontrovertible evidence of the Indian democratic system's failure to represent the interests of the poor, despite universal suffrage and their very large numbers. To some Indians, this failure proves that the vote should not have been given to the illiterate or poor, on the reasoning that the unschooled cannot make sensible political choices.[1] But this is a prejudiced misreading of why universal suffrage has failed the Indian poor. The failure is not intrinsic to universal suffrage nor to the illiteracy of India's masses. Rather, it stems from the nature of the independent India that Nehru and Congress had such a powerful influence in shaping.

The dereliction of the interests of the poor in independent India has its roots in the pre-Independence Congress, which at the time of Independence represented essentially the interests of a range of propertied groups. The Congress' conservatism and pro-property bias is partly understandable, as in the lead-up to Independence suffrage was limited to the propertied, educated and those with at least moderate incomes – the top one-fifth of India's population. Moreover, the colonial setting itself curbed the emergence of a more radical nationalist movement, with the British colonial government routinely outlawing many Communist and other radical groups.[2]

On Independence, by disregarding redistributive land reform in practice (though not in rhetoric), Nehru and other Congress leaders committed the original error that wrecked the emancipation of the poor. They gave the 'masses' the extraordinary gift of the vote, embodying the revolutionary principle of 'one person, one vote', but because this was the sole gain to the poor from Independence, in isolation, without any material assets, the gift was almost worthless. In contrast, radical land reform – the only means of transforming the material conditions of the poor as well as of emancipating them – was systematically shunned.

The Congress then relied on the propertied and powerful in rural India to deliver electoral support and keep it in power. This was the final touch on the conservative superstructure of independent India, damming the emergence of local democracy. The 'socialist pattern of society' that Nehru and the Congress had dedicated themselves to in their 1955 party resolution was nowhere to be seen.

Ram Dass says: *Until Independence, the* Thakurs *were in conflict with the Congress. The Congress was good then, but this ended when the* Thakurs *joined it. These people realized that there was no point being in conflict with the government in power and that instead they should join that party. So they all became important people in the Congress. But at least we got a little more food and more clothes with the Congress. Earlier, in winter, we would just have to double our* dhoti *to try to keep warm.*

*In the first few elections the* Thakurs *wouldn't let anyone from the lower castes enter. They would fill in the ballots themselves. They would force us uneducated people to do what they wanted, to put our thumb print on this ballot paper and not on any other. Usually they made us vote for the Congress.*

*Anyway, earlier we poor people wouldn't care about voting, we'd say who cares who we give our vote to? Who cares if the* Thakurs *force us to do this or that? Who is going to bother to go and vote at all? For us the vote didn't mean anything. We thought, what would we get out of it? All us lower-caste people were asleep. Only Dr Ambedkar was awake.*

*The Congress has always been dominant here. And their people have always been rajas and the upper castes. The MP for many terms was the raja from Pratapgarh. The Kalakankar raja's daughter is now an MP, and he was also an MP for one term. He – Dinesh Singh – even came here to the village once while campaigning! And the MLA for many terms has been Pramod Tiwari.*

The alliance between India's dominant political party and dominant rural groups effectively throttled the chances of the poor rising either materially or in civil and social freedoms. Not unexpectedly, the rural poor (in UP or anywhere in India) have since failed to unite as a class or to emerge as an electoral force. Political power has not shifted towards them despite their numbers.[3] With the superstructure of the state so visibly allied with the propertied and patently arrayed against them, the poor face obvious dangers in attempting to emancipate themselves. In addition, there has been no even moderately-powerful political party committed to their interests. Moreover, the emergence of radical challenges was forestalled by the Congress' nationalist legacy, its unceasing pro-poor rhetoric, and its initiation of land reforms, reservations and anti-poverty programmes, however wanting in intention and impact. And just the vote and parliamentary democracy – embodying the hope that peaceful, orderly change is possible – blunted class tensions.

The realities of rural India also militate against the poor emerging as a political force. The difficulties of uniting across, first, diverse castes – ranging from the multitude of middle castes to the many layers within the scheduled castes – and, then, gradations of poverty – from the small and marginal farmer to the absolutely landless – are enormous. Moreover, in Baba ka Gaon and elsewhere, the poor must concentrate on the arduous battle for physical survival, leaving little time and energy for what seem to be less immediate concerns.

Even for the scheduled castes, the one group within the ranks of the poor which in effect has special electoral representation, electoral politics has not led to significant gains. The scheduled castes have not emerged as a strong political movement, nor has their deprivation relative to other groups lessened. To some degree this is a legacy of Gandhi's defeat of Ambedkar's demand for a separate electorate for the scheduled castes. Under the prevailing reservation system of parliamentary and assembly seats, constituencies are set aside for scheduled-caste candidates but the voters are not separated into scheduled-caste and 'other' electorates. Consequently, candidates must appeal not only to the scheduled castes, but broadly to all voters. This reduces their reasons for representing the interests of the scheduled castes and has also set back the development of independent scheduled-caste parties committed to their interests.[4] Clearly, the joint electorates are better than no reservations at all; without them, there would have been no reason for mainstream parties to have developed a core of scheduled-caste legislators.[5] But, until recently, the scheduled castes have been incorporated into the mainstream parties – usually the Congress – and have had to be content with these parties' limited commitment to their interests.

In UP and at the centre in New Delhi, the Congress system held together in this shape for two decades after Independence. Some of the fissures that emerged in the next decade benefited the poor. Mrs Gandhi's recourse to the poor as a constituency was provoked by battles for power within the elite of the Congress. And in UP, the rich, higher-middle caste farmers of western UP broke away from the Congress in the late1960s, enlarging the scope for competitive politics. The gains to the poor in UP were not substantial, and the Congress, during Mrs

Gandhi's second term and then more decisively under Rajiv Gandhi, returned to bolstering the power of the rural elite. But even these tiny gains – the handkerchief-size patches of infertile land – provided the poor with some weapons in their battle against oppression.

The decline of the Congress in UP, once the land of its glory, was palpably evident by the close of the 1980s. The province's politics have since been polarized between the BJP, an essentially upper-caste grouping, and several parties representing middle and scheduled castes. Scheduled-caste support for the Congress waned in the 1980s, a trend made visible when in the 1989 elections the Bahujan Samaj Party, a scheduled-caste grouping, won two parliamentary and 14 assembly seats.[6]

Uttar Pradesh has since been ruled in quick succession by these parties representing the upper, middle and scheduled castes. From end-1989 to mid-1991, the middle-caste-dominated Janata Dal ruled the province. Then, until December 1992, the upper-caste BJP was in power. After a year of direct rule by the central government, the Samajwadi Party – drawing its support from the middle and some share of the scheduled castes – and the Bahujan Samaj Party allied to form the government, which lasted till rivalry between them ended their rule in mid-1995. Then, extraordinarily, UP had its first scheduled-caste chief minister, nearly two decades after the first middle-caste chief minister and nearly half a century since Independence. The event was even more singular because Mayawati was also the province's first woman chief minister (like many scheduled caste persons, she does not use a last name). But her meteoric rise was brief: by October that year the Bahujan Samaj Party had lost power and the province was placed under direct administration by the central government for nearly two years.

Paradoxically, despite the emergence of the parties representing the scheduled castes and the middle castes, land reform and other redistributive issues did not emerge even briefly on to the province's political agenda in these years. This is because, much like the Congress and the Janata coalitions, the Bahujan Samaj and the Samajwadi Parties, in ideology and practice, also disregarded the primary concerns of the poor. Though the Samajwadi Party is dominated by the Yadavs, a fairly prosperous middle caste, many of its backers are impoverished lower-middle and scheduled castes who would gain from land reform. (A significant share of the scheduled castes, including Ram Dass and his family, in fact tend to prefer the Samajwadi Party to the Bahujan Samaj, the major cause of the bitter rivalry between these parties.)[7]

Shrinath says: *These new parties like the Samajwadi and Bahujan Samaj are better than the Congress. But in all of them the malpractices of the politicians continue. No party talks about land reform except the Communists, who believe in equality. The other parties are full of people who are well off and they do not want to make laws under which they themselves will suffer. The Communists contest the elections but they are never successful. They only get 20 or 22 seats in the whole of UP, and because people know they can never form a government they don't vote for them. Otherwise more of us poor people would vote for them. All the stuff the other parties do is just a lot of show! Cheap theatre! All they do is make tall promises and claims on radio and television. All the laws that they make are laws to benefit themselves. Nothing changes for the poor.*

Hansraj says: *Politicians are all for themselves, to see how much they can loot the people. At elections, they throw a scrap to us – over which we tear each other apart – and then they go and fill their stomachs and, at the next elections, they throw another scrap. None of the parties wants anything but to fill their own stomachs. But it's still important to vote, because sometime something will be of benefit to us poor people. When Indira-ji came to power the first time, some good was done, some land was given to the poor. And now there has been some advantage to us since we've got the right to be* pradhans *through reservations, which Mulayam Singh Yadav* [the Samajwadi chief minister in 1995; see section below] *provided. Now even the upper castes have to treat us with respect because some of us are* pradhans.

Durbhe, their relative, says: *We would be happy if there was a political party which would distribute all the* benami *land. We would vote for them. But the politicians don't want to do anything about land reform because they will have to give up their own land! All they do is that just before the elections, their leaders come and promise you a lot of things but this is all talk. All the politicians from the scheduled castes and middle castes talk only about reservations. But reservations in colleges are of no use to people who don't have the money to study, and reservations in government jobs are no use when you're not educated enough to get government jobs! Even these politicians support the rich, not the poor. We poor people would never speak frankly even to the scheduled-caste politicians if they came here and talked to us.*

The failure of both the Bahujan Samaj and the Samajwadi parties to represent the interests of the poor, who are the primary backers of both parties, is rooted in the fact that the parties are led by the small elite of the scheduled and middle castes that has developed since Independence. While the middle-caste elite developed largely as a result of benefiting from land reform, the scheduled-caste elite grew out of the affirmative-action programmes in higher education and in government jobs. By the early 1980s in UP, there was a core of middle and scheduled-caste officials in the provincial and central civil services. The majority held low-ranking posts, and faced discrimination from the upper-caste officials, who have tended to view the civil services as their exclusive preserve. The Bahujan Samaj, in particular, began essentially as a pressure group to improve the position of scheduled-caste officers in the bureaucracy.[8] Since then, the agendas of both the Samajwadi and the Bahujan Samaj parties have been dominated by the effort to raise the numbers of, respectively, the middle castes and the scheduled castes in colleges, specialized education and the bureaucracy.

Despite the failure to advocate land reform and other measures to aid the poor, the parties have succeeded in evoking popular support from the lower-caste poor. In part, this is because rule by a chief minister of their general caste grouping is a potent assertion of their emancipation, even if this is a symbolic rather than a material gain. There is also a potential tangible benefit: that when the province is ruled by 'their government', the police and bureaucracy will be forced to be less abusive and hostile towards them. Both these are important gains for the lower castes, who have so far always faced an environment dominated in every way by the upper castes. Even when their rule offers no material gain, being ruled by a middle or scheduled-caste party and chief minister (or having more middle and scheduled-caste officials) is an advance over the continuation of upper-caste rule. Thus, despite their dissatisfaction with the limited agendas of these parties, in the 1990s many poor middle and scheduled-caste people backed them strongly.

## The *panchayat* elections of 1995

Though the tenure in government of the Samajwadi and Bahujan Samaj parties was not marked by even the rumour of a possibility that they would consider initiating land reform or other directly redistributive measures, this period witnessed what Ram Dass considers to be the second most important political event of his life, next only to *zamindari* abolition in its impact on his family's emancipation. This was the decision in early 1995 by the Samajwadi–Bahujan Samaj alliance to reserve a large share of the posts of *pradhan* for the scheduled castes as well as for the middle castes. Under the scheme, just under a majority of *pradhans* would be from the scheduled or middle castes.[9]

The decision was revolutionary because it threatened the upper-caste domination of the village *panchayats* and most important, their monopoly on the post of *pradhan*. In Baba ka Gaon, for instance, a single *Thakur* man had been the village *pradhan* since 1952, when the first *panchayat* elections had been held. The *pradhan* post was crucial to the upper castes. There is enormous traditional power associated with the post – literally, that of hereditary headman. Moreover, the *panchayats* had since Rajiv Gandhi's tenure received huge funds for poverty-alleviation and rural development programmes, which went almost entirely into the bank accounts of the upper-caste *pradhan* and his allies. Being ousted from the post of *pradhan* was a hammer-blow to the ancient upper-caste domination of Awadh and to their profitable new role of intermediary in independent India's elite-dominated political structure. The system that under Rajiv Gandhi's dispensation had been a travesty of its professed intention – that of aiding the poor – was being shaped into a form that at least now held this potential.

The prospect led the upper castes across Awadh and UP to try to abort the *panchayat* elections. Independent-minded potential candidates from the middle castes and scheduled castes were warned or beaten so that they would not contest the *pradhan*'s post. For weeks before the elections, rural UP was on the verge of exploding into battles between the upper castes and the middle and scheduled castes. The tensions blazed into violence during the elections: some 70 people were killed, hundreds of re-elections ordered, as well as several dozen elections countermanded. Such violence was unprecedented for *panchayat* elections in UP, which in the past had been non-events in which the upper castes swept most posts uncontested.

The 1995 *panchayat* elections irrevocably changed caste equations in Baba ka Gaon. The village *Thakurs* threatened to kill the former army sergeant from the *Maurya* middle caste who, with the backing of the scheduled castes, decided to stand for the *pradhan*'s post. They then burnt the crops of a particularly militant scheduled-caste man. A week before the elections, in mid-afternoon, a group of *Thakurs* entered the hut of a middle-caste family and started thrashing the wife with their staffs while others pinned her husband down. But for the first time in Baba ka Gaon's known history, the scheduled castes – including Prayaga Devi – and the middle castes hit back at the *Thakurs*, beating them away.

Ram Dass says: *Earlier, I would bear it when the* Thakurs *would hit or abuse me. But now if they hit me I will hit them back even harder.*

The *Thakurs* filed a complaint at the police station, alleging that they had been assaulted by the lower castes. At the local police station, 7 km away, the upper-caste police official abused Ram Dass for being the leader of the scheduled castes and threatened to arrest all of them. Ram Dass's comment, that as the woman had been assaulted in her own house the *Thakurs* were clearly the aggressors, provoked the official further. *You must learn to live peacefully*, he shouted. *Even if the* Thakurs *say something to you, behave like Gandhi-ji and accept getting slapped twice and come and complain to me. What has gone wrong with Baba ka Gaon? There was never any trouble there earlier.*

Ram Dass says: *This was the first time that I've been to the police station. In my 70 years, this is the first time I've been to the police station!*

Though the candidate supported by Ram Dass and the scheduled castes won the elections, the complaint by the *Thakurs* was written up by the police officer with such a bias that a few months later two of Baba ka Gaon's scheduled-caste villagers were arrested and jailed for a week in Pratapgarh prison. Ram Dass comments: *The police will do whatever the* Thakurs *want. The police are theirs, so why should they listen to us? The police are the most corrupt and worst part of the administration. They never record our complaints and they never take action. When they talk to the* Thakurs *they say, 'Tell us what happened, how can we help.' But with us they say, 'Hey, why are you creating trouble?' They blame us for everything.*

*Policemen are like dogs – if you give them food they won't bite you but will bite whoever you want them to bite. If you give them money they consider you a good man, if you don't give them money you are a* goonda [hooligan].

Durbhe says: *In Awadh we have a saying about the police – my mother taught it to me – 'Ghore ke pichhari, aur police ke aghari nahin jana!'* [If you go behind the horse, it will kick you and if you go near the police they will beat you so never go near them.]

## The scheduled and middle castes fail to unite

The alliance between the scheduled and middle castes during the *panchayat* elections was the continuation of a historically complex relationship between these groups in northern India. While the relationship between the upper and scheduled castes has been unremittingly hostile and oppressive – attested to by the vast gaps in social and economic status, and the practices of 'untouchability' – that between the middle and scheduled castes has not been as clear-cut. The middle castes (the former *Shudras* or servant castes) are a very large and disparate group, with enormous variation in their caste status and economic well-being. The lowest middle castes have historically been considered just one step above the untouchables. They are desperately impoverished, and continue to be disproportionately represented amongst the absolutely poor in northern India. But the bulk of the middle castes have always been materially and socially immeasurably better off than the former untouchables.

Leaders of the middle and scheduled castes have often tried to build alliances between the two so as to pose a united front against their mutual oppressors, the upper castes. In UP, the various middle and scheduled castes would together comprise roughly two-thirds of the province's population, far outweighing the upper castes. When united, such as during the 1995 *panchayat* elections, they threaten the foundations of upper-caste domination.

But unity has been rare. Efforts to bring the scheduled and middle castes together have generally been wrecked by differences in caste hierarchy as well as by gradations of poverty. Dismayed by the failure to unite the scheduled and middle castes, Ambedkar wrote:

The reason for this want of solidarity is not far to seek. It is to be found in the system of graded inequality whereby the Brahmin is above everybody, the *Shudra* is below the Brahmin, and above the untouchable. If the Hindu social order was based on inequality, it would have been thrown out long ago. But it is based on graded inequality so that the *Shudra*, while he is anxious to pull down the Brahmin, is not prepared to see the untouchables raised to his level . . . The result is that there is nobody to join the untouchable in his struggle. He is completely isolated. Not only is he isolated, he is opposed by the very classes who ought to be his natural allies.[10]

Shrinath says: *At the time of Independence, there were three national leaders. There was Jinnah, who was the leader of the Muslims. There was Gandhi, who represented the upper castes. And then there was Ambedkar, for us. The middle castes did not have a good leader. And when the debate started about which communities should be given reservations, Ambedkar wished that the middle castes should join with the scheduled castes because then the numbers of the lower castes would increase. But then the upper castes started a movement directed at the middle castes to 'Rise Upwards', hinting that they could become upper-caste. The middle castes were misled into believing that they could join the upper castes and so they left the scheduled castes. And once this happened they were stuck in the middle – they couldn't go into the upper castes nor with the scheduled castes. And it was only the scheduled castes and scheduled tribes who were given reservations. But if the middle castes had at that time joined the scheduled castes, they would have immediately got reservations; they wouldn't have had to wait to get it slowly, slowly as they are doing now. If they had had a leader at that time, they would have joined hands with the scheduled castes and for all of us things would have been better than today.*

Ram Dass says: *Between us and the middle castes there would also be levels of discrimination. All of us were tied into the caste system. The castes within the middle castes would not eat with each other. Nor would people from different scheduled castes eat together. These were traditional restrictions that we just accepted. The upper castes who made the caste system would not allow these castes to eat with each other because if they then got together they would dominate the ones who had begun the system. But progress will only come for us when we are one with the middle castes. Because of this the effort of the upper castes has always been to divide the middle castes from the scheduled castes. They practice the politics of division. Because of this, we have been at the receiving end of the violence, because we were divided and we failed to unite.*

In Baba ka Gaon, relationships between the scheduled and middle castes have in the past century run the gamut from conflict between them to allying against the *Thakurs* and Brahmins. Shrinath says: *The middle castes were always united with the upper castes. They also used to practice things like untouchability because they were totally linked with the upper castes and could even sit and eat with them. Because the* Thakurs *allowed them to share their food, the middle castes followed them.*

*And it's only recently that people like Ram Saran Maurya* [the new *pradhan*, of a higher-middle caste] *and his family, who have lived outside, have begun to not discriminate against us. But they are the exceptions. The other* Mauryas *will still not let the scheduled castes touch their eating and drinking utensils. They will discriminate against the scheduled castes even if we are now vegetarians and the* Mauryas *themselves eat meat and drink alcohol! There is still such a chasm between us. But to my knowledge, there are very few people amongst the middle castes who are not poor. So in my understanding they should get reservations. In the social environment here, middle castes and scheduled castes are almost the same. There is sometimes only a very slight difference.*

Over the last 15 years or so, the scheduled and middle castes in Baba ka Gaon and Awadh have moved closer together, uniting against the upper castes. The unity has been impelled in great part because of a growing rift between the upper and middle castes. The upper castes (including such rich cultivating castes as the Jats and Tyagis) now view the middle castes as challengers to their domination of UP politics as well as competitors for prized government and public-sector jobs. In UP, reservations for the middle castes in government jobs and in education were begun during the tenure of the first middle-caste chief minister, Ram Naresh Yadav, in 1977, and were then expanded in the 1990s under Mulayam Singh Yadav.[11]

Shrinath says: *The upper castes didn't want to give reservations to the middle castes despite the middle castes supporting them. And when Mulayam Singh Yadav came to power, the* Thakurs *and Brahmins started getting worried that the middle castes were taking over UP. The middle castes have become aware of this, that they cannot become upper castes and that the upper castes don't want them to progress. And they have to find some ally, because even though their population is large they haven't had sufficient progress. Our interests are the same and that's why more of them are coming together with the scheduled castes.*

In the foreseeable future, one dominant factor shaping UP's politics will be the relationship between the scheduled and middle castes. How far the outcome will benefit the scheduled castes, as the numerically weaker group, is an imponderable, though the experience of India's peninsular provinces, where the middle-caste movement is far in advance of the north, shows that the needs of the scheduled castes are almost always swamped by those of the more advanced groups.

## The upper castes' appeal to Hindu nationalism

The BJP, an almost exclusively upper-caste grouping, has since the decline of the Congress emerged as the single largest party in UP, winning one-third of the votes in assembly and parliamentary elections since 1991. In an attempt to increase its share of the vote, the BJP has sought to unite all Hindus, including the scheduled castes, through appealing to a resurgent Hindu nationalism. A central part of this emotive appeal is the demonizing of Muslims, who are accused of having ruined Hindu India through their centuries of conquest and rule. At the end of 1992, while in power in UP, the BJP and its allies attacked and demolished a medieval mosque in Faizabad, roughly 150 km from Baba ka Gaon. They claimed that the mosque stood on the site of an ancient temple, marking the birth-place of the Hindu god Ram, which had been razed by the Muslims in the 16th century. The Hindu nationalist appeal made little headway with the scheduled castes, as did the BJP strategem of attempting to portray Ambedkar as a Hindu leader.[12] For the scheduled castes, the BJP is the party of the people whose ancestors invented the caste system and who still try to hold them in this bondage today. They are also inherently suspicious of the BJP's motives and ideology, a legacy of their ancient hatred of Hindu orthodoxy.

Ram Dass says: *The BJP, the Shiv Sena, the Vishwa Hindu Parishad – they are all stoking the religious divides. These people are not religious, their motives are different. In the name of religion they are just destroying and not constructing anything. They want to conquer everything through violence. Does one need to build a temple to take the name of God?*

*One* Thakur *and a Brahmin said to me, 'You are a devotee, so why don't you come to Ayodhya?' and I said, 'What are we to do?' and they said, 'We are to break the mosque and to build a temple in its place.' And I said 'What is the point of breaking anyone's religion, all religions say the same things, and I will not go.' So they said, 'At least on this day, at this time, say "Ram, Ram".' To which I said, 'You say "Ram, Ram", because you never say it otherwise! I say "Ram, Ram" all the time. You people encourage violence and never pray! God is within you and you should keep your sanctity because this is where God resides.' And after I said this, they just went away and never spoke to me again.*

*But the more foolish of the scheduled castes went with them, though none were from Baba ka Gaon. And it was these poor people who got killed, not the leaders. The lower castes were used. This has happened from time immemorial. When the upper castes need to fight against someone they start saying that we scheduled-caste people are Hindus! They are then willing to call you friend, brother, father, but when the battle is over they won't even recognize you and will say 'Get out, idiot!'*

*And it's the same for the Muslims: their leaders start the battles but the ones who get killed are the poor. Those who are sitting in the big homes never lose, it's the ones living in the slums who suffer.*

Durbhe says: *The BJP people came to my college and asked us to come to Ayodhya. I told them, 'Why should I come with you?' They said, 'You should come to liberate the mosque which was built by Muslims and to build a Ram Janambhoomi temple* [a temple for Ram's birthplace].' *And so I retorted, 'The Muslims ruled here for hundreds of years, so will you break everything they built? Why don't you also tear down the Taj Mahal and the Red Fort? Why don't you tear down the whole country because they ruled over it for such a long time? Why don't you also break what the British made?'*

*The Brahmins and* Thakurs *were supporting the BJP and Vishwa Hindu Parishad during the Ayodhya problem. But at that time Mulayam Singh Yadav and Kanshi Ram* [leaders of the Samajwadi and Bahujan Samaj parties respectively] *had an agreement. At our college the BJP people would shout slogans insulting Yadav and Kanshi Ram for joining forces. So we would shout back at them, 'Mulayam and Kanshi Ram have got together and the platform of Jai Shri Ram* [literally, glory be to Lord Ram] *has been destroyed!'*

*There is very little support for the BJP amongst our castes. Some of our people did give them some money but that's only because so many of their people come to your house and start pressuring you that you get embarrassed and can't refuse. All the BJP local officials here just made a lot of money from the contributions for building the temple and then went and built nice houses for themselves. They make suckers out of all the people, in every way!*

# 15

# Conclusion:
# The Perpetuation of Mass Poverty

FOR Ram Dass's family, the past has been brutally harsh, the present is precarious, and the future shows no hope of being better. The limited improvements in their economic and social situation add up to very little. When evaluated by the experience of the many million poor families who have fared worse than Ram Dass's, are still destitute or absolutely poor, and will almost inevitably remain so, the only conclusion can be condemnation of independent India's development record.

Judged by conditions in 1997, the fiftieth year of India's Independence and self-rule, there is little likelihood that Ram Dass's or the millions of families poorer than his will find material or social emancipation in the foreseeable future. India's political economy today is such that even small, incremental gains that would add up to a substantial reduction in the number of the poor cannot be expected, for the very reasons that such gains have failed to emerge since Independence. There is even less probability of the sweeping redistributive change that was in principle possible at the time of Independence.[1]

Nevertheless, despite these bleak prospects, through the 1990s India's leaders continued to promise the poor a quick end to poverty.

This repeated the vow that has been uttered in every decade of independent India's history. In the heady first decade of Independence, Nehru pledged to the 'naked, hungry mass' that they would quickly be freed – because colonial rule had been ended, the princely states and the *zamindari* system abolished, and a 'socialist pattern of society' was in the making. With poverty not having diminished one whit, in the 1960s Nehru and his successors promised to take land from the rich and to redistribute it to the poor and landless. In the 1970s, Mrs Gandhi pledged nothing less than *Garibi Hatao!* – to eradicate poverty. For the 1980s, the far less radical offering from both her and her son, Rajiv Gandhi, was a massive array of poverty-alleviation programmes. In the 1990s, the poor were told that their poverty would soon vanish because India's economy was poised for take-off, for unprecedentedly rapid growth.

The hype surrounding this new elixir reached a peak in 1997, when the world joined India in celebrating her golden jubilee. According to the celebrants, India's prospects had never looked rosier. The sustained economic reforms of the past half-decade marked a new epoch in independent India's economic history: the repudiation of Nehruvian state planning and socialist self-reliance. With the confining superstructure of state control and planning on the way out, India's boundless potential could come to fruition, said the celebrants. The biggest market in the world, with a purported middle class of some 250 million, was ready to boom. The rapid economic growth rates that would result would quickly double or triple average income, and would offer enormous scope for ameliorating poverty, the celebrants pronounced. The lives of India's one billion people would shortly be transformed.

Some part of the celebrants' vision is certainly realizable: fast economic growth. But the growth is likely to make India an increasingly dualistic society and economy, much like Brazil in the 1960s and 1970s, when rapid economic growth barely reduced poverty. However, the growth will not transform the lives of the mass of India's people, unlike the achievements of China and the east Asian 'tigers', where radical land reform and sustained investments in health and education laid the foundations for widely shared growth.[2]

In India, it is a certainty that the top one-tenth to one-quarter of the population, huge numbers in themselves, will benefit enormously in the near future, as the bulk of them have already done from the faster growth of the past two decades. But what of the vast ranks of the poor, still an overwhelming majority of the country's people?

Though unlikely, it cannot be ruled out that poverty might indeed worsen despite accelerated economic growth. This is a possibility if the Indian government further reduces public spending, particularly on agriculture, infrastructure and the social sectors. The risks to the poor will be even greater if the government further loosens land-ceiling laws, as is being demanded by the rural rich and the many votaries of economic liberalization.

It is most likely, however, that in the inevitable absence of redistribution, the poor will neither participate in the economy's growth nor receive the gains of growth on anything like the scale required appreciably to reduce mass poverty. Ram Dass's family and the many millions of poorer ones are barred from participating in economic growth, whatever its pace, because of a myriad disabilities: illiteracy and lack of employable skills, ill-health, gender inequity, social discrimination, political subjugation, and the lack of economic assets such as cultivable land. For much the same reasons, the gains of growth barely trickle down to them. To enable the poor to participate and benefit from economic growth, the Indian government would need to undertake widespread land reform, promote good healthcare and schools, foster gender equity, and encourage local democracy. It has not done so for 50 years. The reasons for that tragic inaction remain unchanged. In the future, as in the half-century past and in centuries earlier, India is destined to remain the land of hunger, want and suffering.

# Notes and References

All quotes from Nehru are from 1989.

## Chapter 1

1. The international comparison is from Shiva Kumar, 1991, pp. 2343–5; see also Dreze & Sen, 1996. Figures for Indonesia are from Ravallion & Datt, 1996, p. 2480.

2. The middle castes – the former *Shudras* or servant castes who come between the former 'untouchable' group and the upper, 'twice-born' castes – are a large and very disparate group. Their caste status and economic well-being vary greatly. The nomenclature used to capture this diversity has expanded enormously, so much so that it defies comprehension by all but experts. To avoid confusion, only 'middle' caste is used here, generally qualified by whether they are towards the higher or lower side of the spectrum. For the small number of castes in UP that are not upper castes but were historically not considered *Shudras* nor suffered caste disabilities – such as the Jats, Bhumihars and Tyagis – the term 'elite cultivating castes' is used in this book. For details see, Shah, 1991, p. 607; Ramaiah, 1992, p. 1203.

3. On the occupational and regional distribution of the poor see, Harriss et al., 1992; Mendelsohn & Vicziany, 1994, pp. 79–83; Dandekar & Rath, 1971, pp. 11–17.

## Chapter 2

1. For an overview of India's experience see Frankel, 1996, p. 483.

2. The discussion of pre-British agrarian systems and the changes introduced by the British are based on the following sources: Reeves, 1991; Neale, 1962; Nigam, 1987; Kumar (ed.), 1984, pp. 36–86; Pandey, 1982, pp. 143–97; Siddiqui, 1978; Dhanagare, 1983; Sarkar, 1983.

3. Quoted in Reeves, 1991, p. 51.

4. Siddiqui, 1978, p. 86.

5. Neale, 1962, p. 205.

6. Kumar, 1984, p. 66.

7. Siddiqui, 1978, p. 15, citing Irwin, *The Garden of India; or Chapters on Oudh History and Affairs*, London, 1880.

8. The description of untouchability is based on the following sources: Beteille, 1972, especially p. 413; Blunt, 1969; Mendelsohn & Vicziany, 1994, p. 69; Singh, 1993, pp. 1070–80.

9. Figures are from Saxena, 1985. The analysis of the linkages between caste and agrarian structures is based on: Beteille, 1972; Dhanagare, 1983; Siddiqui, 1978; Omvedt, 1995.

10. Frankel, 1996, p. 494.

11. The section on the revolt and its failure is based almost entirely on Siddiqui's (1978) extensive work and Pandey's (1982) 'subaltern' reinterpretation of his research. Consequently, they are not attributed further in this section.

12. Reeves, 1991, p. 220, citing Pannikar, K.M. (ed.) & Pershad A., *The Voice of Freedom, The Speeches of Pandit Motilal Nehru*; Bombay, 1961, pp. 512–3.

13. Both points are made by Frankel, 1996, p. 495.

14. Siddiqui, 1978, p. 193.

15. Details of landholding structure in 1947 are from Neale, 1962, pp. 270–1; Kumar, 1984, p. 86.

16. The analysis of India's impoverishment under colonial rule is based on Dantwala, 1973.

17. All figures are for British India, Dantwala, 1973, pp. 23–4.

18. Liddle & Joshi 1986, p. 25.

## Chapter 3

1.  All adjustments to prices and incomes in the book are based on the index numbers from CMIE, 1994.

## Chapter 4

1.  There are no firm estimates of how many people benefited or how much land was transferred. These estimates are from a personal interview with N.C. Saxena, a senior Indian government official, 2 April 1997.
2.  On the importance of land ownership to the rural poor, see: Mendelsohn and Vicziany, 1994, pp. 101–3; Agarwal, 1994, p. 480; Herring, 1983, p. 87. On the inverse relationship between farm size and productivity, Saxena, 1985, p. 13.
3.  Nehru, 1989, p. 113.
4.  Reeves, 1991, p. 307, quoting the National Herald, 18 April 1946, p. 6. This analysis is based largely on the following three sources, and only quotes and other essential attribution is cited after this (other references are cited where necessary): Reeves, 1991, especially p. 27; Herring, 1983; Neale, 1962. For legal details see Maurya, 1994.
5.  Reeves, 1991, p. 228.
6.  Herring, 1983, p. 87.
7.  Reeves, 1991, p. 211.
8.  Nehru, 1989, pp. 534–5.
9.  Ibid.
10. Reeves, 1991, p. 220.
11. Nehru, 1989, p. 58. The conclusions are my own. They are based, first, on the land-holding data from Neale (1962), who analyses the UP *Zamindari* Abolition Committee's data, pp. 270–78. The second data set I have used is Reeve's (1991) analysis of occupational categories, p. 27.
12. Reeves, 1991, pp. 220–32.
13. Quoted in ibid., p. 227.
14. Hiro, 1976, p. 83.
15. Quoted in Reeves, 1991, p. 289.
16. Ibid., p. 286.
17. Quoted in Herring, 1983, p. 154.
18. Saxena, 1985.
19. Uttar Pradesh Government, 1987, p. 108.
20. Brass, 1983.
21. The analysis is based on Kohli, 1987, pp. 52–80.

22. Sarkar, 1983.
23. Frankel, 1978, p. 81.
24. Kohli, 1987, p. 62.
25. Ibid., p. 70.
26. Saxena, 1985, pp. 16–17.
27. Kohli, 1987, p. 64
28. Ibid., p. 227

## Chapter 5

1. Economic and Political Weekly Foundation, 1993, Table 1, pp. 1754–63.
2. Nambissan, 1996, Table 2, p. 1014. Much of the analysis is also from Nambissan.
3. Mendelsohn & Vicziany, 1994, p. 489; Zelliot, 1972, p. 79. This analysis is based on the following works, though specific reference is given where necessary: Ambedkar, 1943; Mendelsohn & Vicziany, 1994; Mahar, 1972, various chapters by different authors; Omvedt, 1995; Frankel, 1996.
4. Spear, 1965; Brass, 1994; Sarkar, 1983.
5. Zelliot, 1972, p. 69.
6. Mendelsohn & Vicziany, 1994, p. 108.
7. Zelliot, 1972, p. 90.
8. Frankel, 1996, pp. 492, 497.
9. Dushkin, 1972, p. 215.
10. Quoted in Mendelsohn & Vicziany, 1994, p. 76.
11. Frankel, 1996, p. 491; Mendelsohn & Vicziany, 1994, p. 76.
12. Omvedt, 1995, p. 47.
13. Rao, 1996, p. 11.
14. Mendelsohn & Vicziany, 1994, p. 102.
15. Galanter, 1972, p. 242.
16. Lynch, 1972, p. 103.
17. Quoted in Zelliot, 1966, p. 199.

## Chapter 6

1. Herring, 1983, p. 32.
2. Veit, 1976, Table 2.13, p. 81.
3. Frankel, 1978, p. 204.
4. Reeves, 1991, p. 323.
5. Zoya Hasan in Frankel & Rao, 1996, pp. 161–2.
6. Herring, 1983, p. 135; Dandekar & Rath, 1971, p. 77.

7.  Herring, 1983, p. 135.
8.  Reeves, 1991, p. 306.
9.  Dandekar & Rath, 1971, p. 79.
10. Figures are from Dandekar & Rath, 1971, p. 72; Hasan in Frankel & Rao, 1996, p. 162.
11. Cited in Veit, 1976, p. 248.
12. This paragraph is based on Varshney, 1995, p. 28.
13. Patnaik & Hasan, 1995, p. 276.
14. Kohli, 1987, p. 74.
15. This interpretation of the Green Revolution – for the following three paragraphs – is based on Kohli, 1987, pp. 73–9; and on Brass, 1994, pp. 277–80 and 309–20.
16. By the mid-1980s, foodgrain production per person was just 7.4 per cent higher than at the beginning of the 1960s. Patnaik & Hasan, 1995, p. 281.
17. Bhalla & Tyagi, 1989, pp. 128–31.
18. Whitcombe, 1980, pp. 156–79.
19. Brass, 1994, p. 326.
20. This section is based on Dandekar & Rath, 1971, p. 137.
21. See Tendulkar, 1992, p. 46; Veit, 1976, p. 233; Kohli, 1987, p. 243.

## Chapter 7

1.  Hiro, 1976, p. 75.
2.  Ibid., pp. 68, 76, 81.
3.  Hardgrave, 1980, p. 231.
4.  Ibid., p. 159.
5.  Vaidyanathan, 1995, p. 334.
6.  Hardgrave, 1980, p. 159.
7.  Frankel & Rao, 1996, p. 506.
8.  Hardgrave, 1980, p. 159.
9.  Brass, 1994, p. 295.
10. Ibid.
11. Herring, 1983, pp. 135–8.
12. Frankel & Rao, 1996, p. 501.
13. Veit, 1976, p. 247, quoting *The Times of India*, Oct/Nov 1972 series on land reform.
14. Kohli, 1987, p. 215.
15. Punekar, 1977: see 'Prime Minister's Broadcast' and 'The 20-Point Programme'.
16. Hiro, 1976, p. 271.

17.  This account is from two sources: Hiro, 1976, pp. 271–3; Sims, 1994, pp. 103–36.
18.  Sims, 1994, p. 125.
19.  Ibid.
20.  Hiro, 1976, p. 273. The Turkman Gate incident is from Hardgrave, 1980, p. 171.
21.  Election results are from Kohli, 1987, p. 193; Hardgrave, 1980, pp. 175–7 and 231.
22.  The section on the Janata is from: Kohli, 1987, pp. 189–222; Franda, 1979, p. 223.
23.  Kohli, 1987, p. 215.
24.  The details on poverty in the 1970s are from: Ravallion & Datt, 1996, p. 2480; Nayyar, 1991, p. 31.

## Chapter 8

1.  There is broad agreement about the magnitude of the decline though analysts differ on the initial and final points. See especially, Sen, 1996, pp. 2459–61, Table 1, p. 2460 and Table 7, p. 2466; Minhas, 1991; Ravallion & Datt, 1996, Table 1, p. 2480.
2.  Sen, 1996, p. 2473.
3.  Kohli, 1987, pp. 309–11.
4.  Nayyar, 1991, p. 85.
5.  Saxena, 1997. However, in some western states, particularly Maharashtra, the rural employment programmes did have an impact in curbing the severity of poverty. Economic and Political Weekly Foundation, 1996, p. 2475.
6.  Kohli, 1987, p. 311.
7.  Vaidyanathan, 1995, p. 336.
8.  This paragraph is based on Kohli, 1987, p. 351.
9.  Bhatia, 1997.
10.  Saxena,1985.
11.  Cited in Chambers, 1989, p. 231.
12.  Need about 12 kg per month for an adult, according to government estimates, 'Starvation Scheme', *The Times of India*, 21 January 1997, p. 10.
13.  Nambissan, 1996, p. 1015.
14.  The figure is for rural and urban combined. Dreze & Saran, 1993, p. 35, footnote 36.
15.  Data and many of the insights in this section are from Dreze & Saran, 1993, and this source is not cited further.
16.  Veit, 1976, p. 58; Hiro, 1976, p. 84.
17.  Tilak, 1996, p. 363.
18.  Dreze & Saran, 1993.

19. Tan & Mingat, 1992, p. 145.
20. Tilak, 1996.
21. Mendelsohn & Vicziany, 1994, p. 82.

## Chapter 9

1. All the data and analysis of the higher education systems failures are from several articles in Chitnis & Altbach (eds), 1993. See especially, Indiresan, J., 'Quest for Quality,' and Chitnis, S., 'Gearing a Colonial System of Education to Take Independent India Towards Development'. Data cited here are from pp. 310, 401 and 314.
2. *Statistical Outline of India*, 1994–95, Tata Services Ltd., Bombay, p. 151.
3. Tendulkar, 1992, pp. 28–31.
4. *Statistical Outline of India*, p. 147.
5. Zelliot, 1972, p. 188; Mendelsohn & Vicziany, 1994, p. 98.
6. Ravallion & Datt, 1996, pp. 2481–4.
7. Ibid.; Sen, 1996, pp. 2463, 2476.
8. Saxena, 1985.
9. Ravallion & Datt, 1995, p. 2.
10. Statistics from Food and Agricultural Organization, 1997; Franda, 1979, p. 96.
11. Tendulkar, 1992, pp. 40–1.

## Chapter 10

1. Agarwal, 1994, p. 345.
2. Dreze, 1990, p. 58; Agarwal, 1994, p. 343.
3. Sharma, 1980, p. 52; Agarwal, 1994, pp. 135–8.
4. Dreze, 1990, p. 63.
5. Chatterjee, 1990, p. 24.
6. Bennet, 1992, pp. 45, 87.
7. Sims, 1994, pp. 105–6.
8. Dreze & Sen, 1990, p. 12.
9. Sims, 1994, pp. 105–6
10. Bennet, 1992, p. 14.
11. Dreze, 1990, p. 124, notes an opposite trend in Bengal, where the upper castes are viewed with contempt and their practices have not been adopted, and consequently women in general are better off.
12. Chatterjee, 1990, pp. 9–10.

## Chapter 11

1. CMIE, 1996; Ravallion & Datt, 1996; Sen, 1996, p. 2459 and Table 7, p. 2466.
2. Editorial, *The Economic Times*, 10 December 1996.
3. CMIE, 1996; the figure for 1993 is Rs 230.
4. These are identified as risk factors by Dandekar & Rath, 1971, pp. 11–17.
5. This section on widows is adapted from Dreze, 1990, and so is not footnoted further.
6. Dreze, 1990, p. 96.
7. Jain & Visaria (eds), 1988, p. 64.
8. Ibid, p. 24.
9. This section is from World Bank, 1997.
10. Uttar Pradesh Government, 1996, p. 4.

## Chapter 12

1. In the area around Baba ka Gaon, an acre of decent land currently sells for roughly Rs 40,000.
2. This data is based on interviews with senior UP officials. Also Vishaarad, 1974.
3. Ibid.
4. Harriss, 1992; Copestoke, 1992, p. 218; Herring, 1983, p. 269, who argues that the changes in land-holding since Independence are more 'apparent' than 'real'.
5. Copestoke, 1992, p. 218.
6. Ibid., p. 219; Bandyopadhyaya, 1986; Bandyopadhyaya, 1995.
7. Nair, 1996; Saxena, 1997, pp. 7, 12–13.

## Chapter 13

1. Mendelsohn & Vicziany, 1994, pp. 90, 107.
2. Ibid., p. 93.

## Chapter 14

1. One advocate of this view is amongst India's most eminent lawyers, Palkhivala, 1997.
2. Kohli, 1987, p. 60.
3. Points in this and the paragraph below are from: Kohli, 1987, pp. 43–5; Saxena, 1985; Frankel & Rao, 1996, p. 501.
4. Mahar, 1972, p. 426.
5. Mendelsohn & Vicziany, 1994, p. 97.
6. Ramaseshan, 1995, p. 73.
7. Chandra & Parmar, 1997, p. 217.

8. Ramaseshan, 1995, p. 75.
9. Twenty-seven per cent of the posts were reserved for the middle castes (Other Backward Classes) and 22.5 per cent for the scheduled castes and tribes, and also 33 per cent for women. Under the central government's *panchayati raj* act, while reservations for scheduled castes are mandatory, state governments decide whether to exercise reservations for the middle castes. The *pradhan's* post in each *panchayat* area will sequentially be reserved for the middle castes, scheduled castes and women, with only once in every four elections thrown open to 'general' candidates.
10. Quoted in Ramaseshan, 1995, p. 74.
11. Hasan, 1996, p. 185.
12. Muralidharan, 1995, p. 75; Chandra & Parmar, 1997, p. 217.

## Chapter 15

1. Many elements of this view are shared with: Kohli, 1987, p. 12; Dreze & Sen, 1996, Chapter 8.
2. For an illuminating contrast between Brazil and the participatory pattern of growth in east Asian 'tigers' like South Korea, see Dreze & Sen, 1996, Chapter 8.

# Glossary

| | |
|---|---|
| *Bazaar* | market-place |
| *Banyaan* | vest, often worn in place of a shirt |
| *Bedakhli* | eviction of a tenant farmer or sharecropper |
| *Begar* | forced – sometimes unpaid – labour |
| *Benami* | illegal – literally without name – implying that its ownership is disguised |
| *Charpai* | a rough wood-and-rope bed |
| *Chawl* | low-cost tenements |
| *Dhaba* | roadside eateries known for their spicy food |
| *Garibi Hatao* | Abolish Poverty; a campaign slogan of Prime Minister Indira Gandhi in the early 1970s |
| *Ghat* | steps built along the river for bathing |
| *Goonda* | hooligan |
| *Hari* | forced – sometimes unpaid – labour, specifically referring to ploughing |
| *Harijan* | God's People, a term popularized in the 1930s by Mahatma Gandhi to refer to the 'untouchable' castes. Scheduled castes is the term preferred by the former untouchables. |
| *Khadi* | handloomed cotton |
| *Kisan* | peasant |
| *Kisan Sabhas* | peasants' associations |
| *Kshatriya* | a broad category comprising numerous upper castes; also a member of the second of the four main Hindu castes, the warrior caste |
| *Kucha* | of dried mud, usually applicable to makeshift huts and roads, opp. of pucca |

| | |
|---|---|
| *Lathi* | a long, wooden stick used as a weapon in India |
| *Lekhpal* | village land records keeper |
| *Lungi* | a loose cloth tied around the waist by men as a lower garment; more common in southern India |
| *Mahua* | the succulent flower of a local tree |
| *Maurya* | an upper-middle caste of northern India |
| *Mela* | village fair |
| *Nasbandhi* | vasectomy or male sterilization |
| *Nazrana* | a levy imposed by landlords on tenants when they wanted to renew or begin leases on agricultural land |
| *Pallu* | an end of the saree that is often used by women to veil their head and face |
| *Panchayat* | village councils; in independent India, *panchayat* members are chosen by universal adult suffrage every five years |
| *Pasi* | a scheduled caste, historically considered 'untouchable' |
| *Patwari* | in charge of village land records |
| *Pradhan* | head of the *panchayat* or elected village council; traditionally, village head |
| *Pucca* | proper or solid; *pucca* road means a paved, good road |
| *Shikmi* | the process of giving sub-tenants ownership as part of *zamindari* abolition |
| *Shudra* | the lowest of the four main Hindu castes, the workers |
| *Swaraj* | freedom, independence or self-rule |
| *Taluqadar* | a Persian term for a range of revenue-collecting intermediaries between the ruler and cultivator; under the British became synonymous with landlord |
| *Vaishya* | a member of the third of the four main Hindu castes, a trader caste |
| *Yadav* | a middle caste of northern India |
| *Zamindar* | like *taluqadar*, a Persian term for a range of revenue-collecting intermediaries between the ruler and cultivator; under the British became synonymous with landlord |
| *Zamindari* | as a system, refers to the landlord-centred agrarian system introduced by the British |

# Bibliography

Agarwal, B. (1994) *A Field of One's Own*, Cambridge University Press, Cambridge.

Ambedkar, B.R. (1943) *Mr Gandhi and the Emancipation of the Untouchables,* Thacker, Bombay.

Bandyopadhyaya, D. (1986) 'Land Reform in India', *Economic and Political Weekly,* June 21–28.

Bandyopadhyaya, D. (1995) 'Reflections on Land Reforms in India Since Independence', *Industry and Agriculture in India Since Independence*, Volume 2, Satyamurthy, T.V. (ed.), Oxford University Press, New Delhi.

Bennet, L. (1992) *Women, Poverty and Productivity in India*, World Bank, EDI Seminar Paper #43, Washington D.C.

Beteille, A. (1972) 'Pollution and Poverty', *The Untouchables of Contemporary India,* Mahar, J.M. (ed.), University of Arizona Press, Tucson.

Bhalla, G.S. & Tyagi, D.S. (1989) *Patterns in Indian Agricultural Development,* Government of India, New Delhi.

Bhatia, S.L. (1997) 'Centrally aided schemes to be shifted to states', *The Economic Times*, 10 April.

Blunt, E.A.H. (1969) *The Caste System of Northern India*, S. Chand, Delhi.

Brass, P. (1983) *Caste, Faction and Party in Indian Politics*, Vol I, Chanakya Publications, Delhi.

Brass, P.R. (1994) *The Politics of India Since Independence,* Cambridge University Press, second Indian edition.

Centre for Monitoring the Indian Economy (1994) *Trends in Inflation*, Bombay, April.

Centre for Monitoring the Indian Economy (1996) *India's Social Sectors*, Bombay, February.

Chambers, R. (1989) *To the Hands of the Poor*, Saxena, N.C. *et al* (eds), Oxford University Press, Delhi.

Chandra, K. & Parmar, C. (1997) 'Party Strategies in the Uttar Pradesh Assembly Elections, 1996', *Economic and Political Weekly*, February 1.

Chatterjee, M. (1990) *Indian Women: Their Health and Economic Productivity*, World Bank Discussion Papers, #109, Washington, D.C.

Chitnis, S. & Altbach, P. (eds) (1993) *Higher Education Reform in India*, Sage Publications, New Delhi.

Copestoke, J.G. (1992), 'The Integrated Rural Development Programme: Performance during the Sixth Plan, Policy Responses and Proposals for Reform', *Poverty in India*, Harriss, B., Guhan S. and Cassen R.H., Oxford University Press, Delhi.

Dandekar, V.M. & Rath, N. (1971) *Poverty in India*, Indian School of Political Economy, Poona.

Dantwala, M.L. (1973) *Poverty in India: Then and Now (1870–1970)* Macmillan, Madras.

Dhanagare, D.N. (1983) 'Agrarian Agitation and Congress Politics in Oudh 1920–2 and 1930–2', Chapter V, *Peasant Movements in India 1920–50*, Oxford University Press, Delhi.

Dreze, J. (1990) *Widows in Rural India*, London School of Economics, London.

Dreze, J. & Sen, Amartya (1990) *The Political Economy of Hunger*, Volume I, Oxford University Press, Oxford.

Dreze, J. & Saran, M. (1993) *Primary Education and Economic Development in China and India*, London School of Economics, London.

Dreze, J. & Sen, Amartya (1996) *India: Economic Development and Social Opportunity*, Oxford University Press, India.

Dushkin, L. (1972) 'Scheduled Caste Politics', *The Untouchables of Contemporary India*, Mahar, J.M. (ed.), University of Arizona Press, Tucson.

Economic and Political Weekly Foundation (1993) 'Poverty Levels in India: Norms, Estimates, Trends', *Economic and Political Weekly*, Bombay, August.

Fiske, A. (1972) 'Scheduled Caste Buddhist Politics', *The Untouchables of Contemporary India*, Mahar, J.M. (ed.), University of Arizona Press, Tucson.

Franda, M. (1979) *India's Rural Development*, Indiana University Press, Bloomington.

Frankel, F.R. (1978) *The Gradual Revolution: India's political economy, 1947–1977*, Princeton University Press, Princeton, New Jersey.

Frankel, F.R. (1996) 'Conclusion: Decline of a Social Order', *Dominance and State Power in Modern India*, Volume II, Frankel, F.R. & Rao, M.S.A. (eds), Oxford University Press.

Galanter, M. (1972) 'The Abolition of Disabilities', *The Untouchables of Contemporary India*, Mahar, J.M. (ed.), University of Arizona Press, Tucson.

Hardgrave, R.L. (1980) *India: Government and Politics in a Developing Nation*, 3rd Edition, Harcourt Brace Jovanovich, New York.

Harriss, B., Guhan, S. and Cassen, R.H. (1992) *Poverty in India*, Oxford University Press, Delhi.

Herring, R. (1983) *Land to the Tiller: The Political Economy of Agrarian Reform in South Asia*, Yale University.

Hiro, D. (1976) *Inside India Today*, Routledge and Kegan Paul, London.

Jain, A.K., & Visaria, P. (eds) (1988) *Infant Mortality in India*, Sage Publications, New Delhi.

Kohli, A. (1987) *The State and Poverty in India: The Politics of Reform*, Cambridge University Press.

Kumar, D. (ed.) (1984) *The Cambridge Economic History of India*, Volume II, Orient Longman, Hyderabad.

Liddle, J. & Joshi, R. (1986) *Daughters of Independence: Gender, Caste and Class in India*, Zed, London.

Lynch, O. (1972) 'Dr B.R. Ambedkar – Myth and Charisma', *The Untouchables of Contemporary India*, Mahar, J.M. (ed.), University of Arizona Press, Tucson.

Maurya, R.R. (1994) *Uttar Pradesh Land Laws*, Central Law Publications, Allahabad.

Mendelsohn, O. & Vicziany, M. (1994) 'The Untouchables', *The Rights of Subordinated Peoples*, Mendelsohn, O. & Baxi, U. (eds), Oxford University Press, Delhi.

Muralidharan, S. (1995) 'New Writing on Ambedkar', *Seminar*, Delhi, January.

Nair, J. (1996) 'Predatory Capitalism and Legalised Landgrab: Karnataka Land Reforms', *Economic and Political Weekly*, 3 February.

Nambissan, Geetha B. (1996) 'Equity in Education? Schooling of Dalit Children in India', *Economic and Political Weekly*, Bombay, 20–27 April.

Nayyar, R. (1991) *Rural Poverty in India: An Analysis of Inter-State Differences*, Oxford University Press, New Delhi.

Neale, W.C. (1962) *Economic Change in Rural India: Land Tenure and Reform in Uttar Pradesh, 1800–1955*, Yale University Press, New Haven.

Nehru, J. (1989) *Jawaharlal Nehru; An Autobiography*, John Lane, The Bodley Head Ltd., London, Oxford University Press, New Delhi.

Nigam, S. (1987) *A Social History of a Colonial Stereotype – The Criminal Castes and Tribes of U.P., 1871–1930*, SOAS, Unpublished Doctoral thesis, London.

Omvedt, G. (1995) *Dalit Visions*, Orient Longman, Hyderabad.

Palkhivala, N.A. (1997) 'A Bizarre Thought', *The Times of India*, Opinion piece, 8 April.

Pandey, G. (1982) 'Peasant Revolt and Indian Nationalism', *Subaltern Studies I*, Guha, R. (ed.), Oxford University Press, New Delhi.

Patnaik, U. & Hasan, Z. (1995) 'Aspects of the Farmers' Movement in Uttar Pradesh in the Context of Uneven Capitalist Development in Indian Agriculture', *Industry and Agriculture in India Since Independence*, Volume 2, Satyamurthy, T.V. (ed.), Oxford University Press, New Delhi.

Punekar, S.D. (1977) *Economic Revolution in India (*edited volume) Himalaya Publishing House, Bombay.

Ramaiah, A. (1992) 'Identifying Other Backward Classes', *Economic and Political Weekly*, 6 June.

Ramaseshan, R. (1995) 'Dalit Politics in Uttar Pradesh', *Seminar*, Delhi, January.

Rao, M.S.A. (1996) 'Introduction', *Dominance and State Power in Modern India*, Frankel, F.R. & Rao, M.S.A., Oxford University Press.

Ravallion, M. & Datt, G. (1995) 'How Important to India's Poor is the Sectoral Composition of Economic Growth', Policy Research Department, World Bank, Washington, D.C., July, draft.

Ravallion, M. & Datt, G. (1996) 'India's Checkered History in Fight Against Poverty: Are There Lessons for the Future?', *Economic and Political Weekly*, Bombay, Special Number, September.

Reeves, P. (1991) *Landlords and Governments in Uttar Pradesh – A Study of Their Relations Until Zamindari Abolition*, Oxford University Press.

Sarkar, S. (1983) *Modern India 1885–1947*, Macmillan, Madras.

Saxena, N.C. (1985) 'Caste and Zamindari Abolition in U.P.', *Mainstream*, 15 June.

Saxena, N.C. (1997) 'Instances of some anti-poor government policies in India', Planning Commission, Government of India, unpublished report.

Sen, Abhijit (1996) 'Economic Reforms, Employment and Poverty: Trends and Options', *Economic and Political Weekly*, Special Number, September.

Shah, G. (1991) 'Social Backwardness and Politics of Reservations', *Economic and Political Weekly*, March, Annual Number.

Sharma, U. (1980) *Women, Work and Property in North India*, Tavistock, London.

Shiva Kumar, K. (1991) 'UNDP's Human Development Index', *Economic and Political Weekly*, 12 October.

Siddiqui, M.H. (1978) *Agrarian Unrest in North India: The United Provinces 1918–22*, Vikas Publishing House, Delhi.

Sims, H. (1994) 'Malthusian Nightmare or Richest in Human Resources?', *India Briefing*, Oldenburg, P. (ed.), Westview Press, Boulder.

Singh, K.N. (1993) *The Scheduled Castes*, Oxford University Press, New Delhi.

Spear, P. (1965) *A History of India*, Penguin, Baltimore.

*Statistical Outline of India, 1994–95*, Tata Services Ltd., Bombay.

Tan, Jee-Peng & and Mingat, A. (1992) *Education in Asia: A Comparative Study of Cost and Financing*, World Bank, Washington D.C.

Tendulkar, S. (1992) 'Economic Growth and Productivity', *Poverty in India*, Harriss, B. et.al. (eds), Oxford University Press, Delhi.

Tilak, J.B.G. (1996) 'How Free is 'Free' Primary Education in India?', *Economic and Political Weekly*, Bombay, 10 February.

Uttar Pradesh Government (1987) *Pratapgarh District Gazeteer*, Lucknow.

Uttar Pradesh Government (1996) *ICDS II Project Proposal*, Lucknow.

Vaidyanathan, A. (1995) 'The Political Economy of the Evolution of Anti-Poverty Programmes', *Industry and Agriculture in India Since Independence*, Volume two, Satyamurthy, T.V. (ed.), Oxford University Press, Delhi.

Varshney, A. (1995) *Democracy, Development and the Countryside*, Cambridge University Press.

Veit, L.A. (1976) *India's Second Revolution: The Dimensions of Development*, McGraw-Hill Book Company.

Vishaarad, M.D., MLA (1974) *Bhoomi Vyavastha Janch Samiti*, Rajaswa Vibhag, Uttar Pradesh Government.

Whitcombe, E. (1980) 'Whatever happened to the zamindars?', *Peasants in History: Essays in Honour of Daniel Thorner*, Raj, K.N. (ed.), Oxford University Press, Delhi.

World Bank (1997) *India New Directions in Health Sector Development at the State Level: An Operational Perspective*, Washington D.C.

Zelliot, E. (1972) 'Gandhi and Ambedkar – A Study in Leadership', *The Untouchables of Contemporary India*, Mahar, J.M. (ed.), University of Arizona Press, Tucson.

# THE POLITICS OF CONTEMPORARY ASIA SERIES

Asia has come to prominence in recent years because of its economic dynamism, despite the dramatic financial collapse of 1997. But the decade-long economic success of this highly diverse continent has been dependent on the maintenance of effective government. It can also lead, as the Zed Books Series on Politics in Contemporary Asia shows, to the downplaying of the region's many political problems in the areas of ethnicity, religious identity, democratic control and human rights.

## OTHER RECENT ASIA TITLES FROM ZED BOOKS

Zed Books has major lists in the fields of Development Studies, the Environment, Gender Studies, Cultural Studies and Politics. Many of these titles deal with Asia to a greater or lesser extent. In addition, a number of them, in addition to our *Politics in Contemporary Asia Series,* deal exclusively with particular countries or regions in Asia. Recent titles include:

War in the Blood: Sex, Politics and AIDS in Southeast Asia
*C. Beyrer*

Capital Accumulation and Women's Labour in Asian Economies
*P. Custers*

In the Land of Poverty: Memoirs of an Indian Family, 1947-1997
*Siddharth Dube*

The Secret Politics of Our Desires: Innocence, Culpability and Indian Popular Cinema
*Ashis Nandy*

Daughters of Development: Women in a Changing Environment
*Sinith Sittirak*

The Traffic in Women: Human Realities of the International Sex Trade
*Skrobanek, Boonpakdee and Jantateero*

For full details of these books and Zed's other titles, as well as our subject catalogues, please write to: The Marketing Department, Zed Books, 7 Cynthia Street, London N1 9JF, UK or email Sales@zedbooks.demon.co.uk

Visit our website at: http://www.zedbooks.demon.co.uk